Democratic Discipline

Foundation and Practice

Randy L. Hoover
Youngstown State University

Richard Kindsvatter
Kent State University

Merrill,
an imprint of Prentice Hall
Upper Saddle River, New Jersey   *Columbus, Ohio*

Library of Congress Cataloging-in-Publication Data

Democratic discipline : foundation and practice / Randy L. Hoover, Richard Kindsvatter.

p.   cm.

Includes bibliographical references and index.

ISBN 0-02-364082-0 (alk. paper)

1. School discipline—United States—Philosophy. 2. School discipline—Social aspects—United States. Classroom management—Social aspects—United States.   I. Kindsvatter, Richard. II. Title.

Curr ✓ LB3012.2.K56   1997

371.5—dc20

96-10559

CIP

Editor: Debra A. Stollenwerk

Production Editor: Alexandrina Benedicto Wolf

Photo Researcher: Nancy Harre Ritz

Design Coordinator: Jill E. Bonar

Text Designer: STELLARViSIONs

Cover Designer: Proof Positive/Farrowlyne and Associates

Production Manager: Laura Messerly

Director of Marketing: Kevin Flanagan

Advertising/Marketing Coordinator: Julie Shough

Electronic Text Management: Marilyn Wilson Phelps, Matthew Williams, Karen L. Bretz, Tracey Ward

This book was set in Bitstream Zapf Humanist by Prentice Hall and was printed and bound by Quebecor Printing/Book Press. The cover was printed by Phoenix Color Corp.

 © 1997 by Prentice-Hall, Inc.
Simon & Schuster/A Viacom Company
Upper Saddle River, New Jersey 07458

Photo credits: pp. 1, 26, 108, and 165 by Barbara Schwartz/Merrill; p. 5 by UPI/Corbis-Bettmann; pp. 16, 29, 63, 113, 123, and 176 by Anthony Magnacca/Merrill; pp. 30, 45, 49, 56, 58, 99, 123, 113, 171, and 185 by Scott Cunningham/Merrill; p. 40 by The Bettmann Archive; p. 70 by MGM (Courtesy Kobal); pp. 88 and 158 by CLEO Freelance Photography; p. 94 by AP/Wide World Photos; pp. 128, 136, 140, and 181 by Anne Vega/Merrill.

Printed in the United States of America

10 9 8 7 6 5 4 3 2 1

Gift
4/00

ISBN: 0-02-364082-0

Prentice-Hall International (UK) Limited, *London*
Prentice-Hall of Australia Pty. Limited, *Sydney*
Prentice-Hall of Canada, Inc., *Toronto*
Prentice-Hall Hispanoamericana, S. A., *Mexico*
Prentice-Hall of India Private Limited, *New Delhi*
Prentice-Hall of Japan, Inc., *Tokyo*
Simon & Schuster Asia Pte. Ltd., *Singapore*
Editora Prentice-Hall do Brasil, Ltda., *Rio de Janeiro*

To America's classroom teachers past, present, and future

Preface

The subject of classroom management and discipline is far more complex than commonly assumed. It is imperative that classroom teachers be afforded a vehicle to facilitate their intellectual and professional ownership of a foundational knowledge base used to illuminate the complexity of causes and inform the spectrum of decisions relating to discipline. In short, teachers need to learn how to think about discipline and become conscious of both the short- and long-term effects of discipline on today's students and tomorrow's citizens.

In this sense, we are arguing for educating teachers for informed practice. The book is intended to give a sense of what is called "praxis" in dealing with students in school and classroom settings. Praxis is a notion that embodies the idea of highly informed practice, action that is based on a strong knowledge base grounded in critically examined theory. It represents the basic idea of reflective thinking because it requires "active, persistent, and careful consideration of any belief or supposed form of knowledge in light of the grounds that support it and the further conclusions to which it tends."*

This means developing a sense of critical practice where discipline activities are conducted with a thoughtful eye on the context of events and a keen consideration of what is proper pedagogically, developmentally, and ethically, given that we are ultimately educating for democratic citizenship. *Praxis is the uniting of the intellectual with the practical; praxis is highly informed professional practice.*

Praxis also requires that we possess knowledge that has utility and efficacy (power) relative to dealing with problems of practice. We want you to recognize that actions must be based on grounded knowledge, knowledge that is carefully examined and reflectively derived, to avoid situations like the myths and fictions of discipline that we present in the first chapter.

KEY THEMES

You will notice several themes in the book that we believe are critical for the professional practice of discipline. These include the following:

---

*Dewey. J. (1933). *How we think.* Lexington, MA: D. C. Heath.

- the weaknesses of relying on myths about discipline
- the value of praxis
- the role of critical reflectivity in being a professional
- the power and utility of grounded knowledge
- the way activities of teaching and schooling shape character and citizenship
- the way that values of our democratic society can be given greater consideration through the activities of discipline

FOCUS OF THIS TEXT

This book has a twofold focus. First, its basis is explicitly and unequivocally set in the foundations and ideals of democratic citizenship. The authors take the position that every discipline-related act must be informed by democratic principles—philosophical, sociological, legal, and ethical—that are clearly present and explained in this text. Second, the book postulates the teacher as an informed and empowered decision maker, a fully functioning professional who translates the knowledge base into effective and democratically formative practices. Informed judgment is the defining feature of the teacher's professional practice. Understanding and grounding practice needs to start early on in all professional education programs. While we are sympathetic to the possibility that early attempts to employ principled and ethical practices of discipline may be awkward, we are convinced that the skill will develop in due time through the persistence of thoughtful and examined practice.

This book attempts to present a comprehensive but balanced perspective on discipline. A glance at the table of contents will give a sense of how we have addressed this. For a more comprehensive view, refer to Chapter 10, which provides the reader with a synthesis of the preceding chapters. As you will see throughout the course of the book, it is our belief that a teacher's approach to discipline is personally constructed rather than externally imposed. We intend this text to aid in the thoughtful construction of democratically and ethically principled belief systems regarding the activities of discipline on the part of practitioners.

Maya Angelou has observed that doing the right thing is conditional upon thinking the right thing. This is the underlying premise of this book, perhaps its most salient feature. Much of the book is devoted to preparing teachers to do the right thing. We address the why of democratic discipline throughout the book, with the latter chapters also presenting the what of discipline in terms of approaches for establishing positive climate, managing the classroom, intervening to terminate misbehavior, and remediating. We believe that the student who reads this book with the facilitation of a committed college professor will be able to proceed with confidence and flexibility in planning for discipline that is compatible with the needs of the teacher and the needs of the students, who are ultimately the citizens of tomorrow.

We have conceived this book as a primary text for courses on classroom management and discipline as well as a supplemental text for either general methods classes and certain foundations classes related to examining democratic perspectives on schooling and teaching. We also believe that elements of this text can be used effectively in a variety of graduate-level professional development courses where the focus is school reform, critical reflectivity, curriculum development, or instructional development.

ACKNOWLEDGMENTS

We would like to thank the following reviewers for their invaluable feedback: John J. Bertalan, Hillsborough Community College; Lowell J. Bethel, The University of Texas at Austin; Annette Chavez, Northern Kentucky University; John Chesky, Gardner-Webb College; Sandra L. DiGiaimo, University of Scranton; Quentin L. Griffey, Pfeiffer College; Barbara A. Illig, Indiana University of Pennsylvania; Jack H. Longbotham, Hardin Simmons University; Jane McCarthy, University of Nevada, Las Vegas; Leonard L. Mitchell, Evangel College; Iris Nierenberg, Ball State University; Virginia Regelmann-Engman, Fort Lewis College; Beverly Schemmer, Taylor University; and Robert L. Shearer, Miami University.

Brief Contents

Contents

Chapter 3

The Role of Educational Philosophy and Ideology in Discipline   40

Chapter 4

Discipline and the Postmodern Student   56

Chapter 5

Understanding the Formation of Character and Democratic Citizenship   70

Chapter **6**

Discipline, Law, and the Constitution   88

Chapter 7

Social Power in the Classroom   108

Chapter 8

Establishing and Maintaining Optimal Classroom Conditions   128

Chapter 9

Discipline-Related Intervention and Remediation in the Classroom   158

Chapter 10

Developing a Discipline Plan 176

Democratic Discipline

Foundation and Practice

Chapter 1

Definitions, Mystique, and Myths of Discipline

❖ Focus Questions

1. As an aspect of teaching, discipline is commonly perceived negatively. How might discipline be perceived as a neutral, even a positive, aspect of teaching?

2. What is your current definition of *classroom discipline*? How does it change as you read this and subsequent chapters?

3. What is the relationship between instruction and discipline?

4. Why do many teachers persist in maintaining an anti-intellectual posture regarding discipline (and possibly other aspects of teaching)?

5. What has been the influence of myths in determining educational practice? How does this compare with the occurrence and influence of myths within other professions?

Discipline is the bane of the teacher! An inherent component of the teaching process, discipline is likely to arouse in teachers feelings of apprehension and self-doubt, more so than the other three major components of teaching—planning, instructing, and evaluating. Instructing—engaging kids in the learning process—is usually the most attractive component of teaching. Teachers tend to be matter-of-fact about the planning and evaluating components; writing lesson plans and grading students' work, although each presents its particular challenges and problems, are generally taken in stride by most teachers. But discipline is commonly viewed negatively and often considered a necessary evil of teaching that must be tolerated.

In this book we present discipline as a neutral concept in and of itself that may have essentially positive outcomes in the classroom. We conceive it to be grounded in human relations as much as in authority. It has the potential to be a source of comfort for kids as they are provided with reasonable structure, treated firmly but fairly, and sense the teacher's genuine concern. It may also be a source of satisfaction for teachers as they feel confident in their ability to keep students productively engaged and emotionally relaxed.

In their teacher education programs, prospective teachers learn about planning, instructing, and evaluating rather straightforwardly. Instructors and textbooks may present the material in varying ways, but there is typically little controversy about these topics. However, the principles of discipline are not as clear-cut as in the other areas. A great deal depends on individual belief systems and their associated frames of reference. Many crucial discipline-related skills are subtly embedded within the teaching act. Prospective teachers can learn only in a limited way from exemplary models, for the best teachers do little that is overtly related to discipline. They teach with an integrated style that homogenizes discipline within the instructional strategies. Teachers who must use frequent overt interventions to restore order are likely to be less competent practitioners and thus are not preferable models.

So how do you proceed to learn about discipline? There is no single endorsed process to which educators subscribe. However, there are guidelines you can follow toward becoming knowledgeable and skillful regarding discipline:

1. Do not expect to find a perfect system already developed for you. The approach to discipline you ultimately take will be of your own design, sharing some aspects with others but bearing the stamp of your belief system, personality, and perceptions.
2. Become clear about your beliefs regarding the role of the teacher, your purposes and responsibilities as a teacher, your assumptions about the nature and development of children, and your respect for students' rights. You must also support your beliefs with a pedagogically sound rationale.
3. Be committed to developing your approach in terms of a systematic, comprehensive, internally consistent set of propositions and strategies based on the most credible information you can obtain from the professional literature and informed teachers.
4. Design a package of mutually compatible and complementary practices in which you have confidence and that address the particular conditions of your classroom.
5. Try out your ideas and become skillful in applying the pertinent techniques in clinical settings and classrooms when opportunities are available. Teacher education students may have to wait until they begin student teaching to apply their techniques; practice will probably extend into the first year of teaching. Be as prepared as possible for it.
6. Consider your discipline plan and practices to be continually developing as they reflect your accumulating experience and professional maturity.

DEFINITIONS OF DISCIPLINE

Most people assume that they know what discipline in the school setting means, and up to a point they are correct. But discipline takes on different shades of meaning depending on the context in which it is used and the frame of reference of the user.

Discipline as a noun is used to refer to noncompliant student behavior, to the rules established in the classroom to effect order, and to classroom order itself. As a verb it usually refers to controlling, punishing, or reforming practices used by teachers. The term also appears as the adjective *disciplinary* and as such frequently has a connotation similar to its use as a verb.

These are limited and pejorative interpretations, accommodating at best only the least appealing part of the whole concept. In a more informed and objective perspective, *discipline* is a neutral term.

Discipline is generally understood to be that dimension of teaching which addresses student demeanor; it is especially concerned with promoting behavior that conforms to teacher expectations and/or changing behavior that does not conform. While this is basically true, it is not very helpful in conceiving effective discipline-related teaching practices. A more functional conception of discipline involves understanding that it has three separate, though not mutually exclusive, aspects.

One aspect of discipline is the external social force that induces order, and as such it is a necessary condition within any group. It often exists informally and tends to remain tacit, as among a group of friends or patrons in a theater. In an industrial setting, a political party, or a fraternity, discipline is more codified in terms of contracts and constitutions. In the military, police force, and school, discipline is highly formalized. This is neither good nor bad; it simply is a feature of these settings. A relatively high degree of conformity is necessary for the latter institutions to accomplish their missions effectively. However, when the institutional need for conformity conflicts with personal desires for freedom and power, stress and negativism result. Applying the principles of discipline in these settings requires intelligence, skill, and sensitivity. When this truism is not appreciated by educators, the price is high.

Another aspect of discipline is the internal inclination of students to comply with classroom expectations. This implies that discipline is a process, that its focus is within the students, and that it is neither good nor bad in and of itself. This definition refutes certain common misconceptions about discipline: that it is an absolute, that it is concerned primarily with rules and punishments, and that it is an essentially negative concept and a necessary evil of teaching. In fact, discipline can and should be a positive and rewarding dimension of the classroom for both teachers and students—for teachers as they conduct class skillfully and meet the academic, social, and emotional needs of students, and for students as they realize the satisfaction of self-discipline and responsible citizenship.

A third aspect of discipline is concerned with the conditions in the classroom, especially the conditions established by the teacher. As the classroom leader, the teacher is responsible for structuring the classroom—that is, for setting standards, formulating rules, clarifying expectations for behavior, and monitoring all of these actions. This is essentially the classroom management responsibility, and it is partially embedded in instruction. *Classroom management* and *discipline* are terms that, in some contexts, have been used more or less interchangeably. However, **classroom management**, in the view of the authors, refers and is limited to teacher behaviors that focus on creating a purposeful learning climate and maintaining classroom order.

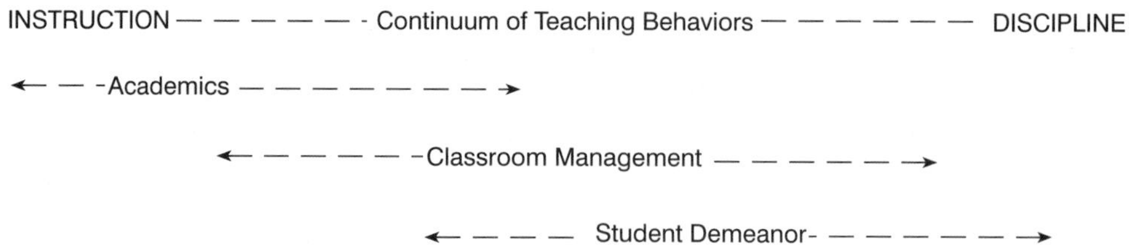

INSTRUCTION — — — — — · Continuum of Teaching Behaviors — — — — — DISCIPLINE

← — -Academics — — — — — — →

← — — — — -Classroom Management — — — — — →

← — — — Student Demeanor- — — — — — →

Figure 1.1

It does not include the intervention and remediation aspects of discipline, nor does it deal directly with the internal motivations and inclinations of students as just described. Figure 1.1 represents classroom management as it relates to both instruction and discipline.

In Figure 1.1, teaching is depicted as a continuum of behaviors from instruction (where the focus is on academics) to discipline (where the focus is on student demeanor). Classroom management, that aspect of teaching concerned with structuring the classroom and monitoring behavior, is linked to both instruction and discipline. When instruction is going well and students are on task, the management function is subsumed within instruction. Students are acting in a manner we describe as *self-disciplined*. As students drift into passive off-task behavior (such as showing a lapse of attention), teacher behavior shifts along the continuum toward more overt management-oriented strategies (such as using subtle eye signals and instructionally embedded cues, like asking a student who does not seem to be attending the discussion to make a comment on the topic under consideration). Should noncompliance escalate from passive inattention to mild disruption (such as pencil tapping or whispering), teacher behavior shifts to more emphatic management behaviors (including using verbal reminders and redirecting students to the learning activity). When openly disruptive behavior occurs, teacher behavior moves beyond management to a more extreme discipline mode in which restoring order through resolute intervention and correction is the single intent.

The most effective teachers, insofar as establishing a positive classroom climate is concerned, are those for whom instructional activities and classroom management techniques are sufficient to evoke orderly behavior. They have little need to employ overt corrective approaches.

THE MYSTIQUE OF DISCIPLINE

As mentioned earlier, although discipline is an inherent part of teaching, it is not always straightforwardly identifiable in terms of either teacher or student behaviors. Discipline occurs tacitly until students engage in deviant behavior and the teacher intervenes to counter that behavior; then it assumes an overt and negative, sometimes emotionally charged, presence. Teachers' inability to control all the factors

involved—in fact, their unawareness of those factors—causes uncertainty and apprehension as they sense that their authority is being undermined. Thus, an aura of mystique is attributed to discipline.[1]

Mystique is a quality attributed to some source by the perceiver even though it does not exist inherently in the source. It has a nebulous, greater-than-reality property. Mystique occurs when one is highly impressed, awed, or intimidated. For example, in an earlier age, humankind viewed eclipses with mystique. Our religious practices often involve a quality of mystique as we submit to spiritual forces that we never fully understand. Places such as Paris and Vienna are often ascribed mystique, whereas places like Indianapolis and Detroit usually are not. Some persons are associated with mystique, such as the brilliant Socrates of antiquity and the ill-fated Marilyn Monroe of the recent past.

Mystique is a quality that is sensed emotionally rather than explained rationally. Reason and objectivity are the antitheses of mystique; when puzzling situations are thought about with reason and objectivity, mystique tends to disappear. For instance, the mystique of eclipses ceased when certain movements of celestial bodies were fully understood; likewise, when the source of the supposed power of the Wizard of

---

[1] The commentary in this section is adapted from Kindsvatter and McLaughlin (1985).

Oz was exposed, his mystique was eliminated. Although mystique is sometimes harmless and even desirable, it is essentially anti-intellectual and gets in the way of clear thinking. Such is the case with discipline. Fortunately, using reason and understanding goes a long way toward eliminating the mystique of discipline. Because mystique exists as a personal perception, not as an inherent dimension of discipline, each teacher must accomplish this task individually.

Emerging from this aura of mystique is a set of beliefs and practices, or educational folkways, that constitutes the conventional wisdom of teaching. These beliefs and practices are not necessarily wrong, and they certainly are not intentionally diabolical, but they remain unscrutinized. They may in some instances be serviceable, but they may just as likely lead to seriously flawed judgment. Raywid (1976) has observed that "the most tyrannical of all our beliefs are those which are persistently unexamined—precisely because they appear so patently reasonable as to be mandated by common sense and impervious to question" (p. 37).

The purposes of this book are to suggest that you develop a posture of healthy suspicion regarding the conventional wisdom of teaching and to encourage your pedagogically sound thinking about discipline. To begin, you should be aware of the contributing causes of the emergence and persistence of conventional-wisdom-based beliefs and practices. These causes include anti-intellectualism, a tendency toward having short-range goals, a narrow view of purpose, and selfish motivations for teaching.

Anti-intellectual Climate

A considerable body of research and theory has accumulated about the nature of teaching and learning. Much of this knowledge, however, has yet to find its way into classroom practice on a regular or systematic basis. For example, the literature has convincingly refuted corporal punishment both philosophically and psychologically for at least 35 years, yet the practice is still condoned by a substantial number of educators (Levine, 1979; Johns & MacNaughton, 1990). The climate among practitioners reflects varying degrees of anti-intellectualism. In an anti-intellectual climate, theory and research are assigned limited credibility. Personal experiences and, inevitably, personal biases are more powerful determiners of teaching practices. Even when preservice teachers learn pedagogically endorsed practices in their university preparation, they soon encounter skeptical veteran teachers, and they are placed under considerable pressure to adopt the prevalent attitudes.

Experienced teachers whose orientation is anti-intellectual make statements to new teachers such as, "The theory you learned sounds great, but here in the real world, you have to do what works." "What works" is not in itself the problem, but in this context it seems to imply that the important consideration is expediency, with the focus more on the benefit of the teacher than on that of the students. We know from research (Brophy & Rohrkemper, 1981) that teachers do not readily recognize themselves as a causal factor of students' misbehavior in the classroom. We may extend this finding to surmise that the limitation of the teacher in translating discipline-related pedagogical principles into practice, more so than inadequacy of the principles themselves, is at the heart of the problem. Therefore, one reason for the tenacity of conventional wisdom is that a sizable population of teachers lacks the competency to apply potentially useful theories and principles effectively.

Short-Range Goals

A second reason for empirical propositions being a powerful influence on classroom control techniques is that in discipline-related matters, teachers usually function in accordance with short-range goals. When misbehavior occurs, most teachers' concern is to suppress it quickly. In and of itself, this is as it should be, for teachers cannot tolerate disruption for very long when it interferes with achieving the learning objectives. However, that is often where they leave it, without follow-up involving the consideration and treatment of causes. Teachers are especially interested in finding ways to control students' behavior and so are quick to adopt expedient means to deal with noncompliance. But an expedient measure, even when justified, is insufficient to carry out teachers' total responsibility for the students' academic and social welfare.

Discipline practices should be conceived primarily in educational terms and only secondarily in control terms. They should be the means by which children learn to cope with the social and institutional expectations they encounter; thus, these practices should have an important long-range educational goal. The short-term measures should comply with this broader concern and not be considered merely momentary expedients.

Narrow View of Purpose

A third cause of the persistence of teachers' reliance on unscrutinized beliefs is the narrow view that many teachers have of their purpose in the classroom—a view that is likely to be reinforced by other school personnel as well. At any level, but especially at the secondary level, many teachers consider their task to be essentially the delivery of subject matter to students. Learning the subject surely is important, and teaching about that subject is the most obvious reason for the classroom activities. However, the students' need to learn about any given subject is predicated and socially defined, not necessarily innate. Only occasionally does classroom learning relate to the basic drives that impel children and adolescents in their behavior. Therefore, when the students become bored or distracted, their behavior interferes with the teachers' intentions. The teacher is likely to be irritated by it and react more angrily than rationally. In this situation the teacher fails to understand the spectrum of factors that is operating (i.e., the attitudes being expressed, the needs being acted out, and the students' hidden agendas that emerge).

Enlightened teachers have a clear sense of purpose and consider that purpose to be broadly based. They realize that for students there are more immediate concerns than passing tests—that classrooms are places where students are really living, not just being prepared for life at some future time. Further, they understand that the subject they teach is more than a body of related facts and skills; it is the vehicle through which they establish a relationship with their students that should contribute to the quality of their students' lives. But when teachers assume that their responsibility is limited to academic considerations, they are likely to use expedient means to maintain order in their classrooms and in so doing to be unduly influenced by specious beliefs.

Reasons for Teaching

A fourth reason why this mystique has become entrenched has to do with why persons decide to become teachers. At least three sources of motivation are involved: the sincere and healthy attraction to young people and an altruistic desire to affect their lives in significant ways; the need for security (teaching is one of the more secure occupations); and the opportunity to exercise power in a very direct and immediate way.

The best teachers are likely to be those who were influenced primarily by the first motive—the attraction to and interest in the development and education of children. If asked, most teachers would likely say (and even believe) that this applies to them. However, the other two motives are undoubtedly powerful factors for many.

Those who strongly feel the need for security are also likely to be those who need certainty in their classroom practice. They will search, largely in vain, for control measures guaranteed to establish and maintain order in their classrooms. These are the teachers who rationalize their shortcomings, blame the principal for not backing up their discipline, and complain that the kids do not seem to learn discipline at home the way they used to.

Regarding the third motive, martinets who find the power potential of the teacher role to be intriguing are inclined to use that power as a featured part of their teaching style. These teachers tend to satisfy their personal need for wielding power at the expense of the students, and because this occurs subconsciously on the part of the teacher it is all the more insidious. Martinets are essentially wedded to suspect tenets of discipline as the basis of their teaching identities. The result is a Catch-22 situation: using flawed practice prevents them from realizing their potential as teachers, but without these practices they lack the crutch that is a crucial component of their confidence.

In this section we have been critical of teachers who employ discipline-related practices that are at variance with the professionally endorsed principles of discipline. The beliefs that underlie these practices are the "myths of discipline," and we will explain the more popular myths in the next section. However, we have the highest regard for teachers whose well-conceived discipline-related practices serve the best interests of their students and mirror respect for the profession they represent.

THE MYTHS OF DISCIPLINE

The mystique that surrounds discipline and the conventional wisdom that provides a quasi-philosophical and quasi-psychological basis for discipline have generated a series of suspect beliefs and practices among teachers. These are considered the **myths of discipline** because they emerge from intuition and supposition and lack pedagogical confirmation. They are deceptive in that they seem to the teachers who subscribe to them to serve a useful purpose. Under critical examination, their flawed logic is exposed. Their effect on teachers' practice and students' learning, as will become apparent, is subversive.[2]

The 20 myths we identify are attractive because they offer simplistic, believable answers to some prickly classroom situations. Acquiring an awareness of the myths is a useful beginning to your study of discipline. With this awareness, you will avoid the temptation to readily accept answers that seem too good to be true (because they probably are too good to be true).

Myth 1

Any student misbehavior is self-evidently the fault of the student.   This is an especially attractive belief to a teacher having discipline-related problems because it implies that the teacher is not responsible for the misbehavior and is therefore the unfortunate victim of circumstances.

Certainly, misbehaving students have chosen to act in their particular ways. However, to consider those acts as isolated expressions of noncompliance blinds one from looking beyond to possible contributing factors. The cause may in some cases lie entirely within students and be the outcome of their respective idiosyncrasies. Students who are hyperactive or who have psychological adjustment problems or social inadequacies may fall into this category. This is not to excuse their noncompliant behavior but to recognize that classroom conditions are not the proximate cause. Misbehavior of this sort deserves to be dealt with in compassionate ways that do not aggravate the problems of already troubled students.

In other instances, however, student **misbehavior**, like the civil disobedience of the sixties, while not necessarily condoned is nevertheless the understandable reaction of outraged persons who are being manipulated by unwarranted forces or conditions. We often fail to recognize that misbehavior may represent student resistance to conditions they experience in schools (such as objectionable aspects of classroom climate, curriculum, instruction, management, and bureaucracy) rather than conditions that lie innately within the students. Educators must be aware of these conditions and accept culpability for them. To ignore them is to allow the blame to be borne disproportionately by the students, while the festering conditions continue unabated.

Myth 2

Discipline implies an adversarial situation that involves a power struggle between the teacher and students.   This belief is attractive to beleaguered teachers because it seems to justify a defensive stance and the blatant use of power. Power is inevitably

---

[2] The commentary on the myths is adapted to a large extent from Kindsvatter and Levine (1980) and Kindsvatter and McLaughlin (1985). Reprinted with permission of the *Phi Delta Kappan* (vol. 61, pp. 690–693, 1980).

involved in the relationship between the teacher and students. But this power need not become manifest in conditions similar to those of a cold war, with the counterproductive assumptions implied by this term. When power is well understood by the teacher and is expressed in terms of enlightened leadership principles, discipline is considered the means by which the optimum learning climate is established and maintained, both in anticipation of and in response to student misbehavior. Students are recognized as complex, sentient, dynamic beings who respond more or less predictably according to established principles of behavior. In other words, power appropriately used is initially concerned with creating classroom conditions that predispose preferred student behavior. Only when prevention efforts are an insufficient deterrent does the teacher use power in the form of an intervention strategy.

Myth 3

Good control depends on finding the right gimmick.   Dreikurs, Grunwald, and Pepper (1971, p. 187) report a study showing that teachers want immediate solutions to discipline problems in their classrooms. Their requests for help often take the form, "What can I do to make the kids pay attention [or quit fooling around or get to class on time or be quiet enough] so that I can teach?" However, teachers must realize that only a part of student misbehavior is wholly spontaneous and unanticipated. The quality of teacher–student relationships, the clarity and reasonableness of the teacher's expectations, the consistency of the teacher's behavior, and the general level of motivation are among the factors that condition student behavior, including misbehavior. These factors become established in the students' minds over time, and changing student perceptions of them in significant ways can also be expected to take time.

Teachers who wish to improve the quality of discipline in their classrooms should first analyze in a dispassionate way the causes of troublesome behavior. Four likely sources of misbehavior are capriciousness, chronic emotional or adjustment problems, students' negative attitudes toward the teacher or the school in general, and volatile intragroup conditions or interpersonal relations. When the sources have been identified, strategies that address the particular misbehavior should be devised and administered. The process is relatively slow and involved. Patience, fortitude, and faith on the part of the teacher are required. Discipline-related practices vary from teacher to teacher based in some measure on personality and teaching style.

Fritz Redl, one of the first modern commentators on discipline, comments thus on the use of gimmicks:

> Administering discipline is a more laborious task than is taking refuge in a few simple punitive tricks. It is just as much more laborious and challenging as is modern medical thinking compared to the proud hocus-pocus of the primitive medicine man. The task of the teacher on his job is to translate the principles of democratic discipline into daily action in the classroom. (1966, p. 254)

Although teachers must take immediate action when misbehavior occurs, formative measures have greater potential for developing the conditions of good discipline in classrooms. They involve establishing a climate of mutual respect, being firm and consistent, and maintaining a dignified but friendly posture even in trying circumstances.

Myth 4

Every teacher can become highly competent in creating the conditions of good discipline. One might assume that if teachers were all sufficiently well trained in effective techniques, they could acquire a high level of competence in managing classroom discipline. The effective techniques, however, exist for all teachers at the level of principles, not practices. It is possible to inform all teachers of the pertinent principles that relate to discipline, but it is not possible to teach them an infallible process for translating them into practice.

The preparation of artists provides an apt analogy. It is surely possible to teach interested persons the principles of balance, composition, and color, as well as certain specific skills such as mixing paints and applying them to canvas. However, no teacher of art would guarantee to produce an artist capable of rendering masterpieces; in fact, guarantees could not be given beyond the technical aspects of art. So it is with preparing teachers to be particularly competent in any but the technical aspects of instruction, for teaching is, in important respects, an art.

Perhaps the most crucial factor determining the teacher's potential for the successful management of discipline is personality. Redl contends that "for the job of establishing good discipline and maintaining it . . . the personality of the teacher is the most essential factor. Under ordinary circumstances the teacher can get along well with a few technical considerations if this one factor of personality is strongly represented" (1966, p. 303). And Dreikurs, Grunwald, and Pepper maintain that "it is obvious that certain personality types have greater difficulty with power-seeking and defiant children" (1971, p. 197).

Effective classroom discipline grows out of the teacher's leadership qualities, group process skills, and the mutual respect that exists in the classroom. However, the extent to which a teacher can be an effective leader, acquire and employ principles of group process, and promote a condition of mutual respect depends on the existence of that potential within the teacher's personality.

Myth 5

The best teachers are those in whose classes students do not dare misbehave. An autocratic approach to discipline, when injudiciously used, assumes an adversarial teacher–student relationship (i.e., it assumes that students will not learn unless they are coerced and will not comply unless they are controlled).

If achieving order and unquestioning compliance is a high priority of an institution, then an autocratic, highly controlling approach to discipline can be justified. In a military or prison setting, it may be the only feasible approach. Schools should be different. Schools should guide students to develop self-control and personal initiative. Relentlessly autocratic teachers tend to induce feelings of repression and impotence.

A martinet may produce compliant students but will inhibit initiative and creative thinking. Further, in an autocratic classroom there is no opportunity for participatory democracy to be modeled or for students to learn the habit and satisfaction of self-discipline. This places an extremely high price on compliance. No reasonable educator takes the position that schools are operated for the convenience of the teachers rather than the fullest development of the students, but the classroom martinet tacitly assumes that position.

In a summary of the research on teacher effectiveness, Sandefur (1970, p. 8) concluded that "good teachers tend to exhibit identifiable personal traits broadly characterized by warmth, a democratic attitude, affective awareness, and a personal concern for students." This finding tends to confirm what most teachers already sense. So why don't all teachers immediately adopt the traits Sandefur identifies? One might as well ask why a swimmer who wishes to break a record doesn't just stroke faster? One doesn't change his or her personality simply by an act of will any more than one might overcome physical limitations thereby. The personalities and related needs patterns of some teachers preclude employing a warm, personable teaching style. This is not to say that teachers cannot have high standards or be demanding and firm when these stances are appropriate; but there is no place in the classroom for teachers who are constitutionally unable or unwilling to establish relationships with their vulnerable, impressionable wards based on kindness, sensitivity, and caring. An Indian proverb poetically expresses this belief: Nothing is so strong as gentleness, nothing so gentle as real strength.

Myth 6

A good classroom is a quiet classroom.   The word *quiet* is one of the most frequently used words by teachers. All of us remember teachers using phrases such as "All right, let's get quiet," "Quiet, class," and "Billy, be quiet," or ones of similar meaning, such as "Let's keep it down," "You're too loud," and even "Shut up," to the extent that we've probably assumed it is not only a normal aspect of the classroom but inevitable. Having a quiet classroom is a condition evidently favored by teachers and administrators. And, of course, there are times in every classroom when quiet conditions are necessary: during a lecture, a test, or supervised study. However, when quiet becomes an end in itself, a method of control more so than a productive learning setting, it violates sound pedagogical principles.

Many effective learning activities in classrooms involve student noise. Some of these are small-group work, projects involving more than one student, and student tutoring. Even open discussions, which should be characterized by respect for each participant, may get noisy as students become passionate about their ideas. Fearful teachers tend to avoid these activities with the rationale that "the students can't handle them." More appropriately, the teacher's role when potentially noisy activities are conducted is to help students learn how to interact responsibly and to monitor the noise level. Effective teachers do this without resorting to constant repetitions of "be quiet" phrases. Overuse of these phrases, including threats of dire consequences, is symptomatic of a classroom where the teacher has failed to establish a climate in which orderly behavior is the student-accepted norm. While the tendency is to blame the students (after all, who is making the noise?), one must also consider why the classroom is dysfunctional. To the extent that boredom, resentment, or teacher style are proximate causes, then the teacher is culpable. Timmreck (1978), after conducting a study of causes of misbehavior, stated that "the causes of discipline difficulties are many and varied; and while the student and the classroom are strong contributors to the problems, the teacher is the major cause of classroom difficulties" (p. 16). So, while a good classroom may on appropriate occasion be a quiet classroom, quietness in and of itself is not a necessary feature of a good classroom. In fact, an unnaturally quiet classroom inhibits learning.

Myth 7

The behavior of teachers can be understood only in terms of their instructional role. The teacher's task, institutionally considered, is to promote student learning. Employing this frame of reference is often useful, but from a personal, human-needs view, teaching is the means a person has selected to satisfy certain basic psychological needs (e.g., for power, security, and self-esteem). Students' unwillingness to comply with teacher directions or expectations undermines the satisfactory fulfillment of those needs. This experience stimulates certain basic negative emotions (such as anger, frustration, and extreme self-consciousness) and behaviors (such as defensiveness and heightened aggressiveness). When acted out, survival instincts are manifested as retaliation or self-justification as the teacher attempts to restore his or her power, security, and self-esteem to a comfortable level. Dreikurs, Grunwald, and Pepper, commenting on teachers' discipline-related behavior, say:

> Many teachers find it extremely distasteful not to respond to the defiance of a power-drunk child. . . . The teacher is afraid for her prestige if she does not try to put the child in his place—regardless of how unsuccessful she may be in the effort. . . .
>
> The first obstacle (to) the solution of the conflict is the widespread assumption that one has to subdue the defiant child and make him respect adult demands. The second stumbling block is the teacher's personal involvement in a power conflict. If one can free himself from such considerations, one can see how amazingly simple it is to resist the power of a child who wants to force us into a struggle. (1971, pp. 40, 197)

Much of what we consider to be teaching behavior is learned rather than instinctive. Rinne has thoughtfully observed that "the natural behavior for many of us is to maintain the kind of control over other people that we feel most comfortable with" (1978, p. 6). Our normal human reactions to threat situations (i.e., achieving "the kind of control we are most comfortable with") are often not appropriate as a classroom technique. The fully rationally acting teacher is one who not only handles the academic aspects of teaching well but also uses his or her emotional energy constructively. Firm self-control and the use of appropriate group process techniques must take precedence over instinctively incited tendencies.

Myth 8

The behavior of students can be understood only in terms of their roles as learners. This myth is the counterpart of Myth 7. The institution predicates the student-as-learner and makes this the basis of curriculum design and learning activities. We assume that what we teach is good for students and that they should be interested and appreciative. In other words, the school program is designed for students as we would like them to be.

But what are students really like? Their preeminent concerns are not for studying and learning as such but for socializing, feeling secure, getting attention, and obtaining evidence of self-worth. In varying degrees, classrooms seem almost purposefully established to prevent students from achieving these basic needs; socializing is discouraged, anxiety often runs high, and individual attention is minimal in groups of 20 to 30. The accumulated effect of these conditions limits students who are neither academically inclined nor natural peer leaders from obtaining much evidence of self-worth.

Students are sometimes confronted with a dilemma, an academic Catch-22. We insist that they be quiet, attentive, polite, cooperative, and generally well behaved; yet, as a psychological imperative, they must pursue the needs they feel. Many students simply cannot simultaneously accomplish both within the constraints of the classroom. Misbehavior on their part is highly predictable. Schools, without due consideration, often establish unreasonable expectations and then punish students for not meeting them. Eventually and inevitably, students develop negative attitudes. The process feeds upon itself until, by the time students reach adolescence, school becomes virtually intolerable for them. Weiner has commented that

> . . . during the peak period of rebelliousness and struggle for maturity (i.e., adolescence), students are being forced into a mold that is scarcely changed from the relatively placid one of pre-adolescence. This is perhaps the source of the most intense current challenge to classroom discipline, and the educational system has barely begun to consider how to accommodate this stress. (1972, p. 29)

Ardrey has posed the plausible theory that every thinking creature has basic drives for identity, stimulation, and security. We add to this the drive for power. Failure to satisfy these drives results in anonymity, boredom, anxiety, and impotence, respectively (1970, p. 91). Our classrooms are likely to become places where these conditions are highly probable unless we make deliberate efforts to provide for students' basic drives. This, as much as anything, may be what good teaching is all about.

Myth 9

Punishment is educational. Students must be made to understand that they cannot misbehave with impunity. They should expect and accept the reasonable consequences of their misbehavior (e.g., being moved if they talk excessively to neighbors or being sent to a time-out site if they persist in disrupting the class). However, in spite of common acceptance, there is virtually no support for harsh punitive practices such as causing humiliation, using abusive language and threats, assigning extra homework, ordering a student to write a phrase repeatedly, scheduling impersonal detention, and inflicting physical pain. Although these techniques are often superficially effective in the immediate suppression of misbehavior and sometimes give the teacher a sense of relief, they nonetheless violate the principles of democracy, have negative long-range effects, and have no intrinsic educational value. They indicate clearly enough to the student that he or she is out of favor with the teacher, but they do not help the student understand the cause of his or her behavior, the standards on which that behavior is judged, or what alternatives are acceptable. Finally, teachers who use these tactics model aggressive behavior for students, and intimidation of the weaker by the stronger is perversely demonstrated to be a seemingly effective means to achieve one's ends.

It is very difficult for teachers who encounter unruly, vulgar, inconsiderate, under-motivated students on a regular basis not to believe they deserve harsh punishment, even when in dispassionate moments these teachers realize that such students need greater understanding and a compelling reason to change their values. Harsh punishment is so much a part of the tradition of teaching that it is difficult to conceive of education without it. It is a carryover from an age when schooling was conducted in a far more simplistic and naive fashion. But to continue to use harsh punishment is to take an anti-intellectual and inhumane approach to managing student behavior. In this purview it is unconscionable. As professional teachers, we should subscribe to the science of our profession and order our behavior accordingly.

Myth 10

A teacher has to use harsh punishment because problem students do not respond to less stern measures. There is no research or professionally endorsed principle to support the use of harsh punishment when students choose not to comply with the teacher's behavioral expectations. Harsh punishment is nowhere consistently related to improved student behavior. When students engage in misbehavior (actually, any behavior), they do so for a reason. The concern of educators is to deal with the causes of misbehavior (except in some cases of chronic behavior disorder) more so than simply to punish it. Teachers sometimes intuitively feel that misbehaving students should "get what they deserve," in the retaliatory sense; that is, they should be made to experience misery commensurate with the seriousness of their misbehavior. From a professional perspective, however, what students actually deserve is teachers' understanding of the causes of their behavior problems and efforts to remediate that behavior. We believe that students need to be made to face the consequences of their behavior, but that those consequences should be conceived in educational terms such that students' misbehavior ultimately has a useful learning outcome for them.

Some students come from homes in which harsh punishment, even abuse, occurs. Such students' experiences and culture do not prepare them to cope with the structure and social expectations of the school. These students attempt to satisfy their personal and social needs in a manner that is unacceptable in the classroom, and they do not respond to teachers' mild interventions to restore decorum. Teachers

search desperately for measures that are effective in dealing with serious misbehavior, and often they resort to harsh punishments, but this simply is not the solution to the problem. Difficult and frustrating as it often is, using compassion and understanding in accordance with the best human relations principles is the teacher's appropriate approach. School officials must realize that teachers, who are not behavioral psychologists and have limited time to deal with severe behavior problems, need support and sometimes relief when they confront these problems.

Myth 11

A teacher's response to misbehavior should always be directly related to the misbehavior.   Misbehavior takes myriad forms in the classroom and throughout the school. The advice that one should make the punishment fit the crime seems quite logical and acceptable initially. Implementing that advice for all the many kinds of misbehavior, however, would sorely tax the most imaginative teacher. What should the teacher do, for example, when a student cheats on a test? Tear up the test paper? But that is retaliation; it has nothing to do with why the student felt he or she had to resort to cheating. Lower the student's grade? That defeats the purpose of the test, which is meant to measure a student's level of achievement; further, it employs grades as a punishment, which is an indefensible use of grades. Preventing cheating in the first place is the preferred approach. However, if cheating is detected, the teacher will certainly want to talk privately with the student to examine the incident from whatever perspectives are pertinent. What are the reasonable consequences? Lower the student's citizenship grade? Not allow the student to be eligible to receive merit points? Notify parents? Assign the student to write an essay pertaining to the incident? Administer a retest over the same material? More than one consequence may be applicable. The special circumstances in each case, prior expectations that have been established, and the teacher's informed judgment will determine the most applicable intervention. The point is that there is no response uniquely pertinent to this and many other types of misbehavior.

Some kinds of misbehavior have reasonable and fairly straightforward consequences, such as moving the seat of a student who talks to his neighbor. But many of the punishments teachers commonly use are suppressive without being corrective and thus have no educational value. To ensure that notable discipline-related incidents result in valuable learning, all teachers should have as part of their general discipline plan a behavior remediation component that employs a systematic approach to help students understand their behavior and its consequences.

Myth 12

The teacher should not smile before Christmas.   Well-meaning veteran teachers often give this advice to new colleagues to help them survive those first difficult months. But the advice assumes an adversarial relationship; it emphasizes teacher authority over human relationships; and it assigns low priority to respect for student dignity and concern for developing self-discipline. The basis for student–teacher relationships in this setting is mutual fear rather than mutual care.

Pleasant and supportive teacher behavior is by no means an admission of weakness or a request for a truce. Surely a teacher can engage in these behaviors while maintaining resolve. And if establishing a warm, comfortable climate is to be managed, then smiles and humor will count for more than affected sternness. Redl speaks eloquently in favor of a sense of humor:

> [I]t is so obviously the most vital characteristic of a skillful handler of discipline problems or tough group situations that its possession must be among the prime requisites for the job. If we had to list with it the one personality trait more injurious to successful discipline, we would pick false dignity (i.e., aloofness and condescension) as our first choice. We know of no other personality trait that causes so much confusion, uproar, and mismanagement as this one. (1966, p. 303)

Myth 13

Students do not know how to behave with decorum.   Some teachers take responsibility for directing students' behavior on the assumption that students are not willing to do it themselves. Yet, given certain situations, youngsters of school age conduct themselves quite admirably (e.g., in church, at a friend's home, at a funeral, and at a formal dance). Young people have sufficient reason to behave with discretion in these settings. Students, therefore, seem not to need to be taught how to behave appropriately nearly so much as they need to be convinced that it really is in their best interest to conform to the teacher's and school's expectations.

Teachers have at least five kinds of power available to them for effecting student compliance: legitimate power—the power inherent in the position; reward power—the power to award meaningful praise or privilege; coercive power—the power to apply sanctions, restrictions, and punishment; referent (personality) power—the socially attractive quality of the teacher; and expert power—the competence of the teacher (French & Raven, 1960, p. 612). Very often we find teachers relying too heavily on the first three of these powers to induce compliance. Research has shown that the long-range effects in these cases are negative. But when teachers are able to use referent and expert power, producing a charismatic aura, students find it a sufficient reason to be compliant and cooperative.

Ideally, students should perceive their classes as places where they and the teacher are partners in achieving worthwhile personal, social, and academic outcomes. If students have this attitude, the likelihood that they will appear not to know how to behave will be minimal. In classrooms where students are kept busy, interested, and psychologically comfortable, there is little reason or propensity for misbehavior.

Myth 14

Students deliberately test the teacher to find out what they can get away with.   Students do test the teacher, but not, in most cases, deliberately. There is usually no conspiracy to gauge the teacher's tolerance. Students are not psychologically comfortable until they know the limits of their freedom in the classroom. For example, students have a strong social drive and will talk to their neighbors if they feel they can do this with impunity. But the teacher expects students to refrain from unsanctioned conversations. The students must determine which of the two forces is the stronger—the internal one for socializing or the external one imposed by the teacher or the classroom conditions.

To the extent that the teacher is inconsistent or the limits of tolerance remain unclear, students will seek clarification. This sort of testing occurs not necessarily because of any inherent mean-spiritedness in students but because, psychologically speaking, they have to know. The more clearly the teacher sets the limits and consequences, and the greater the credibility of the teacher in establishing them, the less need the students have to test.

Myth 15

To remain unprejudiced, teachers should not examine students' records.   The purpose of inspecting a student's record is to obtain information that will be helpful in guiding that student's learning. A well-informed teacher has a decided advantage in that regard. On the other hand, forming negative preconceptions from reading certain records without giving the student the benefit of the doubt is neither professional nor defensible.

Ideally, the teacher should have carefully developed information available dealing objectively, even clinically, with a student's behavior problem. Such information, including descriptions, diagnoses, and effective past treatment, would obviously be valuable. But any pertinent information used with discretion can be incorporated in the teacher's decision making regarding how best to help students whose past behavior has indicated that they have coping or adjustment problems. Needless ignorance is inexcusable unpreparedness, and it could set the stage for otherwise avoidable confrontations. The notion that "every student should start off in my class with a clean slate" has a superficial democratic appeal, but more careful consideration reveals the taint of anti-intellectualism.

Myth 16

Being consistent should take precedence over all other considerations. Consistency in discipline practices is held in high regard among teachers, and rightly so. Nevertheless, the context within which the teacher employs consistency must be considered. The thoughtless application of this guideline is not a virtue. Informed judgment is a higher priority.

The response a teacher makes to a particular sort of misbehavior should not necessarily be identical from instance to instance. To assume that all students should be treated similarly upon the commission of similar offenses is to overlook the unique circumstances—psychological, pedagogical, and social—that impel each student. The child who has a pathological needs pattern or a chronic adjustment problem must surely be treated differently from the student who is merely bored or has a temporary personal problem. Also, a reserved, dependent, usually compliant child will be affected differently by a particular control technique than an aggressive, independent, frequently boisterous child will be.

The humanist psychologist Carl Rogers emphasizes the importance of the interpersonal relationship between teachers and children. He has made a convincing argument for a person-centered rather than a rules-centered approach to classroom interaction. If teachers accept Rogers's viewpoint, they will give higher priority to the quality of the interaction that occurs than to controlling students as an end in itself.

Ralph Waldo Emerson noted that "a foolish consistency is the hobgoblin of little minds." He was not telling us to be inconsistent, but only that consistency needs to be reasoned—that it should be the outcome of a conscious decision.

Myth 17

Keeping students occupied will prevent misbehavior. A self-evident principle of effective discipline is that preventing misbehavior will relieve the teacher from having to cope with misbehavior. Some teachers assume, based on this principle, that any activity that occupies students will serve as a prevention measure. This leads to assigning busy work to students that is intended more as a means of occupying them than leading to purposeful learning outcomes. Much of the seat work assigned to students falls into this category, as do many homework assignments involving rote practice far beyond what is necessary to master the targeted skill or information.

Involvement in such assignments may accomplish its controlling intent for a while after the assignment is given. Compliant students will work diligently at the assignments, no matter how meaningless, and cause no behavior problems. But compliant students are not the ones who most need to be controlled. Students who are not suffi-ciently motivated by interest in the work or a desire to please the teacher will remain on task for a very short time. Their attention will turn to finding ways to relieve their boredom or vent their resentment. This might take the form of relatively harmless behavior such as reading a bootlegged comic book or just doodling on their paper, or it may result in more annoying acts such as pencil tapping or chair rocking. However, the socializing drive is irresistible for many, and surreptitious whispering, note passing, and game playing ensue. Monitoring and intervening increasingly occupy the teacher while productive learning diminishes. Even more serious behavior may occur as momentum builds, and the classroom is reduced to a travesty of learning.

The solution is at once simple and difficult: provide for students' motivation. Teachers who plan lessons with the students' interest and involvement in mind, who inject the class with contagious enthusiasm and a sense of humor, and who provide effective leadership can expect few discipline problems. Their teaching style and the nature of their learning activities are tacit preventive forces. They need not resort to the hidden agenda of busy work to accomplish their classroom management goals. Few teachers are blessed with the natural ability to teach in the style that has this inherently preventive dimension. For most it involves learning and using the endorsed principles of teaching in a competent fashion. When this happens, teaching is very satisfying; when it doesn't, teaching can be an onerous chore.

Myth 18

Students will comply if they are given sufficient incentive.   This myth results from a limited understanding of the nature of rewards. Many persons assume rewards are good by their very nature. What is not well understood is that rewards are of two types, extrinsic and intrinsic. Extrinsic rewards, or incentives, function as a means to an end for the teacher, but they are frequently viewed as ends in themselves by stu-dents. Students may study diligently to learn all the spelling words correctly to get an "A" on the test, yet they have little concern about correct spelling as it contributes to their communication skills. When the goal of learning is short-sighted, the learning itself is subverted by the transposition of ends and means.

Incentives such as grades, teacher praise, and classroom privileges serve a useful purpose by encouraging student involvement in learning activities, but they are never sufficient because they are not related directly to the learning itself. In fact, at the point where incentives are given prior to achievement, rewards take the form of bribes and are as such unconscionable. For teachers, a central concern should be to wean students from focus on incentives and to guide them toward valuing targeted learning as being pertinent and worthwhile for its own sake. The intrinsic reward of such meaningful learning that is internalized by the student enhances the perma-nency of that learning.

The application of the reward principle to behavior is similar to its application to learning. Teachers can provide incentives for desired behavior just as they can for desired learning, but if students comply only to receive the reward, they are essentially manipulating the teacher. Meanwhile, they are learning nothing of social responsibility and productive citizenship. At some point, students need to realize that the predisposition to responsible and considerate behavior is its own reward, and that self-discipline is an important trait to acquire.

Myth 19

Students will behave for the teacher if they consider the teacher to be one of the gang.   Human nature causes all of us to want to be accepted and admired by others. Teachers are no exception. In their classrooms, teachers want to be liked. However, being liked must take its position among our priorities. When being popular with students is an inordinately strong teacher need, as is often the case with new, unsure teachers, we are likely to find them doing things such as encouraging students to call them by their first name, promising no homework in the class, and inflating grades. However, by these very acts they undermine their authority and put themselves in the position of being compromised. Students will sense the vulnerability of the teacher and continue to extend the limits of their behavior beyond acceptable bounds. Control becomes an increasing problem for the teacher and eventually occupies much of classroom time.

Students need, and feel more comfortable with, a teacher who fulfills their image of a teacher—that is, a person in authority who provides strong leadership. When teachers have established credibility with their students, the students sense that the situation is under control and that the classroom is psychologically right. Classrooms should be purposeful but friendly places where, to paraphrase an old Texas line, the teacher is the teacher and the kids are glad of it.

Myth 20

All misbehavior should be dealt with swiftly.   As in several of the myths, enough truth is incorporated in this statement to make it attractive and, for some instances of misbehavior, applicable. When students misbehave in ways that are disruptive, they need to be made aware that the teacher is unwilling to tolerate it and that a penalty (reasonable consequence) may be incurred. Students who, for example, engage in unsanctioned talking, become rowdy, push another student in line, or use abusive profanity must be dealt with promptly in ways that are appropriate and reasonable to restore order. While one might speculate about what is a reasonable consequence in each instance, this is a matter that, in the final analysis, can be determined only situationally. Throughout this book, we take the position that teacher judgment, in accordance with professionally endorsed democratic and pedagogical standards, is the recommended basis for teacher action and that preconceived approaches by persons other than the involved teacher are presumptuous or suggestive at best.

The major problem with this myth is that it implies that all misbehavior occurs apart from other considerations—that is, that it can be isolated and then dealt with simplistically and summarily. As is acknowledged in the preceding paragraph, this is applicable for minor, transitory misbehavior. However, students also misbehave for reasons that are subtle and complex. Such misbehavior deserves the teacher's mature and informed judgment. Misbehavior may signal the student's need for help that can occur only through the sensitivity of a compassionate teacher. Teachers who default too quickly to expedient, largely self-serving, approaches forfeit the opportunity to help students refine their social and coping skills. The remediation that occurs following misbehavior may be the most important learning some students experience in a given class.

These 20 myths are appealing to teachers who encounter the mystique of discipline, along with the anti-intellectual climate it engenders, without sufficient preparation or personal resources. The more that a teacher subscribes to specious beliefs, the less likely is that teacher to enjoy a productive learning climate. The fact that the myths are acknowledged and can be categorized as a body of conventional wisdom is evidence of an anti-intellectual dimension that is entrenched in the schools. Weber (1980) comments that this results in a cookbook approach to the discipline aspect of teaching in which the ends justify the means. This is the antithesis of professional practice.

SUMMARY

In the most general sense, the term *discipline* subsumes all the factors and conditions in the classroom that affect students' behavior. However, to understand discipline and to deal with it in practical ways, it needs to be defined in more specific terms. There are at least three narrower meanings of the term.

First, when we speak of discipline we refer to those aspects of classroom climate that affect the quality of learning and the productivity of the students. In this aspect, discipline is embedded within instruction and the quality of social relationships that exist within the classroom. Orderly behavior is promoted when students are motivated by the learning activities and are secure in their interpersonal relationships.

Second, discipline refers to the students' inclination to comply with the teacher's expectations. Discipline in this context is reflexive; that is, students' behavior is in part predisposed by the personal and social needs of the students. These needs are expressed in a variety of ways by the students, individually and collectively, in response to the evolving conditions in the classroom.

Finally, when we speak of classroom discipline we refer to the structure and expectations the teacher imposes on the classroom to achieve a desirable level of decorum within the group and orderly behavior on the part of each student. For this aspect of discipline, we often use the term *classroom management*, for it includes the rules and regularities that are established to guide students' behavior, as well as the monitoring behaviors of the teacher.

As is evident from considering the definitions of discipline, it is a complex concept. Those who search for a single, practical, comprehensive definition of it will look in vain. In their need to understand it, however, educators tend to oversimplify it and skew its meaning to fit their purpose. In practice, this often results in discipline being limited in its scope to overt controlling and punishing behaviors. Thus, in this popular view, discipline has an undeserved negative connotation, and the practices based on this flawed view are negative as well.

In this chapter, the mystique of discipline was explained to help you understand that discipline, like other components of teaching, has a rational basis in pedagogical principles. However, in the case of discipline there are subtle, emotional, and even insidious aspects that tend to obscure the rational basis. As a result, teachers often abandon reason in favor of more visceral responses to discipline-related problems and allow the perception of mystique to pervade.

The myths of discipline were described at length to inform you of certain suspect beliefs and practices. With this awareness, you may more readily avoid the temptation to use questionable measures. The difficult task of selecting pedagogically affirmed measures that are most suitable for you still lies ahead as you read farther in this book and proceed in your development to become an effective teacher.

LOOKING AHEAD

The myths are intended to raise questions rather than answer them. The quest to become a reflective practitioner, one who can deal with discipline on a rational rather than mythical level, starts with building a foundation of knowledge that informs our judgments and practices. Chapter 2, "Preparing the Foundation for Practice," examines the elemental concepts and principles needed to start the quest for reflective practice. It discusses critical elements of the foundation, such as the relation of theory to practice, critical reflectivity, and the nature of the curriculum. From Chapter 2 we will begin to examine and interpret conditions that affect the behavior of students and the principles needed to understand and deal with the wide range of student behaviors that will occur in your classrooms. We will also give specific consideration to using foundational principles to prevent misbehavior before it occurs.

❖ REFLECTIVE ACTIVITIES

1. Now that you have read the 20 myths of discipline, and perhaps have added some of your own, which of them have you unconsciously or unwittingly subscribed to? In general, how will your approach to thinking about discipline change based on the understandings you have acquired about the myths?
2. As you begin to think about developing an informed approach to classroom discipline, what is likely to be the bedrock principle—the most fundamental proposition—upon which your approach is built? As you proceed in your development, be conscious of whether your position changes.

❖ REFERENCES

Ardrey, R. (1970). *The social contract.* New York: Atheneum.

Brophy, J., & Rohrkemper, M. (1981). The influence of problem ownership on teacher perceptions. *Journal of Educational Psychology, 73*(3), 295–311.

Dreikurs, R., Grunwald, B., & Pepper, C. (1971). *Maintaining sanity in the classroom: Illustrated teaching techniques.* New York: Harper and Row.

French, J., & Raven, B. (1960). The bases of social power. In D. Cartwright & A. Zander (Eds.), *Group dynamics: Research and theory* (2nd ed.). Evanston, IL: Row Peterson.

Johns, F., & MacNaughton, R. (1990). Spare the rod: A continuing controversy. *The Clearing House, 63*(9), 388–392.

Kindsvatter, R., & Levine, M. (1980). The myths of discipline. *Phi Delta Kappan, 61*(10), 690–693.

Kindsvatter, R., & McLaughlin, M. (1985). Discipline mystique and discipline practice. *The Clearing House, 58*(9), 403–407.

Levine, M. (1979). Are teachers becoming more human? *Phi Delta Kappan, 59*(5), 353–354.

Raywid, M. (1976). The democratic classroom: Mistake or misnomer? *Theory into Practice, 15*(1), 37–46.

Redl, F. (1966). *When we deal with children.* New York: Free Press.

Rinne, C. (1978, August). Teaching: The unnatural act. *Thresholds in Education,* p. 3.

Sandefur, J. (1970). *The evaluation of teacher education graduates.* Washington, DC: American Association of Teacher Education.

Timmreck, T. (1978). Will the real cause of classroom discipline problems please stand up! *The Journal of School Health, 48*(8), 491–497.

Weber, W. (1980). Classroom management. In J. Cooper (Ed.), *Classroom teaching skills* (2nd ed.). Lexington, MA: D. C. Heath.

Weiner, D. (1972). *Classroom management and discipline.* Itasca, IL: F. E. Peacock.

Preparing the Foundation for Practice

❖ Focus Questions

1. When we think of discipline, what knowledge are we using to inform what we do? What is your current foundation for thinking about discipline?

2. What does it mean to use good judgment? What is needed for us to make the best judgments possible?

3. We often separate theory from practice. How can good theory affect practice?

4. What does it mean to be critically reflective, and how does being so affect our view of how and why we discipline our students?

5. In what ways are the activities of discipline part of the curriculum? What role does the hidden curriculum play in discipline and learning?

6. How does a reflective practitioner approach discipline, and what is needed to become a reflective practitioner?

PRAXIS AND PRAGMATISM

Before anything of merit can be built, a foundation needs to be constructed that will support it. This idea is equally true of buildings, sports teams, arguments, political campaigns, and, most relative to us, our actions as educators. Indeed, a good knowledge base has the power to give us clear understandings and can serve us in a variety of situations. Historically, teachers have tended to see discipline actions as pragmatic means for controlling students who disrupt the teacher's desired activities. But rarely, if ever, has the foundation for their pragmatism been anything more than the thought that if a discipline action works, it is good. In this sense, we would argue that most acts of discipline are vulgar pragmatisms (Cherryholmes, 1988) in that they are not based on a great deal of rational thought or reasoned value judgments.

There is a good foundation for understanding discipline as both practical and thoughtful. You can begin to understand the purpose of developing a foundation for practice by recognizing that the term **pragmatism** relates to doing the practical and remembering the idea of **praxis** as discussed in the Preface. The spirit of praxis embodies the idea of informed, thoughtful practice (knowing and understanding clearly what we are doing and why we are doing it), but what we do must also be practical. Therefore, through the consideration and construction of a foundation for practice we are developing activities of discipline that are considered critical pragmatisms—they are eminently practical and based in rational, thoughtful understanding.

THE POWER OF A SOUND KNOWLEDGE BASE

As we consider our activities of teaching and discipline, we must recognize the nature of the foundation from which we act. This means coming to grips with the knowledge base we use to determine what we do, when we do it, and why we do it as we work to control, intervene in, encourage, and prevent particular student behaviors.

The more limited our knowledge base, the more limited we are in our choices and options for discipline and management of our classrooms. When we act from the standpoint of limited understanding, our conduct may indeed be shaky. Foundational knowledge empowers us, providing sufficient understanding for us to act in ways that benefit our students. Thus we can transform our students positively rather than alienate them from opportunities to be thoughtful and ethical. The foundations of **democratic discipline** give us the means to understand and arrive at our purposes for discipline. It is like planning a vacation—the more knowledge we have of various places to go, the greater the number of choices we have. Likewise, the more knowledge we have, the more efficiently and effectively we can choose and plan the route to our chosen destination.

KNOWLEDGE AND JUDGMENT

No one doubts the proposition that the more knowledge we have about something, the more power we have in dealing with that "something." However, we often give scant consideration to the idea that most knowledge is actually theoretical knowledge. Very simply put, theoretical knowledge is the kind we use to deal with and manage the uncertainties we face in life. The more power and utility the knowledge has, the better able we are to deal appropriately, effectively, and credibly with uncertainties and problems.

While we may be uncertain about some things such as a batting average or who wrote the Declaration of Independence, these are not problematic because they are questions of fact that can be looked up and verified. However, when we pause to think about most of the decisions and actions we have to make in life, we quickly realize that rarely can we be 100% certain about them.

To deal as effectively as possible with the uncertainties we must face, we engage in making *judgment calls*. Green (1971) explains that the role of judgment "is to get optimum results under less than optimum conditions or on grounds which are less than decisive." A good foundation of knowledge is inexorably connected to good judgment because knowledge is the point around which our judgments turn. The more extensive our foundational knowledge, the more informed we are and the more likely we are to recognize and achieve optimum results from our actions. Good foundational knowledge also enhances the credibility of our actions because it enables us to articulate a rational and reasonable basis for our judgments and their subsequent actions. In sum, the quality and breadth of our repertoire of knowledge determines our ability to know our purpose, inform our judgments, and give credibility to our actions.

THEORY AND PRACTICE

Knowledge is related to judgment as theory is to practice. Theory informs practice through the use of good judgment. Theory without use is intellectual elitism; action without examined theory is mindlessness. In other words, knowledge is related to judgment as theory is related to practice, and theory informs practice through the use of good judgment. Good theoretical knowledge is a foundation that has value and power in developing a clear sense of purpose, interpreting classroom events, recognizing the choices of action we have, selecting the most appropriate alternative, and applying the actions we must take as teachers to manage classes and discipline stu-

dents. When we work from a solid foundation of theoretical knowledge, we achieve informed practice, or praxis.

In reading this book you should begin to understand and value an expanded theoretical foundation to the practice of classroom management and discipline. Further, understanding the basic idea of praxis is essential in using this book effectively. But applying praxis means more than simply acquiring and substituting a knowledge base different from the traditional one and using it to inform practice. It also requires a critically reflective stance toward our knowledge and actions. Reflectivity addresses our willingness to question and critique what we are doing and why we are doing it (purpose, or desired ends), as well as how we are doing it (means). For example, paddling a student for being late to class may achieve the ends of getting the student to class on time. However, paddling as a means to this end is also easily seen as inappropriate, even offensive.

CRITICAL REFLECTIVITY

Reflectivity represents part of the foundation for practice. Essentially, to be reflective means to be able to use good judgment by carefully thinking about all possible aspects of a given decision. A variety of terms is used to describe what is generally meant by reflectivity: *critical thinking, informed judgment, critical reflectivity, thinking skills, scientific method,* and *reflective thinking.* Likewise, definitions vary among authors and disci-

plines. For our purposes, we will use the term **critical reflectivity**. Much of the way we use the term is grounded in the work of John Dewey (1933, 1938). Although Dewey used the term *reflective thinking,* the term *critical reflectivity* better serves today's audiences in that it signifies the role that critique and criticism play in the reflective process.

Generally, people are more used to hearing the term *critical thinking,* which is a concept that represents a very wide spectrum of theories and views of what is good thinking. Being critically reflective means directing our thinking toward developing a keenly conscious awareness regarding ourselves. A critically reflective individual persistently engages in constructive questioning of the validity of knowledge and beliefs and the reliability of judgments and claims. These persistent engagements must be directed at what we personally believe and at what we are told by others. Critique gives us a better sense of the warrantability of various principles, theories, and ideas in terms of the ends they claim to serve. The myths of discipline discussed in Chapter 1 represent professional beliefs that, through critique, are exposed as poor principles for disciplinary judgments.

On a similar note, reflective practitioners are critically reflective in the sense that they recognize and accept the uncertainties of practice. In many ways, classroom management in general and discipline in particular are both conducted within a certain context of uncertainty. The reflective practitioner recognizes that there are no master narratives or policies that can tell us what to do in all cases. Indeed, it is the ability to use judgment in instances of uncertainty that separates the professional from the technician; to use professional judgment is to understand the role of being a professional. In all cases, the actions of a critically reflective individual are thoughtfully considered in light of theory and practice both before and after the actions we take.

We are concerned that you become a critically reflective practitioner and, in turn, educate your students to become critically reflective citizens of our democracy (in Chapter 5 you will see how important critical reflectivity is to the survival of our democracy). Let's consider some of the more basic elements of the concept of critical reflectivity.

Critical reflectivity is a process of thinking that stands apart from ordinary thinking. It concerns our willingness to be intellectually aggressive in searching for truth and tentative in the beliefs we hold. It also holds us to being rational in our analysis and application of logic and values. Being reflective stands in opposition to being superstitious or blindly accepting. At the outset, critical reflectivity is an attitude, a disposition toward seeking to understand the meaning and ramifications of ideas and actions. In the words of Dewey (1933, p. 17), critical reflectivity serves to convert "action that is merely appetitive, blind, and impulsive into intelligent action."

Critical reflectivity is neither a mechanical process nor a set of steps and phases that one can use to be guaranteed of doing the right thing at the right time. The goal of praxis is to be able to take actions that are both practical and intelligent. Therefore, we are searching for pragmatic actions.

However, as we build a foundation for practical or pragmatic solutions, it is important to distinguish between vulgar and critical pragmatisms (Cherryholmes, 1988). *Vulgar pragmatisms* are actions that are practical only in the sense that they are the most expeditious means to achieve what we feel is practical. The vulgar pragmatism results from using knowledge that is not based in good evidence or informed theory, from not thinking through the consequences of our actions, and from being unaware of or ignoring the values being acted upon. The vulgar pragmatism is very seductive. Amid the uncertainty and pressure of teaching we often find it very coherent to take actions that seem to be sound and practical but that are really nothing more than part of the path of least resistance. When you rely on vulgar pragmatism, the seemingly practical action you take is blind to meanings and ramifications, uninformed and without the application of critical thought.

For example, when a student is seen nodding off during the morning math lesson it is often the inclination of the teacher to embarrass or criticize the student in a very direct manner in front of the group. The action certainly serves as a reminder to all that the teacher is the one in a power position. However, it fails entirely to address any consideration of the reasons for the student's action, which may well be caused by illness or home problems. If the teacher were to realize that the heat had been shut off at the student's home and the student was up most of the night trying to keep warm, a very different discipline action might have been taken. Instead of using the vulgar pragmatism, a critical pragmatism would have a very different impact.

Praxis in our sense of the word represents taking actions that represent the critical pragmatism. Critical pragmatism in terms of discipline results from having a sound **professional knowledge base** and giving significant thoughtful consideration to the particular context and ramifications of the actions. Critical reflectivity not only asks us to consider the widest range of possibilities but also demands that we consider the values that motivate the student as well as the teacher.

Critical reflectivity also requires that we examine and critique any knowledge base we are using to make decisions and take actions, whether our ideas come from the teachers' lounge or scholarly books. A major part of acquiring intellectual ownership of the foundational knowledge base that undergirds your classroom actions comes from having thought through the origins, meanings, values, and implications of that knowledge base. In this sense, ownership means that the knowledge base dwells within you and that you are as conscious of its strengths as you are of its weaknesses.

Education is the only profession in which 12 years of observation precede our taking our first professional education course. Because we have attended school, we have observed and learned a great deal about what is done traditionally by teachers in the realm of discipline. From our observation of the activities of discipline, we tend to develop an implicit knowledge base that we see as credible because we have experienced it. As a result, we have difficulty considering that this knowledge base may not be the most appropriate one.

CONVENTIONAL WISDOM

To further understand praxis and the spirit of critical reflection, you should question and critique the body of professional teaching knowledge often referred to as conventional wisdom, or craft knowledge. Indeed, the myths you encountered in Chapter 1 reflect the questionable knowledge base very often used for interpreting and acting upon discipline problems. The conventional wisdom of the workplace, the teaching culture, represents assumptions about teachers and students and means and ends that, while dearly held by many practitioners, afford the conscientious teacher a dubious foundation for interpretation and well-reasoned ethical action.

As you will discover, we are deeply concerned with empowerment of both teachers and students. We lament that conscientious teachers are not given the foundation needed to allow them to envision the opportunities for thoughtful interpretation and well-reasoned action. There is a significant difference between acting from the knowledge base of conventional wisdom and acting from the knowledge base suggested herein. Conventional wisdom gives us only a narrow understanding of the issues, choices, and effects of securing an orderly classroom; our skills are thus limited. Working from a more grounded knowledge base, one that has broader scope and entertains the widest possible understandings, affords us greater skill in constructing meaningful and empowering environments for our students. The more we know about discipline, the better able we are to deal reasonably, selectively, and effectively with discipline-related problems and practice and, ultimately, the formation of human character that is appropriate to democratic citizenship.

Teaching in general and discipline in particular have been decidedly nonintellectual, even anti-intellectual at times. By contrast, we are asking you to consider an intellectual approach to the conduct of classroom management and discipline. Teachers need to be educated in a broad repertoire of knowledge and skills about teacher–student behavior in lieu of relying on cookbook-type recipes, how-to lists, and the myths and fictions often purveyed in the teachers' lounge. Our implicit purpose is to empower you by helping you prepare for intellectual ownership of a knowledge base that will broaden the realm of possible understanding and widen the range of decision latitude you can invoke in dealing with the significant issues of school and classroom discipline.

Our explicit purpose is to help you prepare a foundation of knowledge that will facilitate the activities of discipline as well as the activities of citizenship. We will answer such questions as how does conventional wisdom fall short in empowering teachers? How is discipline embedded in instruction? How do social forces and factors affect student attitudes? How does dominant ideology shape expectations? How do teachers' belief systems shape discipline actions? And how does popular culture contribute to tensions between teachers and students?

One of the major problems with conventional wisdom as the knowledge base for discipline is the strong tendency to see discipline in virtual isolation from the other activities of teaching and schooling. When the foundation of discipline is disassociated from other forces and factors such as those mentioned earlier, the primary emergent principle guiding the teacher is adversarial and often very simplistic. The student is seen as a law breaker who should be punished without any consideration of contributing factors that may well lie beyond the student's control.

For example, from the standpoint of instruction, consider teachers and the learning activities they design to engage their students. What we do instructionally as teachers frames what we interpret as discipline problems, as well as how the students grow to learn about power, authority, and rule breaking as they act in school and society. Too often, rules, expectations, and discipline are used without considering what the students are learning implicitly from them.

Indeed, much of the conventional wisdom of the workplace operates without serious thought about the formative effects that our discipline-related activities have upon the ethical character of our students. In addition, it usually operates without thoughtful consideration of the role schooling plays in developing the values and attitudes that the students will hold and act on as future community members and citizens. Although there is virtually a national preoccupation with student performance in school in terms of academics and behavior, we rarely make the connection that schools affect how students act as citizens. Our knowledge base needs to inform us about how and what students learn from the discipline activities that help or hinder behavior in school and shape their future behavior as citizens in the American democracy.

As discussed in Chapter 1, discipline is too often narrowly conceptualized, encompassing little more than a defense against disruption of teaching plans. In this sense, discipline and related classroom strategies are too often reactive and preventative rather than proactive and formative. We often fail to consider that discipline activities can be perceived other than as negatives, as things teachers do to suppress behaviors they dislike or find disruptive. We will reconceptualize how discipline can be considered as positives embedded within the climate and activities of teaching as well as schooling in general.

Reconceptualizing discipline and classroom management as they shape both the teacher and students ultimately makes the teacher's work easier. We will deal with topics that are rarely given much importance in general discussions of teaching and schooling but are foundational to grasping a keen understanding of the discipline process and outcome. We will deal with concepts ranging from mythology and ideology to popular culture and multiculturalism to help you grasp the complexity of reconceptualizing why students behave as they do. Our argument is simple: To be most effective as educators, we must have a clear and cogent understanding of what shapes student behavior and what choices are possible before we can deal thoughtfully, ethically, and intelligently with that behavior. We must interpret our students' actions thoughtfully before we can act appropriately.

Some words of warning may be in order. Having a good knowledge base does not mean simply having access to recipes or formulas for quick success in any situation. You must also be willing to be reflective, allowing yourself to discover that there are many possibilities and choices. Discovering that you have choices in the performance of discipline activities and understanding what those choices mean ethically, democratically, and practically distinguishes what it means to be a reflective practitioner, a true professional. Understanding and being able to use principles of democratic discipline will facilitate your making educationally sound choices in teaching, facilitate your students' learning, and ultimately prepare them for thoughtful participation in democratic society.

Further, while the teacher may have a good grasp of the knowledge base of discipline, there is no guarantee of resoundingly effective classroom management. To be an optimally effective teacher, you must have leadership ability, good interpersonal skills, and an ethical character. These factors will affect students' acceptance and compliance with teacher expectations.

CURRICULUM

Understanding the notion of curriculum is part of the foundation needed to operationalize effective, democratic discipline. A convenient, simple, working definition of the term **curriculum** is "what the students have the opportunity to learn" (McCutcheon, 1995). Given this definition, we can more easily discuss the wide range of things that students learn (or don't learn) based on their experience of going to school. We can also examine things that are conspicuously absent from their school experience.

Viewed in this way, curriculum refers to much more than what we formally plan to teach. Everything we do as teachers has the potential to serve as an opportunity for students to learn something. Understanding the rudimentary elements of curriculum allows us to more easily discuss the factors that have direct formative effects on what students learn and do not learn. As beginning teachers we are often so preoccupied with teaching our subject material that we fail to realize that students can learn a great deal from the things we model, say, and value. Even our attitude represents an opportunity for students to learn.

We will examine three specific aspects of the overall curriculum: the overt curriculum, the hidden curriculum, and the null curriculum.

The Overt Curriculum

The **overt curriculum** refers to that aspect of the curriculum that is formally stated. It includes material in textbooks, lesson plans, class materials, student codes, courses of study, and workbooks. The content of the overt curriculum refers to what we intend students to learn; it exists whether or not students actually do learn them. If we were to list everything we formally provide students an opportunity to learn, we would have a list of the overt curriculum. Obvious examples of the overt curriculum are such things as $2 + 2 = 4$; Washington, D.C., is the capital of the United States; and $y = mx + b$.

The Hidden Curriculum

The **hidden curriculum** consists of what students have the opportunity to learn but what is not formally stated or necessarily intended to be taught. Everything from learning how to act in class to learning social behaviors falls within the hidden curriculum. For example, our teachers do not formally teach us whom to associate with, how to ask for a date, or how to cheat on an objective test. However, we learn how to play the classroom game and what we can and cannot get away with through the opportunities we experience in going to school. Indeed, when we consider all that we learned in school that was not part of the formal instructional agenda, we begin to see how powerful and extensive is the hidden curriculum. As we shall learn in coming chapters, the formative effect of the hidden curriculum in shaping our character and interactions with others is very powerful.

Much of what students learn through the hidden curriculum is contributed by teachers in the conduct of their classrooms. This includes such things as how we interact with our students, what we say and how we say it, and what attitudes and behaviors we reward and punish as well as how we reward and punish.

The power of the hidden curriculum must not be underestimated. A significant repertoire of values, attitudes, and beliefs is rather unconsciously learned through our experience of the hidden curriculum. Some of these are reinforced at home and in the neighborhood, but most of them are solidified through our schooling experiences. As we shall see in subsequent chapters and particularly in Chapter 5, our vision and beliefs about authority, law, power, position, and citizenship are significantly shaped through the hidden curriculum.

The Null Curriculum

The **null curriculum** is much less obvious to us than the hidden and the overt curricula. It represents that aspect of the curriculum where opportunity to learn something is denied. Put another way, the null curriculum represents the lack of opportunity to learn significant things; it consists of things that are conspicuous by their absence.

Historically, most of the elements of the hidden curriculum were considered taboo—socially unacceptable to be discussed in polite company. For many years such topics as pregnancy, venereal disease, sexuality, and death were considered too inappropriate and offensive to be taught, discussed, or even mentioned in school. Unlike the hidden curriculum, the absence of any formal teaching along with the lack of perceived student need for knowing about these issues precluded any opportunity for students to learn about them in school.

AIDS education is a classic example of an issue once embedded in the null curriculum. The onset of the AIDS epidemic coupled with its association with homosexuality (a topic usually relegated to the null curriculum) generated a homophobic response from many school authorities and policymakers. As a result, the subject, although significant for everyone, was not considered appropriate for the overt curriculum. However, when former surgeon general C. Everett Koop completed his campaign to create public awareness about AIDS, in many schools the topic moved from the null curriculum into the overt curriculum.

Understanding these aspects of the curriculum serves as part of the foundation for interpreting the actions of teachers and students. As Figure 2.1 shows, the rela-

Figure 2.1

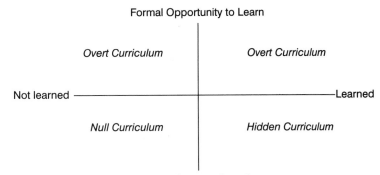

tionships between what we formally claim to teach and what students do or do not have the opportunity to learn play out in different settings. It is important to recognize that the null curriculum quadrant represents significant items that the student has no opportunity to experience or learn about.

BUILDING TOWARD PRINCIPLED ACTION

The last important consideration in recognizing what it means to build a solid foundation for action is understanding the role of guiding principles. Knowledge for knowledge's sake is a dead end both intellectually and practically. Praxis, on the other hand, assumes foundational knowledge to be a repertoire of valuable intellectual tools powered by our willingness to be reflective.

Applying praxis means that we make choices and take actions that are guided by very consciously held principles, which emerge from intellectual activity and practice. Good working principles for discipline are born from the idealism and reality of a powerful and usable knowledge base. Through reflectivity they are refined and particularized as we experience the activities of teaching and engage in the lives of our students.

The principles we work with define the nature of our professional intellectual and ethical character. When we achieve intellectual ownership of a fluid knowledge base and adopt a critically reflective stance, we come to value principled thought and action as our sense of project or mission. But it is important to understand that principles guide us rather than direct us. In other words, our goal is still informed, principled action, not simply the formation of principles as ends in themselves. Reflective practitioners stop short of absolute and strict adherence to principle. They are neither zealots nor preachers of morality but caring human beings who recognize that knowledge must be held tentatively and gently in the service of students. Our principles must always work to frame our own growth and development as educators and ultimately to facilitate the transformation of our students into thoughtful, democratic citizens.

SUMMARY

To be a critically reflective teacher, a true professional, your actions in the classroom must be the result of the exercise of reflective judgments grounded in appropriate theory. Critically reflective teachers understand the nature of curriculum, instruction, and discipline as contributing to the formative development of their students.

Teachers whose professional goal is praxis are willing to critically examine all knowledge about teaching in general and discipline in particular. Professionals who use critical pragmatism are willing to recognize the inadequacies of conventional wisdom (craft knowledge). By acquiring and implementing an expansive professional knowledge base we are better able to engage in discipline activities for the betterment of character and the formation of citizenship in a democratic society. The challenge for new professional educators is to service the needs of a democratic citizenry as well as the academic needs of students by using a solid foundation of professional knowledge in their teaching activities.

LOOKING AHEAD

We have examined the fundamental elements of the foundation for reflective practice. We now need to understand the social mechanisms that form our belief systems and the belief systems of our students. Chapter 3 will discuss these mechanisms as well as power relations between teacher and student, the role of the hidden curriculum, and the problem of cultural reproduction as it affects our behaviors in and out of school. The chapter will help you develop a professional sense of how schools operate traditionally and how you can present democratic ideals in your activities with students.

❖ REFLECTIVE ACTIVITIES

1. How does understanding the notions of praxis, theory, knowledge base, conventional wisdom, and critical reflectivity affect the traditional view of what it means to be a teacher? How have these ideas changed your view of yourself as a teacher?
2. Discuss how judgment relates to reflective practice. How is judgment involved in connecting theory to practice?

3. Examine your own experiences and those of your friends in elementary and high school. What has been the impact of the hidden curriculum in shaping what you have come to believe? What has been the impact of the null curriculum?

❖ REFERENCES

Cherryholmes, C. H. (1988). *Power and criticism: Poststructural investigations in education.* New York: Teachers College Press.

Dewey, J. (1933). *How we think.* Lexington, MA: D. C. Heath.

Dewey, J. (1938). *Logic: The theory of inquiry.* New York: Holt, Rinehart, and Winston.

Green, T. (1971). *The activities of teaching.* New York: McGraw Hill.

McCutcheon, G. (1995). *Developing the curriculum.* White Plains, NY: Longman.

Chapter 3

The Role of Educational Philosophy and Ideology in Discipline

❖ Focus Questions

1. What is empowerment, and how does it differ from traditional teaching and schooling?
2. What is ideology, and how does it relate to philosophy?
3. What is problematic in accepting ideology as a basis for making judgments?
4. What does it mean to have our actions grounded?
5. Why is conventional wisdom inadequate for reflective practitioners?
6. How does the dominant ideology and the goal of cultural reproduction conflict with education for democracy?
7. What are some of the most important considerations one must address in working to become a reflective practitioner?

This chapter describes the relationship between the dominant ideology of our society and educational philosophy as they relate to how we manage classrooms and deal with students who misbehave. Our intent is to show how the outcomes of schooling (i.e., the truth structures that students learn for making sense of their world) are dependent on what teachers portray in their actions toward students.

Educational philosophy and ideology relate to how and what we see as truth, or commonsense realities, about students and classrooms. As a teacher, you should understand the source and nature of the mystique and myths of discipline and the way these notions are connected to the general beliefs of the larger society. When you do not critically examine the roots of disciplinary activities, you are forced to rely on traditional conventions of practice instead of well-thought-out principles consistent with education in a democratic society. As you shall see, reliance on convention places conservative limits on understanding and acting in conscious, purposeful ways.

EMPOWERMENT

The idea of **empowerment** is thematic in this book. Being empowered means having the breadth and depth of knowledge to think and act independently of convention and others' opinions. It refers to being educated in the power of thought (Dewey, 1933) and to having experience in the knowledge structures that yield the most warranted judgments and decisions. We are empowered when we can consider principles, concepts, and ideas in a reflective manner to deal with the exigencies of our lives. Empowerment in this sense is synonymous with liberation, emancipation, and freedom; it allows us to act as intentional, moral, and thoughtful human beings. Teachers must be empowered themselves before they can empower their students.

Teachers who are empowered know why they do what they do. They have a solid sense of purpose embodied in principled actions aimed at empowering their students. Such teachers can perceive and enjoin a less restrained world of greater possibilities than those who blindly adhere to convention. As we examine the basis for tradition and convention in classroom management activities, we are concerned with developing a sharper understanding of the difference between simply knowing how to do something because it's supposed to be done that way and knowing why something is to be done. Likewise for our students, we will begin to see the difference between their blindly behaving the way the teacher wants and behaving appropriately because they know why the behavior is desirable.

Many questions need to be asked if we are to have a more complete and informed understanding of our behavior as classroom managers and disciplinarians. Where do the ideas that govern what we do in classrooms come from? What is the basis of the ideas we study in our education courses? What is the source of the mechanisms of convention that we use in teaching and schooling? How are the myths discussed in Chapter 1 generated, what is their purpose, and how do they affect students?

In answering such questions we need to come to grips with the concepts of educational philosophy and ideology, which are not as distant from classroom practices as they may seem. There is a much stronger link between these concepts and the conventions and myths of teaching than you may believe. We want you to consider these links and the subtle processes by which they are related to practice.

EDUCATIONAL PHILOSOPHY AND IDEOLOGY

Educational philosophy and ideology may be seen as constructs that represent a set of beliefs, or assumed truths, about how the world operates. As human beings in general and teachers in particular, we are driven to make sense of experience because without meaning we feel very unsettled. We invoke our conceptions of truth to make sense of what we experience. We also use these beliefs as guides and explanations for the actions we take.

Within both educational philosophy and ideology there exist content and function. As systems, they contain the substance of values, rules, interpretations, and beliefs (Cherryholmes, 1988) that guide, direct, and frame actions, ideas, behavior, and positions. We use ideology and educational philosophy in three ways: to make meaning (interpret), to make choices (action), and to provide accountability (explain) for what we do. In the classroom discipline sense, we constantly are making interpretations of student behavior and taking actions based on the interpretations.

For the sake of this discussion, we can consider **ideology** the dominant lens or belief system of the society (Pratte, 1983). We can consider **educational philosophy** as a set of ideological elements *that have been formalized and subjected to public discourse* as a generalized system of assumptions and principles that classify, describe, or prescribe human action. The fundamental difference between the two is found in the degree of conscious formality one has about the assumptions and values of the belief system and the degree to which the beliefs are a product of sound judgments made from the tenets of the belief system. However, the distinction between the two may be without significant difference *if one holds a personal and educational philosophy that has not been reflectively derived.* Although the particular educational practices of the teacher may have some historical roots in educational philosophy, rarely does the teacher act according to a reflectively developed set of philosophical principles.

To examine the origin of the myths relating to discipline practices, we will focus on ideology, which is more socially and educationally pervasive than educational philosophy. Educational philosophy might be considered an informal but broadly conceived form of ideology that embodies and legitimizes the day-to-day operating principles of conventional wisdom. This view is not intended to demean or deny the various educational philosophies that have been formally proposed, widely debated, and thoughtfully studied in educational foundations. Certainly, works ranging from Plato and Aristotle, through Comenius and Rousseau, to Skinner and Dewey represent formal and articulate forms of educational philosophy. However, these models are rarely, if ever, held dearly by the typical classroom teachers of American schools. In practice, teachers will articulate personal philosophies of education that are far more related to ideology than to any formal scheme of philosophy as defined by the great educational philosophers throughout our history.

ORIGIN OF THE MYTHS OF DISCIPLINE

Ideology represents rather unconsciously held assumptions about how the world operates—about human nature, political systems, economic conditions, and social relations. In many ways, ideological beliefs are experienced by us as commonsense truths that exist simply as matters of fact or rules to follow. Ideology serves us as a vehicle for making sense of the information, behavior, and events that bombard us every day.

More specifically, much of what we do in classrooms regarding student behavior is based on unexamined assumptions and rules—myths and fictions. We undeniably live in a world of contradictory information and mixed messages where, as Lather (1991) observes, ideology is a means of coping for those who cannot "stop making sense."[1] But, for us as teachers, it is not enough to just make sense of it all; we must come to know how defensible and reasonable that sense is.

Historically, teachers' views of their roles, students, subject matter, curriculum, instruction, and, especially, discipline have been deeply anchored in the dominant ideology of the time. Much of what we articulate as personal educational philosophy is traceable to the social and political ethos of the time—from the "do your own thing" view of the 1960s and 1970s to the "law and order" view of the 1980s and 1990s. While recognizing a blurring of distinctions between personal educational philosophy and ideology, we must understand how the dominant views of our society permeate the expectations, interpretations, and actions we take as teachers regarding the type of classroom management that is operationalized in the schools.

Therefore, to be effective teachers and to understand our interactions with students, we need to realize that our activities as teachers are shaped by our confidence in the validity of how we see the world. As was exposed in Chapter 1, myths often take on a life of their own as they frame our classroom actions. We begin to see these myths as teaching and schooling realities that emerge as guiding ideas for our interpretation of events and for the actions we take with regard to those events.

We tend to accept the legitimacy of these guiding ideas without question because they are so-called truths we have seen and experienced since kindergarten. The myths represent a sort of pedagogical common sense that has become known as the conventional wisdom of the teaching profession. Veteran teachers will often admonish field experience students and student teachers by saying, "You'll learn what teaching is *really* all about here in the trenches, not in those irrelevant education classes." While we applaud those particular veteran teachers in their intent to help beginners, we take strong exception to those who promote an anti-intellectual attitude toward professional thinking and conduct.

EMPOWERING TEACHERS

Teacher induction, your initiation into the profession, is often a time when you learn the myths and fictions as the only reality for guiding you to survive as a teacher. Our purpose herein is to empower you to have a clearly focused and defensible sense of purpose in your actions. You should be able to sensibly interpret the behavior of students and then give greater, more thoughtful consideration to the activities of discipline you choose; being empowered, you will be able to take appropriate action and be reasonable and ethical in your conduct. In your management of discipline, we

---

[1] Lather's reference is to the title of rock singer David Byrne's video/album, "Stop Making Sense." The lyrics are a postmodern commentary on the conditions and ironies of living in a postmodern world.

want you to consider the importance of moving from unconscious reliance on convention to informed, purposeful activity—that is, from reliance on the tenets of ideology to principles of a sound personal philosophy.

It is difficult to begin to question things that we have long taken for granted. As Raywid (1976) observed, "The most tyrannical of all our beliefs are those which are persistently unexamined—precisely because they appear so patently reasonable as to be mandated by common sense and impervious to question" (p. 37). The difficulty becomes even greater when we recognize that, traditionally, the conventional wisdom of schooling has often been formalized in teacher education programs through the agency of teacher educators themselves and through the texts, materials, and research they use.

GROUNDED MEANING AND ACTION

When we, as teachers, build our repertoire of professional knowledge and sense of action on a foundation of unquestioned convention and myth, our grounding is weak. Thoughtful, purposeful action has solid grounding in evidence, examined principles, and critical consciousness. When we consider empowering students through our thoughtfully grounded actions, we first face our own resistance to questioning and understanding the values we hold so dearly, albeit rather unconsciously.

To understand better why students behave as they do, we also need to look at what contributes to how students make sense of the world around them. Although when we speak of discipline or behavior problems we seem to be setting apart the perspective of the teacher from that of the student, little actually separates teachers' beliefs from the beliefs of the majority of students. In fact, the process of schooling, including teachers' expectations that students will conform to the expected principles of compliance and conformity, reflects an effort to get students to accept and promote the belief system of the larger social order in general and the ruling class or establishment in particular. When this process, which is called cultural reproduction (discussed further in the next section), is disturbed by student resistance or refusal to act within classroom norms, we find discipline problems on our hands.

CULTURAL REPRODUCTION

We do not often think of teachers as instrumental in the process of molding students into appropriate social role models. We also do not think of how our standards for classroom conduct reflect particular societal standards. Again, it is often our lack of a clear sense of purpose for doing what we do that creates this problem, which is analogous to taking a trip without having a specific destination in mind. The roads we choose, the decisions we make, are grounded in caprice, or the simple truth of the moment; where we end up may not be a destination we would have chosen had we thought about it ahead of time.

The conventional wisdom of the dominant ideology leads us to believe that society mirrors schooling, when in reality it is far more supportable to argue that schools mirror the social order. This does not mean that it is impossible for schools to graduate students who will significantly alter the society to make it more just, fair, and equitable. It means that, as traditionally conceived and currently operated, schools serve to reproduce the cultural norms, beliefs, and conditions of the dominant social order. For example, we know that grade-point averages, performance on standardized tests, and the levels of classes (e.g., college prep, average, slow, technical, etc.) in which students are placed correlate most strongly with the student's socioeconomic status—that is, the lower the income level of the student's family, the more likely he or she will be rated lower on measures of academic success. Similar effects are seen across race, gender, and ethnicity as well.

As teachers working toward an understanding of our role as molders of the citizenry, we need to acutely understand whether we can effect change within the society. We begin by understanding how we serve to reproduce and reinforce existing cultural relations and conditions and by realizing what is needed on our part as teachers to create positive change in those conditions.

Being a teacher means being a facilitator of what students learn both consciously and unconsciously. However, this raises a two-pronged problem. Are we conscious of what we are teaching through our discipline? And are we conscious of what the student is actually learning through these behaviors? Or, as in the travel analogy used earlier, are we clearly aware of where we are going and where we actually take our students? It is imperative that we move to fully understand the nature of our agency in general and the results of that agency in the arena of discipline in particular.

Again, it is a question of what students learn from our expectations and methods of discipline, from where those ideas come to us, and whether we are conscious of the reality of what we may be teaching and where we are taking our students through our actions.

CONVENTIONAL WISDOM

Common sense, craft knowledge, and **conventional wisdom** are terms that describe the grounding of our actions. As mentioned in Chapter 2, education is unique in that it is the only profession where practitioners have many years of participant observation of the profession prior to entering it; we all went to school, observing the activities of our teachers. Likewise, as students move through the process of schooling from kindergarten to high school, they too accept and adapt many of the values, norms, and expectations of the dominant ideology that legitimize the myths and fictions of their teachers' classroom discipline activities.

Because of this we all have strong notions about what it means to be a teacher and classroom manager; we have experienced it as student observers as we went through school. The problem arises when we accept the behaviors we have observed in our own teachers without examining and questioning their fairness, justice, and legitimacy. For example, it is not uncommon to adopt the classroom management strategies of teachers who impressed us during our stint in school without any questioning of what those actions teach or what they lead our students to believe as truth.

We often fail to ask where the behaviors of our former teachers came from and how and by what they were shaped. There is often a great deal to be discovered about what students learn when we examine the roots of teacher behaviors. We find that we are often teaching students ideas and principles that we really do not believe in ourselves. For example, we may not believe in the use of physical force (violence) to solve interpersonal disputes but we support corporal punishment to deter students from fighting. In this case, we fail to realize that using corporal punishment may be teaching the students that physical violence is acceptable for solving problems. Likewise, the students may be inferring principles of behavior, power relations, and norms that work against democratic principles such as justice and fairness.

Again, we need to examine what ideology and philosophy are and how they play themselves out in schools and classrooms through the behaviors of teachers and students. We can make a strong argument that the myths and fictions constituting conventional wisdom are the rationale and principles used to explain and defend our actions in the classroom. Also, every experienced teacher knows that fads periodically occur in education. Discipline-related fads in the form of packaged formulas and recipes for classroom discipline usually take the form of cookbook approaches for dealing with unruly or nonconforming students. But, as with the unexamined professional knowledge we pick up from having been in schools ourselves, these fads are soon seen as having little effect once the newness wears off. When the fundamental principles undergirding most of these cookbook packages are examined, the same old myths and fictions are exposed. We quickly see that they are grounded in the same unquestioned assumptions and beliefs that undergird the common sense and conventional wisdom that dominate too many of today's classrooms.

Regardless of whether our commonsense notions of classroom behaviors come from ideology or educational philosophy, we are often imbued with attitudes that we have acquired unconsciously and hold dearly without ever having critically examined them. These attitudes and assumptions can have toxic effects on our students without our even knowing it. For example, when we punish students for some offense to our rules by requiring them to do extra schoolwork, such as outline a chapter or do extra homework, we usually show that we have failed to consider what it means to use our subject matter as punishment and how that shapes a student's attitude toward the knowledge we teach.

Equally, we often fail to examine closely the rules we invoke for our classes and the assumptions undergirding those rules. In fact, the basic stance we traditionally take toward students is one that subjugates them to the power of our position. Our traditional stance considers them to be unworthy, entitled neither to make any of their own decisions nor to have even the slightest input regarding the structures and rules that prescribe their behavior because we are the choosers and they are the learners (Bowles & Gintis, 1989).

This position leads us into a classroom management trap that defines and limits the teacher–student relationship in terms of power relations alone. For example, most teachers will claim that the grades they give students reflect the students' academic proficiency. However, it is not uncommon for those same teachers to lower grades or take away points from students who violate certain rules of behavior. In other words, there is a teaching convention that allows many teachers to base academic grades on the students' willingness to be subordinate to the teacher's rules regardless of the students' academic performance or the fairness of our rules. When this often traditional frame of reference dominates, an adversarial teacher–student condition ("us against them") dominates classroom management and discipline. As we shall see, when we take this type of attitude, we reflect behavior that is well rooted in both ideology and the conventional philosophy of our workplace.

POWER RELATIONS

One way of examining the degree to which dominant ideology shapes personal educational philosophy is to consider classroom management and discipline through the lens of power relations. When we reexamine some of the myths discussed in the first chapter, we see an amplification of the "chooser–learner" relationship. For example, when we adopt the stance defined in Myth 1, which says that student misbehavior is self-evidently the fault of the student, we manifest the commonly held ideological belief that respect for authority is sufficient reason for being law-abiding citizens.

The phrase "law and order" as a moral imperative of the ruling class is directly reflected in a teacher's intransigence about any behavior violation being solely the fault of the student. The myth rests on the belief that those who do not have authority must submit their wills to those who do. This assumption is the basis for the adversarial relationship between teachers and students. Likewise, when we hold this view it becomes a common denominator for interpreting and assessing student behavior at the expense of our considering other interpretations.

In reality, it is easily seen that various social conditions—such as poverty, abuse, hunger, and alcoholism, among others—contribute to increasing crime rates in the society at large. As certain economic, social, and political conditions that are beyond the control of the individual become more oppressive, the frequency of law breaking increases. Likewise, in our classrooms those same social conditions often contribute to our students' misbehavior and resistance to our demands. Also, what we say and do through the activities of our teaching and the particular force of our personalities often contribute to students' resistance to compliance with our demands as authority figures. Just as the economic and social environment of the student's home life affects attitudes, values, and behavior, so does the classroom environment created by the teacher.

The reality of the myth of student blame falls apart when we begin to consider our own culpability and recognize that respect for authority for authority's sake is a great illusion in the building of a democratic society. Before we blindly accept the commonsense notion that students need to be trained to respect authority and to blindly accept that our authority as teachers should never be challenged because of who we are, let's examine the position opposite to the authority myth.

When we contrast the idea of *respecting authority* with the idea of *questioning authority,* a very different classroom picture emerges. Emerging first is the striking absence of support for questioning authority within the mainstream of our society; today it is not a widely held cultural value, although it has been greatly valued at different times in our history, such as during the American Revolution and the civil disobedience of Thoreau and Martin Luther King Jr. At the very least, no one would argue that American schools do not function to provide students with the abilities to thoughtfully question authority.

The point here is not to debate the appropriateness of either idea as an educational outcome but to become more conscious about the substance and process of ideology as it relates to cultural reproduction through our assumptions about discipline. If (and the emphasis is on the "if") students were to be engaged in the critical examination of authority and the traditional power relations that emanate from an emphasis on uninformed respect for authority, both students and teachers would be quick to see that traditional classrooms would have to be conducted with a very different management style.

DEMOCRATIC IDEALS VERSUS DOMINANT IDEOLOGY

Democratic philosophy as it embodies the ideals of equality, freedom, and justice for all tends to be lost or supplanted when teaching convention is grounded in the dominant ideology of the times. If we accept the notion that schools ought to perpetuate democratic philosophy, then we must give consideration to whether our classroom management and discipline actions serve to teach and reproduce those democratic ideals. We should contrast traditional classroom management activities with the activities that promote democratic ideals of participation, fairness, equality, and justice and ask ourselves how they compare with authority-based practices.

HEGEMONY AS A TACIT SOURCE OF ATTITUDES

Earlier we mentioned cultural reproduction, the process by which schools mirror the values and conditions of society. Stated very simply, cultural reproduction is the actual function or implicit purpose of schooling. In the case of discipline, we can see that the standards for conduct, dress, and speech, as well as such elements as attitude, effort, and values, are those of the dominant culture. Likewise, the knowledge that is valued, taught, and expected of students is that of the dominant culture. In this sense the activities of teaching and schooling serve to reproduce all aspects of the dominant culture on the part of the students. Those who reproduce it well will succeed; those who reproduce it poorly will fail.

To better understand our role as teachers in the process of cultural reproduction, we must understand our location as teachers within the education process. To do so and to foreshadow the power of classroom management behaviors, we need to give special consideration to the term **hegemony**. This term historically has been used to refer to the influence a large, powerful nation exerts over smaller, less powerful ones. Similarly, the term is also applied to the *noncoercive* forces and factors that are powerful in shaping and influencing students' behavior and beliefs.

In the teaching sense, hegemony refers to the implicit power of the teacher, rules, norms, and peer pressure to shape attitudes, values, and behavior. The significance of the concept is in the idea that hegemony, while very powerful, is noncoercive; it does not involve physical force nor the threat of physical force. It is simply the presence of powerful expectations for conformity to certain behaviors, values, and beliefs of the dominant culture that most teachers take for granted. However, we need to understand that many of our students do not bring the cultural values of ruling-class America to school with them.

Either as teachers or as ordinary citizens, we may find it difficult to come to grips with lenses we have acquired for interpreting, judging, and acting because we are not aware of our actually having acquired them. This reflects the power of hegemony, which, unlike the experience of physical force, is not memorable. But, in understanding how we come to hold our own general views of proper student behavior and appropriate discipline measures, we need to come to grips with how we ourselves experienced hegemony as we went through school.

Understanding hegemony as a concept allows us to begin to understand our often unwitting agency in the process of cultural reproduction. As students in primary and secondary schools, we unconsciously adopted the generalized normative behaviors expected of us by the schools. This is especially true if we were reared in the cultural tradition of the white middle or upper class; these norms are generally accepted as representative of the expectations of white, upper-middle-class males. They are found across discipline, instruction, and extracurricular activities. They frame what we learn as acceptable or unacceptable behavior from students.

ENFLESHMENT OF IDEOLOGY

Our often unwitting participation in classroom management activities that deny student empowerment is perhaps best understood using McLaren's (1991) notion of **"enfleshment."**[2] McLaren speaks to how we unconsciously come to identify and personify the values and norms of the dominant ideology. To enflesh the lenses of interpretation and action is to hold them as deeply personal, as truths that determine our attitudes about the behavior of others. When we enflesh, we are extremely confident

---

[2] The notion of enfleshment captures the idea that we embody such particulars as values and attitudes to the point that they become part of the very essence of our being.

in those attitudes even to the point of self-righteousness about our power. This enfleshment is the outcome of hegemony; we really are unaware of the process of acquiring the attitudinal trappings of our sense of truth.

To understand discipline, we need to understand that our own experience in school happened within a context of norms and values that we soon came to take for granted (i.e, we enfleshed them) and usually continue to take for granted as we study to become teachers. Most particularly, they revolve around the condition of superior–subordinate relations between teacher and student, respectively.

CONVENTION IN THE HIDDEN CURRICULUM

Recall our definition of the hidden curriculum presented in Chapter 2. It consists of what students have the opportunity to learn but what is not formally stated or necessarily intended to be taught. This hidden curriculum almost completely shapes our frame of reference for judging student behaviors. We can begin to circumscribe the context of the hidden curriculum by looking at the words and phrases that typically describe the so-called best students: *respectful, obedient, loyal, quiet, patient, dutiful, hardworking, diligent, neat, punctual, nice, consistent, reliable, trustworthy, smiling, eager to please, good citizen, doesn't talk to neighbors, does own work,* and so on. These behaviors need to be seen from the perspective of their function to please the teacher. That is, as students, if we want to please the teacher, these are the behaviors or images we work to acquire because they are the ones that are rewarded. At best we can see these as charming attributes, characteristics that seem reasonable and even desirable. However, as collective descriptors for students, they represent a picture that changes when critically examined. For example, while it may seem pragmatic to have compliant students who allow us as teachers to conduct our activities without interruption, we must ask what this produces in the long run. What kind of citizens do our students become? What kind of values will they hold? What kind of teachers would they be?

Purpose, or outcome, is given scant consideration when we talk about teaching and schooling in general and virtually no consideration when we talk about the hidden curriculum or classroom management in particular. Classroom management, rather than being conducted with an educative sense of purpose, is usually conducted on the basis of convention. Convention refers to the mechanisms we use as teachers and to the expected behavior of our students. For example, starting each class with a review of the homework is a convention of teaching; having students sit in rows or raise their hands before speaking is a convention demanded of our students. The basic idea of convention has a negative connotation in that it implies doing something the way it has always been done, without conscious consideration of its purpose or effect.

MOVING TOWARD ENLIGHTENED PRACTICE

When we rely on convention, we avoid having to be accountable for thinking through our actions and the long-term effects of those actions upon our students. Jung (1954b) puts it well when he writes, "The mechanism of convention keeps people unconscious, for in that state they can follow their accustomed tracks like blind brutes, without the need for conscious decision" (p. 179).

The myths discussed earlier represent convenient explanations for conventions that are consistent with the dominant ideology. The myths give us a way of making sense of the day-to-day world we experience as teachers; however, they do so without serious consideration of the purposes of teaching and schooling. Unfortunately, the perpetuation of myth often precludes our coming to deeper, more warranted understandings of school phenomena. Likewise, while myths may give us a feeling of coherence and confidence regarding our actions, they fail entirely to address either the ethical or educational consequences of those actions.

SUMMARY

We have now come full circle, from ideology through hegemony and enfleshment to convention and its supporting myths. In summary, we can now see that the myths are profession-specific mental structures that function in particular school settings the way ideology functions across more general societal settings. The two are inexorably connected.

We can also begin to see how hegemony is the very subtle but powerful and often spurious process of acquiring the tenets of ideology that we come to enflesh with confidence and certainty. Last, we can see how convention relates to traditional teaching behaviors and how the idea of myth allows us to defend what we do as we use the mechanisms of pedagogical convention.

Our assumptions about culture and values are not necessarily good for the enhancement of a democratic society in general. The ideals of democracy are not inherent in traditional institutional and classroom management practices because we ourselves have been hegemonized. Likewise, as the demographics of the student population change, it is expected that by the year 2000 the majority of public school students will be those whose race, social class, and ethnic background are not that of the white middle class. The tensions between the experiences of these students and the traditional classroom management style of the middle-class teacher will be striking. The next chapter, "Discipline and the Postmodern Student," deals with some of the issues of cultural diversity, the nature of today's students, and the role of the teacher in discipline strategies.

LOOKING AHEAD

We have just examined some very significant insights about how schools function in the acquisition of our belief systems. Understanding ideology and the process of its acquisition is vital to our understanding the values that motivate our actions as teachers. We have discussed the reproduction of the dominant culture in schools. Now we move to a discussion of the students of the postmodern generation and the way their experience and understanding result in their having values that are very different than our own. Chapter 4 will discuss the forces and factors of popular culture and diverse social conditions and the effects they have on the students we will encounter in our classrooms.

❖ REFLECTIVE ACTIVITIES

1. How are belief systems affected by the ideological aspects of schooling? How does this work against our efforts to form an enlightened citizenry? How does critical reflectivity serve both teachers and students in combating the acceptance of ideology as truth?
2. Discuss the common notion that society mirrors schooling by arguing that schools mirror society. How does this discussion suggest that significant changes in schooling are usually difficult and slow to occur?
3. How did going to school shape some of your own cultural values and beliefs? How have those begun to change as you reflect on what you have read about ideology, hegemony, and cultural reproduction? What is the primary problem for the citizenry when cultural reproduction is the primary outcome of schooling?

❖ REFERENCES

Bowles, S., & Gintis, H. (1989). Can there be a liberal philosophy of education in a democratic society? In H. Giroux & P. McLaren (Eds.), *Critical pedagogy, the state, and cultural struggle.* Albany, NY: SUNY Press.

Byrne, D. (1984). *Stop making sense.* Burbank, CA: Talking Heads Films, Inc.

Cherryholmes, C. H. (1988). *Power and criticism: Poststructural investigations in education.* New York: Teachers College Press.

Dewey, J. (1933). *How we think.* Lexington, MA: D. C. Heath.

Jung, C. G. (1954a). *The development of personality* (R. F. C. Hull, Trans.). Princeton, NJ: Princeton University Press.

Jung, C. G. (1954b). *Psychology and education* (R. F. C. Hull, Trans.). Princeton, NJ: Princeton University Press.

Lather, P. (1991). *Getting smart: Feminist research and pedagogy with/in the postmodern.* New York: Routledge.

McLaren, P. (1991). Schooling the postmodern body: Critical pedagogy and the politics of enfleshment. In H. Giroux (Ed.), *Postmodernism, feminism, and cultural politics* (pp. 144–173). New York: SUNY Press.

Pratte, R. (1983). Ideology and schooling. *Review Journal of Philosophy and Social Science, 8,* 25–45.

Raywid, M. (1976). The democratic classroom: Mistake or misnomer? *Theory into Practice, 15*(1), 37–46.

Discipline and the Postmodern Student

1. What factors shape the values and attitudes of the postmodern student?
2. What special awareness does the teacher need to deal fairly and effectively with the postmodern student?
3. Why is it important for reflective teachers to consider their own cultural views to understand the nature of the postmodern generation of students?
4. How does the cultural diversity of our student population contribute to the necessity for new perspectives on student discipline?
5. How can we work toward greater inclusion across diversity to the betterment of all?

As we move toward the 21st century, we face two very different conditions than teachers faced 10 years ago: cultural and demographic diversity. This chapter explores the basic nature of **postmodern culture** and the social composition of classrooms as we face the new century. We will discuss how the emerging postmodern cultural conditions affect our students and how the changing cultural demographics will affect future student–teacher relations in the classroom.

POSTMODERN CULTURE IN BRIEF

A great deal has been written about the changes culture and society have undergone in the last few decades. Most of what has been written, however, has been in philosophy, literary theory, architecture, social theory, and communications. To grasp the significance of the effects of cultural and social conditions on discipline is not an easy task for teachers. Yet, understanding postmodern effects is a very important step toward understanding how and why the attitudes and expectations of students and teachers differ.

Our current cultural condition is referred to as the postmodern. At the risk of oversimplification, the postmodern is closely associated with the effects of technology and media on society. It concerns the information people receive and the meaning they make of what they see and hear; the postmodern is rooted in sensation and stimulation more than it is in reflection and suspension of belief. As a crude example, MTV is one window that looks onto the postmodern landscape. The technology that brings us laser disks, instant television coverage of current events, computer games, interactive video, high-tech athletic shoes, and Nintendo and Sega also brings a strong inclination to the abandonment of delayed sensual gratification in favor of immediate fulfillment of the senses.

The postmodern era began in the late 1950s with the launching of the first satellite and mass production of the first rock 'n' roll music. The former Soviet Union's launching of *Sputnik,* the first satellite to orbit the earth, brought about massive amounts of funding for the development of advanced technology. Rock 'n' roll influenced a popular culture aimed at young people's desires as it ignored the outrage of the adult population. Elvis Presley created more adult criticism than singer Madonna does now, even though Elvis's brand of rock music seems tame and dated today. In the fifties, a young actor named James Dean, who embodied adolescent qualities of defiance, rebellion, and independence, was adopted as the symbol of youth's disenchantment with the established culture of adults. Today, the culture of MTV's "Beavis and Butthead" is a benchmark of the cultural baggage our students bring to our classrooms.

Overall, many students of the postmodern era are motivated by values and attitudes that differ significantly from those of mainstream, middle-class American adults and from teachers who are rooted in the values and expectations of traditional schooling. Likewise, the size of the cultural generation gap often puts parents in a quandary about what goes on in schools as well as within the minds of their children.

But what does this have to do with teaching? How does beginning to understand the nature of today's youth in a postmodern culture help us teach more effectively? To answer such questions, we must give thoughtful consideration to the factors shaping the attitudes students bring to our classrooms. Few would disagree that the greater our understanding of the lives of our students the easier it is to communicate and to teach.

To prepare for classroom management and discipline that embody democratic ideals such as justice and fairness, we need to recognize two cultural conditions that shape tomorrow's classrooms: popular culture in postmodern times and the expansion of cultural and ethnic diversity as the population changes. On the one hand, the effective teacher needs to realize how the common experiences of popular culture such as TV and music affect our students; on the other hand, we need to know how the different experiences of growing up in separate minority, ethnic, or single-parent homes create additional impediments to understanding each other. Whether we like it or not, the challenge of these tasks is elemental to establishing fair and democratic principles for managing classrooms and working with students.

THE POSTMODERN STUDENT

The condition of popular culture in postmodern times involves the lived experience of the children who have encountered a culture strikingly different from that of the previous generation. Essentially for our students, postmodern culture is one of sensation rather than reflection, MTV rather than books, and immediacy rather than deferred gratification. While the analysis and definition of what *postmodern* means is the subject of hundreds of scholarly works across philosophy, literature, language, and educational theory, for our purposes we need only to make a case that the sights, sounds, and sensations of your students' generation are radically different than those of the previous generation and have shaped a background of experience that affects the attitudes students bring into your classroom.

The generation gap between adults and children involves the differences between what the two generations see as appropriate school behavior. Usually, the gap is a result of selective forgetting on the part of the adult, but, occasionally, changes in social conditions that affect children's experiences result in a change in their attitudes and values. Most cultural theorists agree that our society has undergone a major cultural shift and that our cultural condition is much different than that of just a short time ago. Analogous to the significant changes in cultural conditions between the agrarian and industrial periods, we now face the major cultural shifts caused by our move from the modern into the postmodern era.

The postmodern student is much more a product of sensation and stimulation than were previous generations. Today's students have grown up experiencing cable television, computers, video games, Walkmans, CD players, MTV, VH1, which bring into their lives explicit sexual material, the commercial attention of advertisers, slasher films, Howard Stern, Madonna, and open discussion of many previously taboo subjects, such as condoms, AIDs, and homosexuality. "Beavis and Butthead" has the highest ratings of any MTV offering. Today's students have also come of age in an era of rampant materialism, where the sensation of immediate gratification and the creation of self-identity through the ownership of everything from high-priced tennis shoes and team jackets to BMWs and hot tubs have been dominant.

One very distinguishing characteristic of the postmodern generation is that today's children have not been sheltered from adult realities. No more than a generation ago, access to certain topics, issues, and experiences was quite unavailable to children in their formative years. Television programming just a few years ago consisted mainly of idealized, noncontroversial subject matter. Shows such as "Little House on the Prairie," "Star Trek," and "American Bandstand" were the main fare of what was accessible to developing children. Scenes of explicit sex, extreme violence, unrestrained abuse, and serious drug use were essentially inaccessible from either television or film. Neither did rock 'n roll music, while containing lyrics offensive to conservative adults, provide general access to these subjects.

Through the windows of technology provided by cable and network television, CD-ROM and the Internet, and rock videos and lyrics, we have access to a very wide variety of what was once considered adult fare. Moreover, the pervasiveness of so-called adult images, acts, and speech has arguably lessened the sensitivities of parents toward them. Not long ago it was relatively common for parents to avoid discussions of adult topics in the presence of children; parents considered many subjects taboo. Parents of even a generation ago were able to filter what children experienced to a much greater degree than is possible today.

Our point is not to argue that we must return to a time when children were protected by adults who filtered what they discussed and debated. Nor is our point to criticize the programming of television, the lyrics of popular music, or absolute freedom of Internet. On the contrary, our point is to help you recognize that there are significant differences between what you may have experienced and what today's children are experiencing. Our intent is not to judge the rightness or wrongness of the effects of postmodern cultural conditions on today's kids but to attempt to raise your awareness that the so-called baggage your students bring into the classroom is real in that it shapes their expectations, interpretations, and understandings of what you do to and with them, both psychologically and socially.

One visible symptom of teachers who do not have a grip on effective classroom management is often overheard when they blame students for their lack of proper attitude. They often carp about rock music, television, video games, style of dress, reading material, drug culture, slang, and anything else they cannot associate with the popular culture of their own times. While there are many origins for the different attitudes students bring to the classroom other than popular culture, it becomes problematic when teachers throw up their hands in frustration and disparage the students because of their own inability to deal with the students' popular culture.

EXCLUSION VERSUS INCLUSION

As teachers, we cause problems when we show open disdain for the attitudes shaped by the postmodern popular culture. No one likes to be demeaned for tastes and attitudes held both real and personal. Schools and teachers traditionally have been slow to react and accommodate all sorts of generational changes brought on through popular cultural values. Indeed, one can argue that school rules and policies traditionally have functioned to exclude values, attitudes, music, dress, and language that are not accepted by the white, middle-class segment of the society. Consider the relatively strict dress codes and hairstyle policies enforced even a generation ago.

While America has been a pluralistic, multicultural society, equal and democratic treatment of all people has not been a reality in either the legal system, the workplace, or education. Traditional classroom management has not been shaped by democratic ideals that stress inclusion. Indeed, much of what has shaped the rules and policies of schools has been a narrowly conceived set of standards that exclude any deviance from accepted middle-class norms of dress, attitude, and conduct on the part of all students regardless of the influences of the specific life factors experienced by them.

When the wearing of jeans became popular, when girls and women began wearing pants instead of skirts, when T-shirts became vogue, when hats (worn backward) became popular, schools were consistently slow to allow these forms of popular culture to invade the corridors and classrooms. They were considered disruptive to the orderly process of schooling. But when we give pause to exactly what was disrupted, we soon discover that the disruption was to the narrow sensibilities of the teachers and administrators rather than directly to the educational process. The differences offended school personnel.

Rather than blindly monitoring students' seemingly outrageous affectations, attitudes, and tastes, educators should first scrutinize the motives for their own responses to the student behavior. Teachers then begin to build a basis for discriminating between what is personally offensive and what is truly disruptive to the process of schooling. In this way, schools become more inclusive of diversity and exclusive of true disruption to the educational processes.

One traditional educational mission has been to appropriate and exclude the elements of popular culture that students hold as part of their identities (Aronowitz & Giroux, 1991). School boards, administrators, and teachers might hold educational values that do not accommodate or even accept as legitimate the values and interests students hold for their popular culture. The prime directive has been geared toward maintaining the status quo. Our education system has established the adult policymakers in the role of choosers and the students as learners who are disallowed any decision latitude in the development of their own identities unless that identity is in accord with the model the choosers have adopted (Bowles & Gintis, 1989). Just as we discussed earlier that schools have functioned through the hegemonic process to appropriate values and beliefs into the dominant ideology, the denial of value and identity through popular culture is part of the same process.

The denial and exclusion of students' cultural interests and values are, again, part of the schools' mission of cultural reproduction (denying any popular arts that question or resist the dominant culture, such as Ice-Tea's "Cop Killer" or MTV's "Beavis and Butthead"). Few would argue that, in general, teaching and schooling function to reproduce in the younger generation the dominant culture, especially the values of the ruling class. The closer we are as educators to enfleshing the dominant culture, the more difficult it is for us to see any legitimacy in the seemingly radical departure of today's youth. We are often egocentric (e.g., we hate Metallica, Michael Jackson, or Madonna because we like Barry Manilow, Garth Brooks, or Elvis) and ethnocentric (e.g., we hate black rap because we prefer white rock) about our popular culture values.

We all have a tendency to fear the unfamiliar because it threatens our own sense of coherence and security. The greater the disparity between what we know and what we don't know, the greater the fear. Rod Serling once observed, "The major ingredient of any recipe for fear is the unknown" (1964, p. 403). Today, we live in a world where difference is made more conspicuous than sameness, where the spectrum of events (from the bombing of Iraq to the beatings of Rodney King by the Los Angeles police and Reginald Denney by Los Angeles rioters) is seen in a constant stream of traces across television screens. Just as radical art and diverse music thrive in today's world of media and entertainment, so do religious fundamentalism and political conservatism, which focus on differences by denigrating and excluding what they disagree with from the allowable or speakable in schools.

When we work under the assumption that schools should cultivate democratic values, that high school graduates ought to be well prepared to act as thoughtful citizens in a democratic nation, we quickly realize that discipline needs to be thought of in a very different light than in the past. Traditionally, discipline has been thought of as more preventative and reactive rather than formative and proactive. Terms such as *classroom management* and *discipline* connote control techniques used consciously as defensive (reactive) strategies to prevent the disruption of our plans and activities. These techniques are employed to keep us on task.

The only formative function has been to try to shape students to be more like us in their values, attitudes, and behavior. This is known as the "great melting pot" notion—that schools should function to standardize and normalize their clients in one image. In the postmodern world, where there is great diversity across race, class, gender, ethnicity, disability, and life-style preference, social homogeneity is impossible to realize in America. The idea of this country as the great melting pot has proven to be a fantasy.

Little consideration has been given to helping students learn and understand democratic attitudes and values that will serve them well in their role as citizens later in life. The formative function in terms of preparing students for thoughtful citizenship must be seen as proactive and embedded in the nature of what we do throughout the activities of teaching in general and particularly in our approach to discipline. (Chapter 6 will deal with many of the specifics of proactive, formative classroom management ideas that serve the ends of democratic citizenship.)

We need to be vitally aware that we are working with students who come from a society that focuses more on difference than on similarity, more on exclusion than on inclusion, and more on individuality than on community. Such conditions neither facilitate nor embody the basic principles of democratic citizenship, nor do they make classroom discipline easy to understand, all of which necessitates greater reflective analysis.

It becomes increasingly difficult to show concern, care, and tolerance (a topic given substantial coverage in Chapter 5) toward those who hold attitudes, values, and tastes that seem so radically different from our own. As teachers and students are bombarded with news stories, art, and music that seem unfamiliar, distant, and alien, it becomes easy to write off the views and tastes of others. We tend to reject, dislike, or punish students for being different. Today, more than ever, cultural alienation on our part is poised to exclude a large segment of our student population from constructive, formative, and educative opportunities in school.

The driving force of our acts of discipline is exclusive rather than inclusive. When we act in an exclusionary way, we polarize our relationship to students through our demands for reproduction of our own (usually the dominant) cultural values. While cultural reproduction serves to devalue or cleanse students of the artifacts of their popular cultural interests, it also serves to deny and devalue racial, ethnic, and gender interests that are basic elements to education for democratic citizenship.

We must be willing to accept students regardless of how they have been shaped by the culture of their lived experience and be willing to work to empower

them to be thoughtful in their choices and generative in creating the lives they desire. We need to constantly remember that we had no more control over the factors that shaped our own popular culture experience in childhood and adolescence than today's postmodern students have. We are not suggesting that students never go terribly astray, that teachers and administrators should never intervene, but rather that we should try to discern actions that are hegemonic or coercive in the service of cultural reproduction and disdainful of students' legitimate right to have identities different than our own. (In the next chapter, we will examine principles of behavior and intervention that facilitate students' being able to make intelligent choices about their futures within the framework of democratic schooling and a democratic society.)

SOCIAL AND PEDAGOGICAL CONDITIONS

Disdain for a student's cultural experience because it is so different from our own is just as problematic for teaching as is disdain for the role of parents in shaping today's student. A common complaint from teachers is that today's parents fail to instill in their children any respect for discipline and learning. But we need to recognize, again, that our job is to work with our students as clients who are what they are through circumstance more than choice. In the postmodern generation, the role of helping kids develop (parenting) is often as problematic for teachers as it is for parents and guardians.

Less than a generation ago, headlines were made when a gun was found in a student's locker. Today, many schools have regular searches with metal detectors as students enter the buildings. Students are stabbed or shot for team jackets, tennis shoes, or gang affiliation. School districts that were once considered suburban, middle-class bastions of safety are now vulnerable to incidents of violence that were unheard of only a generation ago. But there is great danger in believing that violence, disrespect for teachers, and chaos reign freely in America's public schools; they do not. To begin to understand the context for more thoughtful and inclusionary classroom management principles, we need to understand that violence has increased but that the increase is not across the board nor in every American school and classroom. To begin to constructively manage our classrooms, we need to remember that our students are shaped by the conditions of their environment and culture and that schools essentially only reflect what is happening in the broader social order. Schools do not create the living conditions of the student, though they may be seen to mirror them. We believe that, through educators' thoughtful consideration of the relations between school and society, schools can be a more constructive force in the formative development of our future citizenry. We can concern ourselves with how teachers and schools contribute to discipline problems, how we deal with problems students bring into our classes from the street, and how teaching and schooling can contribute positively to social change.

In the next chapter we will examine some of the principles for decreasing the likelihood of conflict originating from differences between teachers' and students' values and attitudes. We will begin to conceptualize formative elements of classroom management that can serve citizenship in a democratic society.

COMPOSITION OF AMERICA'S CLASSROOMS

As we race toward the 21st century, the demographic scenery of classrooms is changing from that of a white, English-speaking middle-class to that of a more varied and culturally diverse population. Likewise, less and less often do students come from so-called traditional homes, where both parents are present, the mother and father have high school diplomas, and the parents are in their late 20s or 30s.

America is undergoing a population distribution change where, according to the Population Reference Bureau, by the year 2035 more than half the population under 18 years of age will belong to minority groups. Eighty-two percent of educators responding to the Survey of the American Teacher (Metlife Teachers' Survey, 1993) agreed on some level that students are coming to school with so many problems that it is difficult for them to be good students. This underscores the link between being a member of a minority group and being in a lower economic class. The survey notes that teachers in schools with larger proportions of minority or lower-income students were significantly stronger in their responses.

While the racial and ethnic composition of the student body is changing, the composition of the teaching force continues to remain essentially the same. As the racial, cultural, and ethnic gap between the lived experience of teachers and students continues to widen, renewed consideration of management principles of inclusion becomes even more vital.

While the student composition acquires greater diversity across race, class, and ethnicity, nothing pedagogically purposeful can change without the critical examination of the interpretive lenses we use to make sense of students' academic and behavioral actions. Adherence to the traditional practices and expectations of mainstream American classrooms constricts what is allowable because it limits classroom activity to a narrow set of culturally, rather than pedagogically, defined possibilities. More and more students will bring to school values and attitudes alien to those taken for granted by teachers raised in the middle-class tradition. Teachers who subscribe by default to unexamined myths and fictions of discipline will become the progenitors of unnecessary tension between themselves and their students.

Reflective reality tells us that when the lived experience of children differs from that of teachers and as the demographics of the two groups become more disparate, teaching becomes more difficult. Cultural incongruence foreshadows the basis for the growing problem of dealing with the factors of diversity in working for democratic ideals. The lack of cultural, racial, and ethnic understanding between teachers and students results in, at worst, student disengagement, alienation, and eventual withdrawal from school (Willis, 1977) and, at best, subtler resistance behaviors (Giroux & Simon, 1983; McLaren, 1989; Solomon, 1992).

These findings are not so surprising when we think about how alienating it is to find ourselves in unfamiliar surroundings. We feel ill at ease when we are forced into environments that we have not encountered before. As teachers working for educative classroom management, we must consider that the cultural norms and mores we take for granted may not be ones that our students are familiar with.

DEMOGRAPHICS OF DIVERSITY

The following data point to the problematic conditions we face as America and its schools move into the 21st century. This information needs to be seen in light of how traditional schooling serves its population and in light of the preceding discussions. (We have summarized the data primarily from Hodgkinson [1992], as well as other sources as noted.)

- The typical family consisting of a working father, at-home mother, and two children of school age is long gone. Data suggest that less than 6% of American families fit this description.
- About 82% or more of school-age children have working mothers, and about 60% of preschool children have mothers who are employed outside the home.
- In 1989 alone, 13.7 million children lived in families with the mother the only parent and the median income $10,982.
- By 1990, one in five children were living in poverty, one in four were born to unmarried parents, and one in four had no health insurance.
- A study of at-risk students by Metlife (Metlife Teachers' Survey, 1993) shows that 28% of 9th through 12th graders from two-parent homes and 43% from single-parent homes are considered to be high-at-risk students.
- Six states will have youth populations in which the number of nonwhite youth will be greater than 50% by the year 2010.
- From 1980 to 1990 the number of people in U.S. prisons rose 139%, which establishes the United States as having the highest percentage of its population in prison of any nation in the world.
- Eighty-two percent of prisoners are high school dropouts.
- In grades 8 through 11, 85% of girls and 76% of boys report being victims of sexual harassment, according to a 1992 American Association of University Women poll conducted by Louis Harris and Associates (Metlife Teachers' Survey, 1993).
- Fifteen percent of students in grades 6 through 12 said they had carried a handgun to school at least once in a given period; 59% reported that handguns were easy to obtain.
- Violence and gun use were not confined to urban school settings. Forty percent of students in urban settings knew someone killed or injured by guns, compared with 36% in the suburbs and 43% in rural areas.

- The American Psychological Association (Metlife Teachers' Survey, 1993) reports that students carry an estimated 270,000 guns to school each day, twice the estimate made by the National School Safety Center in 1987.
- Teens are 2.5 times more likely to suffer violence than those over age 20, with most of the violence occurring in or in close proximity to schools.

Whether we speak of traditional democratic ideals of equality, equity, and opportunity or of the emergent democratic ideals of empowerment and emancipation as the conscious and purposeful outcomes of schooling, we must face the critical reality of our own cultural experience and bias. As the demographic data foreshadow, many American schools in the future will consist of even greater varieties of cultural, economic, social, and family backgrounds than today. The challenge at the professional level for teachers is in dealing with diversity while simultaneously working for inclusion. But the initial challenge is at the personal level.

Our personal blindness to the traditions of cultures other than our own binds us to convention, to the belief that there is one standard of conduct for all. It influences us to believe that the American dream is open to all who submit to its standards and that the level of cultural reproduction is the measure of academic proficiency and moral conduct.

We are initially motivated by sets of values that we acquire during our upbringing. One small but significant way to begin to come to grips with our personal level of response to diversity is to first examine and try to discover the values that motivate us as people and as teachers. As well, we need to more clearly understand that even some of our most mundane normative behaviors are culturally conditioned. For example, in mainstream white American culture, it is expected that a child being reprimanded look the teacher in the eyes as a sign of respect; however, in other, nonwhite American cultures the same behavior is considered a sign of disrespect.

Many teachers tend to see multicultural education courses as simply being exercises in becoming familiar with and understanding that different cultures do different things because they hold different values and attitudes about life. What is missing in this view is the element that facilitates the practice of grounded discipline. The key element in working in multicultural settings and simultaneously working for democratic ideals is understanding that we may well be as much a part of the problem as is any different cultural representative. Again, consciously understanding what values motivate us as teachers and why they motivate us is requisite to understanding the values that motivate others.

For example, rugged individualism has been a prized value in mainstream American culture since the origins of our country. In terms of education, we thus expect students to do their work on their own, to compete with other students, and to keep to themselves. However, in Native American culture, children tend to be group oriented and to value working cooperatively in the tasks and activities of their lives. Hence, as the diversity of a teacher's classroom expands to include Native American students, the potential for discord is increased when the teacher insists they work alone and reproaches them for cheating when they interact during an assignment.

In another example, a dominant cultural norm requires that individuals in an audience show respect for the speaker by remaining silent during a presentation—to speak out in such a situation is considered rude. But in the African American culture, individuals in an audience often speak out to affirm the speaker's message. The negative reaction of mainstream white teachers to the spontaneous utterances of students during their lectures is predictable and a likely source of conflict.

The list of differing values that teachers potentially face goes much further than the examples just noted. However, the teacher who seeks to understand the values of his or her students is able to avoid misunderstandings that have the potential to lead to classroom conflicts.

SUMMARY

Teaching today means dealing with a truly significant generation gap that cuts across diversity, cultural experience, economic polarization, and popular culture. The backgrounds and formative experiences of our students are strikingly different from our own in just about every imaginable way. At this time in our history, concerted reflective analysis and understanding of both the values that motive us and the values that motivate our students are critical to developing proactive discipline plans. Without a concerted effort, we further polarize our students from ourselves and further alienate them from the opportunities for empowerment in our schools. Indeed, if teachers do not give significant consideration to what their activities of discipline mean, serious problems can arise concerning the roles today's students will play as future citizens shaping our democracy.

LOOKING AHEAD

By now we have argued how students are shaped by factors not usually considered by teachers. We have seen how schools themselves act to reproduce dominant cultural values in students. We have also seen how diverse economic, social, and cultural experiences affect student values and attitudes and have given consideration to the effects of postmodern culture on shaping our students in ways very different than we experienced.

We will now examine how we can work to shape a democratic citizenry from the students in our own schools and classrooms. Chapter 5, "Understanding the Formation of Character and Democratic Citizenship," addresses the key considerations we must face if we are to turn things around, so to speak, and work proactively and reflectively toward the development of good character and citizenship in our students.

❖ REFLECTIVE ACTIVITIES

1. Recognizing that as we grow through childhood and adolescence we acquire most of our values and attitudes, as well as our disposition toward others, without realizing it (i.e., we take them for granted), why is it especially important for teachers to critically reflect upon these enfleshments?
2. How do the lived experiences of the students you face in your classroom differ significantly from your own? What is the teacher's responsibility in recognizing and dealing with the formative effects of these different experiences?
3. How can you prepare for teaching students with radically different cultural, generational, social, and economic backgrounds than your own?

❖ REFERENCES

Aronowitz, S., & Giroux, H. (1991). *Postmodern education: Politics, culture, and social criticism.* Minneapolis: University of Minnesota Press.

Bowles, S., & Gintis, H. (1989). Can there be a liberal philosophy of education in a democratic society? In H. Giroux & P. McLaren (Eds.), *Critical pedagogy, the state, and cultural struggle.* Albany: SUNY Press.

Giroux, H., & Simon, R. (1983). *Popular culture, schooling, and everyday life.* New York: Bergin & Garvey.

Hodgkinson, H. (1992). *A demographic look at tomorrow.* Washington, DC: Institute for Educational Leadership/Center for Demographic Policy.

McLaren, P. (1989). *Life in schools.* New York: Longman.

Metlife Teachers' Survey. (1993). *Survey of the American Teacher.* New York: Metropolitan Life.

Serling, R. (1964). *The fear.* In M. Zicree (Ed.), *The twilight zone companion.* New York: Bantam Books.

Solomon, R. P. (1992). *Black resistance in high school: Forging a separatist culture.* Albany: SUNY Press.

Willis, P. (1977). *Learning to labor: How working class kids get working class jobs.* New York: Columbia University Press.

Chapter 5

Understanding the Formation of Character and Democratic Citizenship

❖ Focus Questions

1. What is the role of the school in the formation of character, and what is the significance of character to citizenship?

2. What distinguishes democracy from other types of social organization, and how does this affect the activities of teaching and schooling?

3. Why is it important to give consideration to a democratic ethic in the education of a democratic citizenry?

4. What is the relationship between having loyalty to one's country and being a good citizen?

5. Why is the concept of inclusion important in making rules?

6. What is the link between the teaching of values and the effects of our discipline activities in terms of character and citizenship formation?

In Chapter 2 we discussed briefly the idea that good, well-informed discipline should be proactive and formative rather than reactive and preventative. The key principle underlying this idea is the notion that what students learn from our disciplinary activities can significantly shape their future behavior as citizens in our democratic society. While it is common for teachers to consider the academic activities of teaching as preparation for the future, rarely do we think of the activities of discipline as contributing to the formation of future character and citizenship.

In a broad sense, when we speak of discipline we are talking about the idea of character education, or character development. Disciplinary activities have a formative effect on our students' future behavior both ethically and morally regardless of our level of awareness of those effects. Our actions shape not only aspects of how students will behave interpersonally but aspects of how they will behave socially, politically, and legally. Understanding the idea that discipline has powerful formative effects involves grasping key interrelationships among morality, **ethics**, and democratic values and the way they relate to what students come to believe about the nature of human conduct from their experience in school. Therefore, it is very important to understand the multiplicity of roles that schools can and do serve.

First and foremost we must understand that schools do have a formative effect on the intellectual, social, and moral development of all students regardless of whether the school personnel consciously realizes it. Most traditional American schools relegate social and moral development to the aspects of the hidden curriculum rather than to the overt curriculum. As to the formative effects schools have on the development of citizenship, a somewhat different problem exists.

In the next section we discuss how democracy is much more than simply a form of government—it is a way of living. We shall see also that citizenship formation is very much related to character formation—that one's moral-ethical dimensions are directly connected to one's civic dimensions. Let's briefly examine the considerations schools give civic education in light of the considerations we have just discussed regarding character education.

CIVIC EDUCATION

Civic education is addressed, like character education, traditionally through the hidden and null curricula. But, unlike character education, civic education also has formal status in the overt curriculum. Schools usually teach subject matter across the social studies curriculum, and high schools usually teach a specific course in government. Civics courses, however, stress students' learning declarative knowledge of simplistic notions and the technical and formal aspects of how our democratic national government is organized and operates.

Traditionally, students are asked to memorize such things as the preamble to the U.S. Constitution, the Articles of the Constitution, and the branches of government. They are usually asked to tell how a bill becomes law, how a person becomes president, and why the Articles of Confederation were not as good as the Constitution. What is conspicuously absent from these curricula is the intent to instill in students a disposition to think critically about the process and products of government and efforts to instill a disposition toward acting and behaving democratically.

Formatively, what does any student gain from civics courses that reduce the elements of democracy to the memorization of the technical details of our government? How can we begin to educate students if they are not empowered to think reflectively about their character, their citizenship, and their government? When we can accept the idea that schools have formative effects in the social and moral dimensions as well as the intellectual, we can realize how issues of citizenship and character must be overtly dealt with in the curriculum.

GOOD MANNERS, GOOD CHARACTERS, OR GOOD CITIZENS?

Ordinarily, teachers speak of discipline in terms of a good student–bad student continuum. Good students are compliant to our wishes, dutiful in their performance of our assignments, respectful of our authority, and unquestioning of our motives, rules, and procedures. Bad students fail to meet one or more of these good-student criteria, the worst students being those who violate all of them.

Our first-order concerns usually relate to basic classroom manners. We want our students to be silent when others are talking, to use proper forms of address, and to show general respect for all rules, regulations, and activities we choose for them. Our second-order concerns are those of character; we want our students to be honest, to do their own work, and to respect other people and their property. The concern for citizenship is likely important to most teachers but is usually given the least amount of consideration. Generally, we believe that if students are compliant in our classes and well mannered in school, they will be good citizens. What this belief misses is the understanding that being good (as in obeying laws, showing respect, and voting) is only one very small aspect of being a responsible citizen of a democracy.

Being a citizen of a democracy goes far beyond a law and order view. Democracy is significantly more than a form of government or a system of laws that should be obeyed; it is a way of living that brings individualism and community together in very active, participatory ways.

Democracy needs to be pervasive, entering into the conduct of group activity from the level of the national government through the state and local governments into the activities of groups, organizations, and institutions. When we begin to view democracy more as a way of life for its citizens than simply a form of government, we see how democracy is distinctly different from other forms of societal organization and forms of government.

In general, *citizenship* refers to how people interact as members of a given community and how well they uphold the standards of the spirit and intent of certain laws and rules. Most commonly, citizenship is thought of as how a person acts as a member of a nation. However, one may be a citizen of a town, a community, a nation, and a school. How we act to facilitate the goals, standards, and values that have been set by the ruling body determines how good a citizen we are. That is, good citizens work for the benefit of the collective standards rather than for only their individual well-being.

However, in this general sense, good citizenship is a function of the type of government at hand. One can quickly recognize that being a good citizen of the People's Republic of China or Iraq can be considered vastly different from being a good citizen of Canada or the United States. The most immediate difference between totalitarian and democratic governments is seen in how the citizens act to uphold the spirit and intent of the laws and rules. Where the rules are arbitrary and dictatorial, the citizens are expected to follow them without question, regardless of what citizens of a democracy consider to be fair or just. The rules and laws in the totalitarian systems are chosen by the ruling elite to serve only the interests of the ruling class. The citizens, while they may willingly follow the rules, are given no choice in deciding what the nature of those rules are.

A second difference is less conspicuous. Democracy holds individualism and individual rights as important to the general good of all citizens. The basic ideals of the Bill of Rights—protection of minority and individual freedom and rights—recognize two very important foundations for freedom: the ideal of balance between the good of the community and the good of the individual and the protection of minorities from the tyranny of the majority. Further, the spirit of our democracy assumes and strives for intelligent and thoughtful participation on the part of the citizenry.

As well, good character is inexorably connected to good citizenship in a democracy. Character formation deals with issues of ethics and morality, whereas citizenship deals more with issues of law and legal codes. Simply put, morality and ethics begin where legal codes end. However, in a democracy, ethical behavior may be seen as the great facilitator of true democratic citizenship. This interaction of character and citizenship is the focus of civic responsibility.

CIVIC RESPONSIBILITY

To develop a sense of civic responsibility requires that educators understand the formative power of what students experience in schools. The communal and interpersonal relations students experience in school have a tremendous impact on their role in enhancing or inhibiting democratic dispositions later in their lives. Civic responsibility in a democracy is not something someone can be trained to blindly follow. As discussed in Chapter 3, the enfleshment of the dominant ideology (the holding of unwarranted beliefs) is the only possible outcome of such training. Rather, civic responsibility requires civic education—that is, education in ethics and citizenship that involves students actually experiencing and reflecting on their experience in the context of schooling.

Pratte (1988) has written one of the most powerful discussions of the notions of civic responsibility as the energizer of democracy. He stresses the fundamental importance of reflective thinking on the part of the citizenry and the value of a common ethic as cornerstones for having a lived democratic experience, one that can reach the ideals of allowing for individualism while still having a fair and just community.

According to Pratte and others such as Dewey (1916); Mosher, Kenny, and Garrod (1994); and even de Tocqueville (1838) in the 19th century, one of the greatest threats to realizing a fair and just society through democracy is the overemphasis on individualism at the expense of the collective. The arguments are easy to understand: the more individuals choose to do their own thing, so to say, the greater the likelihood that the rights of others, especially the less powerful, will be abused or eliminated. This is particularly so when the power disparity between the rich and poor is great.

The fundamental function of our democratic system is to enable a very large group of very diverse people to live with fairness and justice for all. For our society to err either by blindly following the dictates of government, by allowing the unchallenged policies of special interest groups to formulate law, or by insisting on extreme individualism (where doing one's own thing without regard for the collective is the norm) is to negate this fundamental function of our democracy. When the basic purpose of our system is violated, the violations play themselves out across race, class, gender, ethnicity, disability, age, and life-style preference. In this condition the government is no longer by, for, and of the people but a government by, for, and of only the powerful people, who gain at the expense of others.

We know that certain rights are protected by the Constitution in general and the Bill of Rights in particular. However, this protection has far more to do with restricting the activities of government that would abuse the less powerful than ensuring common civility and inclusion by individuals, institutions, and nongovernmental organizations. The Constitution and our legal codes offer prescriptions and limitations that are formal and often technical in nature rather than being principles shared, valued, and consciously enfleshed by the citizenry. The question, then, for teachers is how can we educate for dispositional knowledge of both the legal and ethical aspects of democracy?

When we speak of character and citizenship formation, we are speaking of educating for a civic responsibility that animates and powers our democracy. For Pratte (1988), this is articulated in the form of a "civic obligation" consisting of "concern, care, and tolerance," which we shall examine closely in the next section. We also must understand that those who have a disposition toward being concerned and caring are more than just nice, polite people.

When we graduate students who share a set of common civic values, which cut across the diversities of race, class, gender, and life-style, we have helped develop a populace that shares a common interest. This forms a connection among all members of the collective, and the common thread begins to connect a wide range of diverse elements in our democracy.

The connection that is possible with a simple but powerful shared civic ethic can serve to reduce the fragmentation of interests across our social order. Education for a disposition toward a civic ethic not only serves the behavior of students in our schools and classrooms, it also serves as a significant contribution toward reestablishing a democratic spirit in the school and, later, the social order.

The following section sets a tone for our behavior and creates a framework within which our students can delineate their behavior in the community of the school. Obviously, this implies our direct involvement in planning and teaching the elements of care, concern, and tolerance as part of the overt curriculum.

THE CIVIC OBLIGATION

Education for civic responsibility has historically been placed in a course of study (e.g., on government, problems of democracy, or civics) separated both from other subjects and from the lived experience of the students. Dispositional knowledge comes from experiencing, not from admonition, lecture, coercion, or a course or two. If we are to educate our students to be disposed to act and behave democratically, we must give consideration to *what* should be taught and *how* it should be taught.

Pratte (1988) suggests that the values of "concern, care, and tolerance" can serve as powerful subject matter for informing the dispositions necessary for animating democracy in our postmodern society. Concern, care, and tolerance are actually ethical predispositions for thoughtful, participatory citizenship. We believe that by holding such predispositions and thinking reflectively, democracy will become the guiding principle for our entire diverse social order in the 21st century.

Concern

The civic value of **concern** represents a motive state toward issues of fairness and justice. We all understand how we can have mundane concern—we may be concerned about taking an upcoming test, paying for car insurance, or getting a job. In any case of concern, we have *conscious interest* regarding something. Very simply put, anytime we are concerned, we are interested and motivated about something.

Although not explicitly dealt with by Pratte, concern as interest or a motive state refers to the state of mind required for thinking reflectively about anything in general and about our agency as citizens in particular. Dewey (1916a, 1916b, 1933) explains how interest is identical with concern and how it is a necessary condition for critical thinking.

As a civic value, concern represents a conscious interest in particular aspects or issues directly connected to the well-being of someone or some group. For example, we might have a conscious interest in such things as justice, integrity, fair play, and equal opportunity; the focus of our civic concern targets the treatment or condition of individuals or groups within the context of these democratic ideals. The civic value of concern is held for individuals as well as for the collective and can include a concern for balancing the treatment or rights of the individual with those of the collective.

Concern is also our immediate psychological reaction to something we find perplexing, unsettled, or incoherent—disturbing in some manner. At the gut level, many things can be disturbing to us. We are not suggesting that civic concern is simply a matter of having an instinctive gut reaction. We believe that it occurs as a result of civic education, which involves making meaning of experience. It involves coming to know oneself and others, especially the differences in the conditions under which others live. Through civic education, students learn of conditions based on advantage and privilege compared with those based on oppression and denial. Students gain a sense of one's civic obligation to be aware of diversities and what they are based on. As students learn about civic education, they should gain personal wisdom, based on their own experience, about who they are and what living a civic life means.

Care

The next element in the trinity of civic obligation, **care**, relates to the actions we take based on our concern. It involves valuing others such that we are willing to serve them in a manner that settles our concern and thus addresses the civic interest we hold for them. In the sense of citizenship, care may be embodied in government policies that address our concerns. For example, our concern for the health and well-being of our senior citizens resulted in the government entitlement policy of Medicare, which is a service that addresses one of our civic concerns.

For Pratte (1988), care in the civic sense is directed toward the property of "human dignity." Just as in the noncivic sense, we may care for our plants or our cars, in the civic sense we care for the dignity that democracy and morality tell us humans are entitled to. Care as service to others, as a democratic ethic, results in service to the democratic system—the action of service embodies the ideal of allowing diverse people to live together with dignity irrespective of cultural, racial, or other types of differences.

Just as civic concern is related to the preconditions for thinking reflectively about our democratic condition, civic care also relates to the action, participation, and service we perform in caring for conditions within our democratic system. Further, such performance is rooted in our thoughtful and critical reflections concerning our democratic institutions. We are the caretakers of the institutions that frame and operationalize our democratic system.

Understanding the interconnectedness of civic concern and care as civic empathy and service is critically important to understanding how they stand as values. But

it is equally important to understand their interconnectedness with democracy as a lived experience. Pratte puts it succinctly when he writes:

> The ethics of service and social responsibility are intimately interconnected in the life of a democratic community. Being predisposed to care for all others is an ethical obligation, an ethical disposition of commitment and conscientiousness, which must be connected to political judgment in the impersonal, logical, objective sense, across a wide range of civic matters. (1988, p. 70)

In this sense, the very heart of civic concern and care involves not only behaving ethically but also thinking reflectively, applying ethical principles across the range of civic issues and problems.

Tolerance

Tolerance, the third principle in the trinity of Pratte's civic obligation, represents a powerful yet usually misunderstood concept. As a civic virtue, tolerance governs our unreflective and often ego- or ethnocentric urges to demand that everyone behave, dress, and believe as we do. It has a very stipulative meaning that is often lost in common use of the term. To be tolerant is to consciously allow something that you do not consider to be right, proper, or correct and that you have the power to prohibit or hinder. We can exercise tolerance only over what we have some ability to affect; we cannot be tolerant about something over which we have absolutely no control. For example, we cannot be tolerant of such things as the weather, the performance of our favorite professional baseball team, or the deadlines publishers or professors give us for our work. We cannot exercise tolerance because, even though we do not consider them to be proper or appropriate, we are powerless to have it any other way. We can, however, exercise tolerance over many things we do not personally approve of but over which we can have some effect in preventing or at least hindering.

Not to be confused with the term *permissiveness*, tolerance as a civic virtue differs significantly in two ways. The first difference, as Pratte notes, "is in permissiveness being a simply behavioral description, whereas tolerance involves both moral judgment and some sort of response" (1988, p. 71). We need to place the notion of tolerance in the context of moral judgment, by which conscious and thoughtful consideration is given to our own values and those of others, which may be significantly different from ours.

The second difference between tolerance and permissiveness is that tolerance involves moral and reflective judgment, whereas permissiveness involves neither morality nor reflectivity. Care and concern as we have discussed them are involved in making a judgment to be tolerant. For example, we may decide to be tolerant because we have concern (interest) for the quality of the democratic experience of others and because we care for others' ability to have such experience. Permissiveness certainly has some of the same outcome characteristics as tolerance does, such as enabling others to act without restraint or limitations, but permissiveness is the result of nonthoughtful or indifferent behavior rather than the highly thoughtful and conscious behavior needed to exercise tolerance.

The act of being intolerant may also be exercised with equal civic concern and reflective thought to achieve ends that protect human dignity and the democratic experience. For example, we might choose to intervene in stopping a bully from extorting lunch money from a student. Based on our grounding in civic virtue, we act in this way because we have thoughtfully decided that, morally, we cannot tolerate the activity.

All decisions regarding toleration are determined reflectively and informed by the civic virtues of concern and care. Together, civic concern, care, and tolerance represent a moral or ethical stance indicative of having moral character both individually and collectively. The power in this trinity of civic obligation is in how it serves as the strong fiber of a democratic society's moral fabric. Without a unifying civic ethic, the motives and activities of our citizenry have no guidelines or frame of reference for acting democratically. Given our society's diverse and pluralistic composition, we cannot have a viable democracy and protect each other's rights without having a common connecting ethic or creed to link each other as citizens. This point has been argued by others—namely, Broudy (1981), Dewey (1916), Green (1971), and Pratte (1988). Pratte expresses this point cogently when he writes:

> It is important to grasp . . . that democratic practices would be impossible if divorced from a viable social ethic. A democracy requires both an ethic of obligation and an ethic of civic service practiced so that citizens are bonded in an affective way. Civic institutions require the exercise of civic service, for in this ethic resides democracy's real cohesion and consequently its strength. (pp. 77–78)

We see Pratte's "civic obligation" as a straightforward, reasoned combination of civic virtues that are simple yet powerful. In a society where many individuals and interest groups flinch when any mention of schools engaging in the teaching of values or civics beyond rote technicalities is made, we believe that these three civic and moral values are hard to oppose as unreasonable.

SETTING THE STAGE FOR PRACTICE

How can we educate using democratic discipline to achieve a viable democratic system? First we need to consider the current practices of teaching character and civic education. The operational definition teachers give to the term *citizenship* is usually implicit rather than explicit. When all levels and types of students seem to get along well in our school's setting, we tend to accept it without considering why it is so. Sometimes the terms *school climate* or *classroom climate* are used to refer to aspects of citizenship. However, little consideration has been given to planning climates that engage students in the practice of democratic citizenship. Indeed, the hidden curriculum of most schools and classrooms teaches students little about democratic ideals while teaching a great deal about nondemocratic, authoritarian governance and, worse still, ways to beat the system without getting caught.

Historically, there has been vulgar pragmatism at work in schools and classrooms, motivated by the values of control and containment of students to ensure order and discipline for the smooth operation of the management of large groups, administrative duties, and public image. Little has been done to include experience or participation in democratic conventions as a regular, planned part of the curriculum. It is one thing to frame our expectations for student behavior in terms of what facilitates our own desires and comforts (the vulgar pragmatism), and it is quite another to consider that we are instrumental in the formation and development of character and citizenship for adulthood in a democratic society.

The citizenry (including parents and policymakers) has always demanded that schools and teachers play a certain role in the formative development of citizenship. However, that traditionally prescribed role has been one of insistence and distance. It has been insistent in the demands for such things as requiring that students recite the Pledge of Allegiance, mandating the study of state governments, requiring a senior-level class in government, requiring the placement of flags in classrooms, and, in some cases, mandating prayer in the classroom.

Across the curriculum there has been virtually nothing that has promoted or sustained reflectivity or a real sense of engaging students in the practice of being moral and informed citizens. Indeed, the efforts that schools put forth, particularly ones that policymakers and special interest groups (such as fundamentalist churches, the National Rifle Association, and the American Legion) make, are ideological and emotional. Most images of citizenship are of unquestioned loyalty and patriotism produced through hegemony rather than through dialogue, discourse, and thoughtful analysis of values and interests framed by the ideals of democracy.

In many communities and certainly within many conservative interest groups, there is tremendous opposition to lessening the distance between the expectations of the school and the lived experience of students. Throughout our history those who have powerful influence over school policy have steadfastly refused to accept any efforts to educate students for a critically thinking citizenry. Yet since the founding of our democracy many have written about schools serving the purpose of educating for democracy; many of those, including Dewey, argued for an enlightened citizenry as an absolute necessity for the survival of democracy.

No group would argue publicly against the idea of the need for an enlightened citizenry to sustain democracy. However, the operational definition of the term *enlightened* is interpreted very differently across various groups. Fundamentally and foundationally, the operational definition of the term has meant, in a curiously perverted way, having the ability, nonreflective and nonthoughtful, to reproduce dominant values, attitudes, and beliefs in students. Being a good citizen has been far more often associated with unquestioning loyalty than with any sense of reasoned civic ethic or obligation. Although the problem with this stance is quite obvious if we advocate intellectual empowerment, there is another troublesome aspect to it. Those who promote unthinking loyalty have significantly different goals than those who promote the notion of think-

ing loyalty. Pratte (1988) comments that "a thinking loyalty, rather than an unthinking loyalty, is fundamental to producing a *just* democratic society" (p. 8, italics added). The term *just democratic society* represents the significant difference between the two aforementioned groups. Indeed, we can even begin to see the role that civil disobedience plays in seeking a just society as a thinking loyalty to democratic principles.[1]

Again, as in Chapter 3, we face the fictions and illusions of democracy when it is allowed to be framed only by the special interests of the ruling class. Specifically, the ruling class portrays anyone who attempts to generate curriculum for thoughtful critique of the activities of our democracy as anti-American, radical, liberal, or even communist.[2] What is missing in this position is the recognition that there is a reasoned middle ground that sees discourse, debate, critique, and even criticism as positive for the health of our system because it is reflective patriotism. The urgency of dealing with the marginalization of the advocates of a thoughtful foundation for democratic citizenship is very precisely stated by Pratte:

> We must avoid at all costs a civic education that fails to question persistently the central and political traditions of the nation-society, on the one hand, and on the other hand promotes an overly zealous and critical attitude toward the organization and operation of modern governmental institutions, so that civic distrust and negativism result. (1988, p. 8)

---

[1] Critical to understanding the role of civil disobedience is an understanding of the willingness of the protester to admit to breaking the rule or law and to accept the consequences in the name of justice.

[2] In 1968, the work of Jerome Bruner and others resulted in a public school curriculum package called *Man: A Course of Study*. Part of this program engaged students in the examination and discussion of conflicting cultural and social values. The project was strongly attacked by a variety of conservative and religious groups as being everything from secular humanism to socialist propaganda.

Pratte's thought strikes at the heart of our guiding principle in writing this book: Educating for an ethical, reflective, critical, and informed citizenry is the best guarantee for realizing the ideals of a truly democratic society. When we ask what we want our students to act like as future citizens, and when we decide to educate for future citizenship, we begin to establish the agenda for the formative development of our students.

Likewise, when we explore and examine the core issues of character—such as integrity, honesty, care, concern, and tolerance—we also begin to set a formative agenda for character development that connects ethics and morality to the health of our political system. As educators, we begin to understand both our responsibility and agency in the promotion of our democratic system and accept the notion of a viable civic imperative. When we are willing to accept consciously a role in the formation of character and citizenship, we begin to postulate ourselves not only as keepers of order but as shapers of citizens as well.

CHOOSERS AND LEARNERS

Part of the problem surrounding the failure of schools to take an active role in the formation of democratic values in students has been associated with the prescribed roles for teachers and students. As discussed in previous chapters, Bowles and Gintis (1989) frame the problem of prescribed roles well when they describe the traditional school setting as one where the teacher's role is that of a chooser and the student's role is that of a learner. While at first glance there seems to be nothing unreasonable about these roles, Bowles and Gintis comment that in practice the two roles are clearly partitioned such that choice or democratic exercise is disallowed for the learners at all meaningful levels.

When discipline is framed by the chooser–learner partition, teachers tend to consider discipline only in terms of control and punishment; that is, they see discipline as something they do to, not for, students who act in ways that violate rules or expectations for conduct. The problem here is one of power relations in the sense that we hold students accountable for rules and expectations over which they have had no decision latitude. A deeper analysis of the relationship between accountability and decision latitude highlights the root of the problem and gives us tremendous insight into an element critically necessary for democratic discipline to work.

We are not advocating that the fox be charged with guarding the hen house. Just because we see the students as omitted from participation and decision making does not mean that students should make all the rules all the time without the participation of teachers or administrators. We are proposing that teachers consider the viability of the middle ground between the absolute authority of the educator and the absolute authority of students. Legally and traditionally, educators have the final responsibility for policies and rules, but the process of developing those rules can be much more participatory than it typically is.

ACCOUNTABILITY AND DECISION LATITUDE

The analysis of the relationship between accountability and decision latitude shows us that true accountability is a direct function of decision latitude. To hold someone accountable for something, the person being held accountable must hold decision latitude over the condition he or she is being held accountable for. For example, if a friend is holding you accountable for repaying a loan, it is easier to accept the accountability if you have more than enough money from this week's pay to cover the debt. If you simply do not have enough money from the week's pay to cover the debt, holding you accountable is moot because you hold no decision latitude over whether to pay up. There is a greater sense of owning up to our responsibilities when we hold decision latitude—that is, when we have options. It is far more difficult to own up when we have little or no control over the circumstances to which we are held accountable.

We begin to see now that, in the chooser–learner partitioning of schools and classrooms, excluding students from any role in rule making makes holding them accountable more unrealistic and difficult. We have held students accountable for our decisions about rules and expectations with no input from them. The problem is exacerbated, particularly in secondary schools, when students travel from classroom to classroom, to different teachers with differing expectations and rules, none of which the students participated in making.

As a general rule, the more decision latitude individuals have over something, the more they can be held accountable for their performance and actions. Axiomatically, democracy is a system that, ideally, is predicated on vesting individuals with optimum decision latitude regarding their conduct, where accountability is a function of individuals accepting responsibility for the decisions they have been empowered to make. The legal code also holds individuals responsible for their actions (this is where the trite but true adage that "for every freedom, there is a corresponding responsibility" becomes relative). Therefore, if we are to educate for democratic citizenship and enhance the cooperativeness of our students, we need to ask how and in what form students have latitude regarding decisions that affect their own community within the school.

If we value character and citizenship formation, we must consider how we can provide students with the opportunity to practice the behaviors and decision making that lead to their understanding of morals and democracy. Democratic citizenship is participatory; democratic character is moral agency. Both require that students practice to acquire and hold consciously the values and understandings necessary for their realization.

WHOSE RULES?

There are serious implications for developing democratic citizens through schooling if we accept that there is a chooser–learner partition. The primary implication is that students do not have the opportunity to make choices and that adults in the roles of teachers, administrators, and policymakers establish and enforce the rules. The central idea of democracy is the ability of those governed to participate in making the rules, yet the rules and expectations for governing students are imposed from outside their community.

Imagine what the public outcry would be if suddenly all the adults in America were forced to live under laws that were chosen by a group of people from another nation without any input from us. We would no longer consider the laws of our nation to be our laws; they would be mandates we neither own nor accept. Indeed, the basis for the American Revolution was grounded in such a circumstance.

When democracy prevails, ideally we have laws that we believe in and understand. The ideal condition in a democracy is that we obey laws because we understand them and accept them as consistent with our own purposes as ethical human beings. In other words, the central vision of a democracy is to have laws and rules that are not arbitrary but are instead consciously internalized and believed in by the citizenry.

The mainstay of democracy is the idea that the rules are society's rules, not simply narrow vested interests. Democratic rules are those we understand, believe in, and own through our sense of knowing what is right. In the case of schooling and especially discipline, we need to ask what is the formative effect on students when rules and policies are chosen by someone outside the student community.

There is a humorous story of a first grader who was told by his teacher to put away some materials that the student had been using. The student responded by asking why they should be put away, whereupon the teacher commented that those were the rules. The first grader then responded, with some insight, that those were her rules, not his. Aside from the humor of the situation, this story holds important insight from the exchange about the formation of democratic citizenship. People of all ages will behave more reasonably if they feel and think that a rule is important and valuable. The situation of the first grader takes on new light when we recognize that what is problematic is not the rule itself but the child's inability to value the rule as beneficial to the classroom community (returning materials to their proper places benefits everyone in the class).

At this point we begin to distinguish between two important views of rules and laws. On the one hand, we may accept rules and follow them because we are afraid of sanctions; on the other hand, we may accept and follow rules because we believe them to be valuable. Social conventions are usually based on the latter motivation. There are hundreds of unwritten rules that guide our general social behavior, such as shaking hands when introduced to someone, helping someone who has fallen down, or knocking on someone's door before entering.

Similarly, there are many laws that, like social conventions, we follow because we understand and value their purpose. With many laws, if not most, we feel also that we have had representation in the establishment of the law. We also know as citizens that through the actions of our government representatives or through petition and referendum we can eliminate or alter laws we deem unjust or unfair. This is not to say that every citizen agrees with every law, but generally most citizens respect laws and understand that they are for the good of the collective. It is important for us to recognize that schools and classrooms do not require the complexity of laws that a state or nation requires.

However, the principles that apply to why people obey rules is important in considering who formulates the rules and what the likelihood is that they will be followed.

There are two goals at hand for the teacher who wishes to foster formative development of democratic citizens. The first is allowing student participation in developing rules of governance; the second is having the students consciously and critically understand and value the rules they develop. In one important sense, democratic citizenship and the ethics of being a good person are predicated on our seeking to personally understand the question Who am I and who are we? Participation in rule making and personally valuing the rules that we create leads us to deal with the interrelationship of the individual and the collective in a manner that promotes and protects the well-being of both.

CREDIBILITY

Conscious and reasoned rules arrived at through democratic consensus become operational principles for behavior thoughtfully accepted by the group participating in their development. They are not someone else's rules. On the contrary, they are credible.

The last significant consideration in our understanding of democratic behavior is *credibility*. Credibility represents the motive behind adhering to a law or rule. Broudy (1981) explains credibility as a most critical element in assessing or judging someone's behavior. For example, when we hear the CEO of a major business claim that "minimum wages should be held in check because it is good for the country," we may accept his claim as valid simply because he is successful and sounds reasonable. However, when we pursue the question of credibility by reflectively questioning the motive behind his statement, we may well discover that by keeping wages at the current minimum rate his company will gain greater profits regardless of whether doing so is "good for the country." Hence the claim lacks credibility based on its self-serving, rather than civically principled, nature. However, if this CEO were to declare that raising the minimum wage would be good for the country, reflective questioning of the claim would produce much greater credibility because the self-interest of his corporation would not be enhanced.

Motive is central to the integrity of what we do. Thus, the issue of credibility relates directly to notions of a thinking loyalty (a loyalty reflectively arrived at) to our political system and of participatory involvement of students in governing their school environment. Students may follow a rule simply because they are dutiful, because the rule does not interfere with their desires, or because they fear the consequences of breaking the rule (deterrent). Any of these three motivations may facilitate our classroom management, but what formative effects do they have on the moral character and civic values of students if they go unchecked or unexamined?

The motivation for following rules and obeying laws ought to be credible in the sense that the individual following the rule understands and values the rule and the ramifications of breaking it beyond convenient and expeditious reasons of selfishness.[3] Civic care, concern, and tolerance are far more credible motivations if we are committed to building a foundation for democratic ethics and consciousness. One can follow rules either blindly or with conscious understanding. Blind adherence to any rule or principle can be problematic because it denies or precludes any rational explanation or discussion as to the rule's effect and desirability. Just as motive is important in understanding why someone breaks a rule, it is equally important in a democracy to understand why someone does not break a rule.

SUMMARY

The discussion in this chapter has tremendous implications for practice. Giving consideration to creating curriculum and instruction for civic education is, for the most part, novel, if not radical, in light of the historically conservative direction of traditional teaching and schooling. However, the current state of affairs regarding the failure to overtly consider civic education as a combination of personal ethics and the ideals of a 200-year-old political system is not the fault of teachers either past or present. The fault lies with a combination of elements and groups, most of which we have discussed herein.

Teachers should not be held responsible for the problem of the lack of teaching for democratic citizenship. Practicing teachers can do only what they know how to do based on their experience either as students having observed what their teachers did or as learners in their teacher education programs. For practice to change, beginning educators need to be able to conceptualize their impact on character and citizenship formation in a manner vastly different than that of their predecessors. Discipline must be reconceptualized to accommodate the formative effects it has on students. When we can accept that everything we do, whether in our planning books or in our demeanors, has such definite effects on our students, we can begin to be consummately purposeful in our academic and disciplinary activities.

To educate students to hold dearly a civic obligation and sense of mission about their individual roles in the realization of democratic ideals is ultimately the choice of the teacher. We make choices regarding what we do in our own classrooms and how we act with our peers to influence the political and social climate of our schools. In no small way, we are moral agents whether we accept the responsibility or not.

LOOKING AHEAD

This chapter presents what we must consider in the quest to be reflective practitioners working to educate for democracy in our schools. Chapter 6, "Discipline, Law,

---

[3] The issue of credibility in ethics and law was brought to the forefront of democratic considerations by Harry Broudy in his 1981 book, *Truth and Credibility: A Citizen's Dilemma.*

and the Constitution," will take us to the heart of our democratic principles in addressing how we might develop an initiative to compare the U.S. Constitution and Bill of Rights to the real-world experiences of today's students. The chapter will discuss the key principles of our democratic system of law, ways they are interpreted, and ways their significance can be part of the activities of teaching and schooling.

❖ REFLECTIVE ACTIVITIES

1. What distinguishes the role of citizens in a democracy such as ours from the role of citizens in nondemocratic societies? What does this distinction mean for the role schools and teachers play in the lives of students in a democratic society?
2. Discipline is a major activity of teachers. How do nonreflective approaches (as compared with reflective approaches) to the activities of discipline affect the formation of character and citizenship in our students? How can we be teaching values even when we do not formally plan do so?
3. Why is it important for a democracy of diverse peoples to have a common thread of connection to each other? What role does a sense of civic obligation play in uniting diverse peoples? What does a democratic ethic have to do with making democratic living better for everyone?

❖ REFERENCES

Bowles, S., & Gintis, H. (1989). Can there be a liberal philosophy of education in a democratic society? In H. Giroux & P. McLaren (Eds.), *Critical pedagogy, the state, and cultural struggle*. Albany: SUNY Press.

Broudy, H. (1981). *Truth and credibility: A citizen's dilemma*. New York: Longman.

Bruner, J. (1968). *Man: A course of study* (social studies curriculum project). Cambridge, MA: Educational Development Center.

Dewey, J. (1916a). *Democracy in education*. Englewood Cliffs, NJ: Merrill/Prentice Hall.

Dewey, J. (1916b). Interest and effort. In *Essays on philosophy and psychology*.

Dewey, J. (1933). *How we think*. Lexington, MA: D. C. Heath.

Green, T. (1971). *The activities of teaching*. New York: McGraw Hill.

Mosher, R., Kenny, R., & Garrod, A. (1994). *Preparing for citizenship: Teaching youth to live democratically*. Westport, CT: Praeger.

Pratte, R. (1988). *The civic imperative: Examining the need for civic education*. New York: Teachers College Press.

Tocqueville, Alexis de (1838). *Democracy in America*. New York: G. Dearborn & Co.

Chapter 6

Discipline, Law, and the Constitution

1. How have Supreme Court interpretations of the Constitution changed the conduct of schooling?
2. Why is it important to view freedom and individual rights on a continuum rather than in absolute terms?
3. How can understanding the basis for Supreme Court rulings inform our efforts to create democratic discipline? How can this understanding, along with an understanding of the key principles of the Bill of Rights, lead us to create mechanisms by which students can learn to live democratically?
4. What considerations beyond the law, the Constitution, and the Bill of Rights must be given to establish workable democratic mechanisms within schools and classrooms?
5. What is the relationship between understanding the mechanisms of democracy and having a disposition toward acting from a sense of democratic ethics?

Understanding discipline from the perspectives of ethics, philosophy, and critical practice is incomplete without recognizing the roles that the local, state, and federal governments play in shaping our ideals and realities concerning discipline. All three levels of government affect the rights and responsibilities of students and teachers.

We also need to understand the principles embodied in the law if we are to engage our students in experiencing the realities of learning to live democratically within the school community. Democracy is much more than a system of laws and rules—it is a way of living, embodying democratic principles. We must see the connections between the legal principles that govern our democracy and their application to the experiences students have in schools and classrooms.

This chapter will first examine the basic relations of local, state, and federal law as they most generally relate to the issues of schooling. We will then focus on the initiatives of constitutional law in terms of how several key Supreme Court rulings have shaped the climate of democracy in schools and classrooms. If educators are truly passionate about creating a foundation for democratic discipline and citizenship, they must capture the democratic initiative started by the courts. We will attempt to show that certain constitutional and legal principles can be used to inform our initiative to have students experience democratic principles within the school community.

LOCAL, STATE, AND FEDERAL CONNECTIONS TO SCHOOLING

The most substantial contributions to the body of laws that govern how schools operate emanate from the individual states rather than from the local or federal levels. In the U.S. Constitution there is no specific empowerment given to the federal government to directly regulate schools. Hence, Washington's ability to regulate schooling is indirect. On the local level, communities and school districts can regulate schools only within the specific framework of the body of school law created by the state government. Indeed, one of the problems we encounter in the study of school law is that all 50 states have different sets of laws governing the operation of schools.

Further, the body of state laws that govern the operation of schools is much broader in scope than most people first realize. State school law covers virtually everything schools do, from funding processes to pupil personnel regulations, proficiency testing, teacher certification and licensure, tenure and dismissal procedures, retirement plans, and corporal punishment permissibility. Certainly in most cases, state school law codes give decision latitude to local districts, but that latitude can be used only within the limits set by the laws of the particular state.

However, states may not make any law abridging the U.S. Constitution. Further, the Constitution provides certain guarantees to all citizens and provides principles for the conduct of all institutions, particularly for public-sector institutions such as schools. The general constitutional principles are just that, general principles to guide fair and just treatment of citizens and to protect individual rights. Whereas the Constitution does not specifically address issues regarding schooling, the federal court system, which culminates in the Supreme Court, determines how the general constitutional principles may apply to the specific activities of public institutions.[1] In this manner, the entire range of school regulations, from state law to local building policy, falls under the potential scrutiny of the courts as they may examine the constitutionality of any policy, requirement, or law as it may affect individual rights.

---

[1] The emphasis here is on the word *public*. Public school policy is viewed differently than private school policy, particularly in the application of the principles of the Fourteenth Amendment, which is concerned with individuals' rights to due process. Before generalizing the application of constitutional law or court rulings to private school venues, we should check the validity of the application.

CONSTITUTIONAL LAW AND THE ACTIVITIES OF DISCIPLINE

Schools and teachers were once able to operate much as they pleased regardless of constitutional principles. The legal concept of in loco parentis protected their actions from constitutional challenge—educators were viewed by the courts as acting in the place of the parent when applying discipline. Because administrators and teachers were seen in this way, the courts deferred from making judgments regarding the constitutionality of their actions. Students, as children, were not viewed as having the same constitutional rights as adult citizens.

Over the past several decades, the principle of in loco parentis has weakened substantially, although it still remains viable in diminished form. As the principle diminishes, the principles of constitutional protection of the rights of the student increase.

In the most general sense, the courts use the principles expressed in the Constitution to adjudicate issues of rights that are related directly to three core democratic values: freedom, equality, and justice. Freedom refers to the right to act or speak in a protected manner; equality refers to fair distribution of benefits and requirements; justice refers to fair procedures of treatment. In other words, the courts have granted students some degree of constitutional guarantees to freedom of speech and expression, equal opportunity and access, and the right to due process.

In terms of what we have discussed in the previous chapters, the role of schools in the process of forcing students into compliant acceptance of dominant norms and values has diminished as the legal doctrine of in loco parentis has weakened. This is not to say that the courts have ruled that students are entitled to full and comprehensive constitutional rights, nor that schools are to be bastions of democratic entitlements. As we well know, schools and classrooms are not places where democratic constitutional rights are conspicuous by their presence. We consider this a travesty in U.S. schools.

In the following section we explain several court-decreed applications of constitutional principles to the conduct of discipline-related issues and activities.

FREEDOM OF SPEECH AND THE EXTENSION OF CONSTITUTIONAL PROTECTIONS

The *Wooster v. Sunderland* (1915) case concerned the expulsion of Earl Wooster from a California high school for his refusal to apologize publicly for a speech he had made regarding unsafe school facilities. The court upheld Wooster's expulsion on the basis that his refusal to apologize was indicative of serious misconduct that deserved discipline. In other words, the court essentially ruled that Wooster's refusal to be compliant made his expulsion necessary to maintain school discipline. What we see in the *Wooster* decision is the widely held view of the time that public school students had no entitlement to constitutional protection of the rights granted to adults, in this case the specific right to free speech.

In another case, *Tinker v. Des Moines* (1969), the Supreme Court took a large step forward in its interpretation of how the basic rights of the Constitution apply in school settings. The *Tinker* case involved a group of high school students in Des Moines, Iowa, who had worn black armbands to school in protest of the Vietnam War. The high school had a policy, known to the protesting students, that prohibited the wearing of armbands because such display could cause a disturbance. When the students were suspended for their protest, they took the case to court, arguing that their right to free speech had been violated. The court ruled in favor of the students.

The contrast between the rulings in *Wooster* and *Tinker* is significant in two ways. First, and most obvious, is that the *Tinker* ruling represents the court's view that students have a degree of constitutional protection of the basic rights granted to the adult citizenry. Second, just as the *Wooster* case ruling is indicative of the beliefs of the time (remember, in 1915 women had not yet been granted the right to vote), the ruling in *Tinker* represents how beliefs and interpretations of the applicability of democratic principles change over time.

For our purposes in examining the foundations for democratic discipline, the majority decision in *Tinker* represents a major milestone in the argument that democratic principles must be thoughtfully integrated into the activities and policies of schooling. Justice Fortas, in writing for the court majority, explicitly argued that schools educate for citizenship and that they must integrate the vital principles of constitutional rights "if we are not to strangle the free mind at its source and teach youth to discount important principles of our government as mere platitudes" (*Tinker v. Des Moines Independent School District*, 393 U.S. 503, 1969).

Historically, the courts have examined the interests of the state (the policy body governing schools as exemplified by either the U.S. government, state government, local government, or the school board) against the interests of the individual. The courts thus wrestle with the issue of interests and how compelling those interests are in adjudicating disputes over the rights of the individual versus the rights of the collective. Essentially, the court asks whether the governing body has a **compelling interest** in restricting the rights of the individual to protect the welfare of the group. As we can see from the striking contrast between the decisions in *Wooster* and *Tinker*, the answer to the question of compelling interest is entirely a function of the majority view of the court and can change radically over time.

The compelling interest legal question notwithstanding, the guiding thesis of this book moves the question into the arena of education, most specifically regarding teachers as they develop a consciousness about discipline in terms of philosophy, ethics, and citizenship. In one sense, our argument is for educators to pre-empt the courts' determinations by giving thoughtful consideration to discipline plans that incorporate constitutional principles as part of the lived experience of our students within the community of the school.[2] When we examine how schools may create

---

[2] Forrest Gathercoal has incorporated this argument in his book *Judicious Discipline*. We believe that it is well worth reading for a detailed analysis of how constitutional principles, particularly those of the Bill of Rights, can apply to school settings.

Figure 6.1

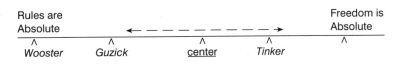

democratic communities that afford students the opportunity to experience democracy, we need to recognize that the judicial processes used in the interpretations of the constitution inform the process.

As we draw from the experiences of constitutional interpretations of school policy and law, we see that a continuum emerges where, on one extreme, discipline is determined by a set of absolutes where the rules exist for their own sake and, on the other extreme, freedom is absolute and students can do anything they choose. Figure 6.1 represents this continuum with three court decisions located in terms of their relations to the two extremes.

From the placement of *Tinker*, we infer that the courts did not rule that students have absolute freedom of expression, which is correct. The *Tinker* decision was not as radical in granting freedom of action to students as many thought it to be. The court used the principle of compelling interest in giving explicit consideration to student conduct in terms of the degree to which it "*materially* disrupts classwork or involves *substantial* disorder or invasion of the rights of others [italics added]." Whereas the court ruled that antiwar armbands did not materially disrupt nor cause substantial disorder, it also made explicit that freedom of speech is not license to do anything regardless of its effects on others.

The court's rejoinder that freedom of speech is not license to put others at risk was affirmed in *Guzick v. Drebus* (1971), a case similar to *Tinker*. This case involved a Cleveland, Ohio, high school rule that banned students from wearing buttons and badges that made reference to racial positions. The court upheld the ban because the wearing of these symbols had led to fighting between white and black students. The relative placement of *Guzick* on the continuum shows its contrast to both *Wooster*, where the courts saw students as having no entitlement to constitutional protection, and *Tinker*, where the courts saw a clear entitlement to constitutional protection.

DUE PROCESS AND THE EXTENSION OF CONSTITUTIONAL PROTECTIONS

Due process is another area of constitutional law that has direct ramifications in the realm of discipline. The Fourteenth Amendment speaks to an individual's right to procedural and substantive due process of law. Very simply put, this refers to one's right to fairness in the application of official actions and the freedom from being treated arbitrarily in a discriminatory or unreasonable manner. (For the most part, the distinctions between procedural and substantive due process are very technical and, as

specifics, have little direct bearing on the activities of teaching and learning for democracy, whereas the general principle has a great deal to do with such activities.)

As with freedom of speech and expression, the courts traditionally held the primacy of school policy and refused students any constitutional protection of due process rights on the basis of in loco parentis. However, in the case of *Goss v. Lopez* (1975) the court extended the constitutional principle of due process to students. This case involved the suspension of several high school students, including the plaintiff, Dwight Lopez, for alleged acts of violence. Certain students' acts were clearly documented, but the acts of Lopez and other students were not. None of the students were given a hearing regarding their suspensions, nor were they informed of the charges against them. The Lopez claim was that the students' right to due process was violated; the court agreed.

The *Goss* decision was grounded in the same principles as in *Tinker:* students do not lose their constitutional rights when they enter a public school. Just as in the *Tinker* decision, two important points were made by the court. First was the immediate granting of due process rights to students; second was the reaffirmation of the general principle in *Tinker* that extended constitutional protection to students.

In some ways the *Goss* decision has more immediate ramifications for the integration of democratic principles into the process of schooling than does the *Tinker* decision because it specifically recognizes the right of the student to a fair hearing and the right to be able to respond to charges made. This recognition gives citizenship rights that protect the students from arbitrary action on the part of school officials that can deprive them of good reputations and the right to be schooled. The ruling serves to protect students from being punished for charges unknown to them, a right fundamental to any democratic community.

Just as in *Tinker,* the court recognized that the *Goss* decision was not an absolute. *Goss* does not give students the absolute right to full-blown legal hearings in every case of alleged student misconduct. Indeed, the court was very considerate of the application of due process as a function of the extent of the charges, the immediacy of the transgression, and the severity of the proposed punishment. In other words, the extent to which the student is entitled to a formal hearing varies considerably.

School officials are not bound to the formalities of due process in the more mundane or trivial aspects of discipline. Such routine acts as serving detentions, assigning extra homework, and sending students to the principal's office are not sufficiently significant to warrant due process procedures. The procedures are needed in reasonable degree in more serious situations, such as suspensions and expulsions. In normal suspension situations and the like, while the courts recognize that elements of due process must be present, the court in *Goss* explicitly recognized the problem that escalation of formal procedures creates in paralyzing the effectiveness of operating a school.

Although the specifics of the court rulings regarding such issues as freedom of speech and the right to due process are extremely important constitutional principles, more significant here is that the court rulings have legitimized and grounded the foundations for democratic discipline. However, we need to understand the distinction between the imposition of certain democratic principles from the outside and the creation of democratic principles from within the school community. Simply because a court has decreed that students are entitled to certain constitutional rights is not a guarantee that students will be educated in democratic principles.

CAPTURING THE CONSTITUTIONAL INITIATIVE

While it is certainly significant that the courts have extended limited constitutional protections to students, it is too easy to overestimate the significance in terms of its ramifications for shaping a future citizenry. To begin with, the vast majority of students is unaware of either the principles involved or the application of the principles to their living democratically. It is one thing to be given due process in a discipline hearing or to exercise free speech in a school setting—it is quite another thing to be motivated by those same principles in the conduct of one's behavior within the school and community.

Living democratically requires understanding the particular democratic principles and being consciously motivated by those principles as key values behind our actions. In other words, one needs a certain sophistication to act democratically in any consistent manner that is more than simply self-serving. We know that the ideological-philosophical character of the Supreme Court changes. As the court becomes more politically conservative, the likelihood of the once-liberal extensions of constitutional protections being reduced is very real. If the extensions are reduced, who will protest from within the school community if no one understands nor values their entitlements to constitutional protections? Why was the democratization initiated by the courts and not by educators nor large numbers of students?

The answers to these questions relate largely to the intellectual sophistication required to understand the complexities of democratic principles and the commitment to value them enough to be motivated to seek their integration in the activities of teaching and schooling. Clearly, as we have discussed earlier, certain ideological and philosophical positions value control and cultural reproduction more than the formative development of a reflective democratic citizenry.

Capturing the **constitutional initiative** refers to educators as the prime movers in making constitutional principles part of the overt curriculum of discipline. It means that teachers should no longer wait for court decisions to include constitutional principles in their disciplinary actions. Capturing the constitutional initiative requires our being motivated by a **democratic ethic** and being consciously concerned that our students experience the basic legal principles of democracy as articulated within the Constitution. To prepare to capture the initiative, we must be willing to work to fluently understand the implications that the principles of the Constitution hold for developing a curriculum for democratic citizenship.

SETTING THE STAGE

As we see in *Tinker* and the other court cases, there is a continuum along which the rights of the collective are balanced with the rights of the individual. The principle of compelling interest is reflected in this continuum.

When the courts consider the compelling interest that the school-governing body has in restricting individuals' rights to ensure the health, safety, or well-being of the group, they are in effect considering the necessary degree of restriction (in contrast to the degree of freedom) granted under the Constitution. In general, the courts will also consider the setting in determining the degree of interest: the more public the institution, the more the rights of the individual are protected. For example, the courts will extend more constitutional coverage to public institutions such as public schools and government agencies than they will to private institutions such as private schools and business establishments.

Where the courts historically have looked at the constitutionality of individual rights as a function of how much peril a particular right puts the community in, we must do likewise as curriculum developers. We must recognize that working for democratic climates in schools and classrooms is not a matter of either–or. It is extremely important to grasp the notion that the application of the principle of compelling interest will be different in its application to the rights of children and adolescents in school settings than it is in its application to adult settings. In other words, while we agree that students cannot be given freedoms identical to those that adults have, we believe that students must have more access to the rights and procedures of justice, freedom, and equality than currently available in traditional school settings. We are working toward the formative development of a critical democratic ethic and understanding. We are not working to simply entitle students to constitutional rights but to develop knowledge of constitutional rights and responsibilities through creating explicit learning experiences directly connected to those rights and responsibilities.

We need to cogently understand the principle of compelling interest for two other fundamental reasons. First, it will enable us to communicate to and convince school authorities and parents that the plan will not be a threat to operating an orderly school. Second, it will allow us to truly balance the interests of the school with the interests of individual rights.

For students to learn and experience the elemental principles of the Constitution, we must be willing to work in every possible way to construct opportunities that push the limits of freedom while maintaining the order necessary for the general activities of teaching and schooling. Gathercoal (1990) speaks directly to this issue when he writes:

> We are now at the core, the very heart and soul of the question facing educators in public schools today. *Is there a way to establish and maintain an effective learning environment in our schools, while teaching and respecting student rights of freedom, justice, and equality?* [italics added] (p. 17)

In other words, what principles can facilitate our construction of a democratic school community that will not seriously jeopardize the compelling interest of the state (i.e., school authorities) to maintain an orderly and effective school operation? Addressing this question directly and seriously helps us overcome our fears of anarchy within the school, a vestige of our own untested belief system that seduces us into seeing things in absolute terms. Further, it brings us back to the idea of a continuum that speaks equally to the principles of compelling interest and freedom and control. We seek a framework against which our decisions about a democratic curriculum can be made. The continuum, as shown in Figure 6.2, can lead us to secure an appropriate balance for the level of students we are teaching.

As mentioned in Chapter 2, a good working definition of *curriculum* is McCutcheon's (1995) notion of "what the students have the opportunity to learn." With this definition in mind, we begin to plan our foundation for a democratic curriculum by first considering the fundamental constitutional principles that can be applied to the school community. Then we choose the types of situations that will afford students the opportunity to experience these principles. This is a major part of the process of how we, as educators, capture the constitutional initiative.

Figure 6.2

Rules are Absolute		Freedom is Absolute

Control ← — — — — — — — — — — — — — — — → *Anarchy*

(Compelling Interest)   (No Compelling Interest)

STARTING POINTS FOR THE CONSTITUTIONAL INITIATIVE

Although the rulings of the Supreme Court are limited in their direct application to discipline, they deal essentially with freedom of speech and due process as well as the generalized notion that students are entitled to constitutional protection. Even though students' freedoms may be more limited than those of the general citizenry, the basis for such entitlements resides within the framework of the Constitution. When we revisit the idea of discipline as creating opportunities for the formative development of democratic citizenship, we realize the importance of students' experiencing the very basis of our democracy as framed by the Constitution.

The Constitution itself must be viewed as foundational in guiding our plans for democratic discipline. The articles of the Constitution provide a framework for creating mechanisms for democratic experience. The basic framework consists of the following:

- Statement of intent and mission (Preamble)
- The organization and responsibilities of the legislative branch (Article I)
- The organization and responsibilities of the executive branch (Article II)
- The organization and responsibilities of the judicial branch (Article III)
- The means for changing the framework (Article IV)
- Enumeration of the basic rights and guarantees of the citizenry (the Bill of Rights and the amendments)

The U.S. Constitution serves as the framework for the organization of state and local governments, with appropriate technical modifications needed as the size of the collective to be governed lessens (e.g., the specific manner in which representatives are elected, the length of time they serve, the way courts are organized). Because this is a book about democratic ideals as they affect the formation of democratic citizenship and character, we address the fundamentals of the Constitution in their idealized form. The following articles and amendments to the Constitution suggest experiences that need to be developed as part of our students' opportunity to experience fundamental elements of our democracy.

Article I: Establishment of the Legislative Branch

The ideas of representation and participation in rule making are most fundamental to democracy. In its ideal form, the legislative facet works as an advocate of the voice of the people it represents. Further, the legislature comprises a cross-section of the larger population it represents. The implications for schooling are vast when we draw from Article I. The purpose of a legislative branch is to provide a forum for the development of rules that represent the will of the people they will live under.

In the case of schooling, Article I speaks to what we have traditionally seen in the form of student and class councils. However, these councils usually serve in only a token manner. Rarely do they actually operate as bodies that legislate school and

classroom rules. In the ideal form, the legislative component of the democratic experience for students can be an exercise in participatory democracy.

Participatory democracy refers to the ideal of having as much involvement in rule making and ruling as possible on the part of the citizens. Most student councils reflect only the technical aspect of the democratic experience. They are made up of elected representatives who rarely do anything other than organize special activities—rather than engage the spirit of democracy through discussion of rules, conditions, and decisions made by school authorities that affect the student community. As we look at the spirit of Article I, as well as the spirit of educating for democratic citizenship, we must consider providing the technical mechanisms that give students an effective voice in the decisions governing their lives within the school.

Article II: Establishment of the Executive Branch

The idea that an elected leader is needed to carry out the activities of government reflects the notion that the people are free to choose a credible representative of the interests and issues most important to the quality and character of the type of life they desire. Article II guides us to consider a form of elected representative leadership that is more than simply the exercise of a popularity contest. When we actively provide students (be they class presidents, student council presidents, or school presidents) with guidance and a framework for democratic citizenship, we must help them frame the executive role as one of substance regarding the issues concerning student life as well as one of leadership regarding those issues.

Article III: Establishment of the Judicial Branch

The judicial side of democracy relative to the school experience is probably the most often disregarded and misunderstood aspect of our democratic ideals. Just as the framers of the Constitution knew that freedom, justice, and equality can never be realized without a fair system of courts, we need to incorporate students into the process of adjudicating some of the complaints and offenses of student affairs. While student courts need not be as formal, technical, and complex as those in the larger system, they should be an elemental facet of the lived democratic experience.

Through the creation of a student court system, students are able to learn a great deal about the subtleties of democratic systems. Likewise and equally important, students can begin to learn about the relations between the individual and the collective in terms of fair play and the responsibilities of holding power.

The creation of a student court system provides students opportunities to learn three general lessons that relate to democratic rule and democratic ethics. First is the opportunity to learn the processes that protect the citizen from unfair trial and punishment (e.g., the notions of the accused being innocent until proven guilty, of having the right to face witnesses, of having the right to not have to testify against oneself, and having the right to a jury of one's peers).

Second, students can learn about the notion of having a punishment fit the crime. The rehabilitation of the offender can be a guiding ethic for the dispensation of justice through the student court.

The third lesson regards the notion of participatory democracy. Depending on the type of student court system implemented, there are many opportunities for significant numbers of students to participate in the various roles required. Participation is expansive in the sense that much of what the court would deal with would be rules established democratically by the student legislative body. In this sense, students begin to learn the real-world consequences and responsibilities connected to living within the law they create.

The Bill of Rights

The Bill of Rights was developed as a group of key democratic principles intended to define the basic freedoms to which citizens are entitled. The following amendments of the Bill of Rights serve as principles necessary for fleshing out the framework within which the democratic experience is guided.

Amendment I: Political and Religious Freedoms
The First Amendment guides us in establishing the legitimacy of free speech and the right of citizens to be active in their efforts to establish rules under which they live. For schools, the amendment gives explicit entitlement to living freely in a responsible manner.

Amendment IV: Freedom from Unfair Searches and Seizures
The Fourth Amendment speaks to the right to be secure in one's property and possessions when the authorities cannot produce a just reason for searching for and taking

something a citizen possesses. In the case of schooling, this may well be seen as a very controversial item, given that many schools have problems with weapons and drugs being brought to school by students. However, since the courts have ruled that schools may engage in random locker searches, drug tests, and the use of drug dogs, the principle here is one of guiding the students and school authorities toward a shared view of what kind of reasonable policies are necessary for the protection of the school community. It encourages that such policies be owned and understood by the students they are designed to protect rather than simply be imposed from above.

Amendment V: Freedom from Unfair Accusation and Self-incrimination

The Fifth Amendment refers to three key principles related to democratic freedom. The first requires formal accusation based on evidence before being held for trial; this principle guards against accusing someone of a crime without a basis in evidence. The second principle publicly establishes that those accused cannot be forced to testify against themselves. The third principle guarantees that we cannot be deprived of liberty, property, or life without due process of the law.

In the case of the first principle, it certainly has application to a student court system. Citizen-students need to understand that just as in our national legal system, charges must be substantiated before holding someone to trial for breaking the law. The second principle helps keep us free from being bullied into confessing something we did not do. Historically, this item has been formalized to prevent authorities from coercing and threatening confessions evoked from fear rather than from the truth. This aspect of the Fifth Amendment is comparatively unique to our legal system and serves well to lessen abuses of power. The third principle establishes that all actions taken to deprive anyone of freedom or possessions must be performed through the proper application of the legal system, a substantial foundation for a student court system. This third principle is reinforced by the Fourteenth Amendment.

Amendment VI: The Right to Trial by Jury and the Disclosure of Witnesses

There are three important elements of democracy in the Sixth Amendment. First is the right to a trial by jury, second is the right to a defense, and third is the right to confront all witnesses for the prosecution. Through its entitlements, this amendment essentially underscores the principle derived from English common law of innocent until proven guilty. While the Constitution is silent on the issue of the jury being of one's peers, the principle is derived from English common law and is reaffirmed by the Supreme Court.

Amendment VIII: The Right to Nonexcessive Bail and the Right to Noninfliction of Cruel and Unusual Punishment

The Eighth Amendment addresses bail money and punishments. While bail is not particularly relevant to our school settings, the notion that punishments should not be cruel or unusual can lead students to understanding better how penalties must be judiciously derived and appropriately applied. If we are to shape students' ideas of punishment as being more than revengeful, we need to extrapolate from the implied principle of the Eighth Amendment that suggests that the punishment should fit the offense. Sometimes, by reflecting on the nature of the misbehavior, we can derive a punishment that serves as a learning experience for the student. For example, a student who is guilty of writing on a desk will probably learn more by being sentenced to wash all the desks in the classroom than if he were sentenced to several days of detention.

Amendment XIV (Section 1): Equal Protection and Due Process

The Fourteenth Amendment was ratified after the Civil War (1868) as a result of overt efforts in the South to deny the rights of citizenship to African Americans. The first section of this amendment was generated to prohibit states from abridging rights and freedoms guaranteed to U.S. citizens by the Constitution. Further, it restates that all citizens are to be treated equally by the law with the reaffirming of the right to due process as elemental to the equal protection of the law. The Fourteenth Amendment is the basis for many legal arguments regarding issues of civil rights. The concepts of equal protection and due process are pivotal in students' learning to be effective citizens.

Reflecting on the Constitutional Initiative

The constitutional initiative as presented represents our efforts to be prime movers in creating the opportunities for students to dwell within the democratic experience. In the sense of McCutcheon's definition, we are curriculum developers for democracy. The perspective of the courts, the principles they use, and the relevant principles of the Constitution provide the framework around which we develop mechanisms for student opportunity. In a collateral manner, the balance between the rights of the collective and the freedom of the individual reaches different levels along a continuum as a function of a variety of variables.

POSSIBLE MECHANISMS FOR DEMOCRATIC OPPORTUNITY

The following ideas represent mechanisms and activities that can afford students opportunities to live the democratic experience within the school community.[3] The list is not exhaustive, nor are the experiences associated with the various mechanisms sufficient to meet the needs of developing democratic and ethical students. We believe that they can contribute significantly to developing a foundation upon which students can enflesh the values, principles, and processes of democracy as well as understand its weaknesses and problems.

---

[3] For a detailed explication of specific ideas and experiences regarding democratic teacher education, see John Novak (Ed.), *Democratic Teacher Education: Programs, Processes, Problems, and Prospects* (Albany: SUNY Press, 1994).

These student endeavors must have substance and a vested level of power in their conduct. Token student councils and figurehead class presidents miseducate students and, rather than enhancing the formative development of citizenship, deny it.

• *Student government:* Ideally, students can operate more than just a token governmental body. In its most effective form, student government consists of four basic elements: (1) a constitution that contains its charge (or mission) and its scope of operation (including involvement in decision making with related administrative, parent, and teacher groups); (2) an executive branch; (3) a representative or legislative body of elected student members; and (4) a student court or discipline panel with power to adjudicate. A valid, operating student government teaches the realities of governing, using power, and trying to balance the needs and interests of all those involved in the school community.

• *Town meetings:* Town meetings model the classic assemblies of New England. All participating citizens of the school or class community are present. Such meetings are predicated on open discussion and participation. Like student governments, a community constitution or by-laws of operation facilitate the workings of the body. They are especially valuable in developing a democratic sense of affiliation and participation. While the town meeting mechanism has been used effectively for entire schools, it is particularly effective in classroom settings, especially at the elementary levels. The town meeting concept greatly enhances the students' opportunity to experience what it means to live and participate in a community.

• *Student advisory groups:* Student advisory groups can function well at a variety of levels. Their primary function is to provide input and critique for teachers and administrators regarding issues that affect students but that are usually exclusively determined by the adults. One example might be a high school physics class where the teacher meets with a small group of students each Friday to discuss how the teaching and learning went during the week and what the upcoming lessons will entail. The students can provide the teacher with valuable insight while gaining a sense of participation and shared responsibility for the direction of the course. This activity not only increases the sense of community the students have, it also provides them the opportunity to learn how to share ideas for the betterment of all concerned.

• *School or class service duty:* Service duty involves providing students with the opportunity to learn and develop the aspects of civic obligation (concern, care, and tolerance) so vital to establishing a democratic ethic. Certain students dedicate time and effort to improving conditions within the school and local community to benefit the quality of life for the more disadvantaged. Within the school, the service duty might entail tutoring less academically successful students, working with younger students, mentoring new students, or working on projects to improve the overall school climate. Outside the school, students might work with underprivileged groups such as the homeless, the elderly, the poor, and persons with disabilities to improve some aspect of their quality of life.

These types of activities provide students with a sense of participation and obligation. They give students an opportunity to learn that the quality of life in a community is a function of all members of that community, regardless of privilege or disadvantage.

• *School–community partnerships:* Partnership activities are similar to service duties but represent working with specific community groups in serving a particular mission. One example is having a group of students work with the established neighborhood improvement group of the area in which the school is located to improve neighborhood conditions. Another is having students work with the school's parent–teacher group to deal with specific school problems or projects. Such activities facilitate students' learning the value of collective activities while teaching them how to be involved and responsible in working with others for the benefit of all.

• *Discipline councils/student courts:* Many schools have formed groups in which students actually hear cases and make recommendations regarding the misbehaviors of other students. These groups function to facilitate the students' sense of ownership for the conduct of each other as peers in a school or class community. They give students the opportunity to operationalize several key facets of democratic constitutional principles, such as due process, innocence until proven guilty, and reasonable and appropriate penalty. Although this type of activity requires educating students in the meaning and process of judicial hearings, it makes the vital elements of our Constitution come alive. To work most effectively, such groups need to be framed within a discipline code or code of conduct that has been developed, agreed to, and implemented by the students.

• *Safety patrols:* At the elementary school level, the tradition of the safety patrol can be a source of opportunity for students to learn the value of service to others rather than, as is often the case, the thrill of power and control. When the implementation of a safety patrol is accompanied by guided discussions of the service function, care, concern, and tolerance can be the focus of the mission as perceived by the students.

• *Honors classes:* Although honors classes have existed for a long time in many schools, they usually place their emphasis on giftedness or academic achievement. Honors classes that are open to students of all academic levels can provide students with the opportunity to learn responsibility for self-determination rather than elitism and group cooperation instead of individualism and competitiveness.

• *Study groups/focus groups:* Study groups can be designed to follow particular current event issues that relate to particular democratic processes. They function by selecting an issue determined to be relevant to democracy and engaging the students in open discussion and dialogue regarding its meaning to citizens of a democracy. For example, the Rodney King beating or the O.J. Simpson trial and verdict could serve as a focus topic to examine race relations in addressing the significance of the events for the students as citizens. These groups can provide students with the opportunity to understand and clarify their own values and those of others and the significance of such understanding for living in a population of diverse citizens.

These mechanisms will vary across age, level, school, and classroom according to the needs and limitations of the particular unit. For example, the mechanisms we create for a fifth-grade, self-contained classroom will probably differ greatly from what we create for a large suburban high school. But while the actual mechanisms will differ, the principles that guide the experiences will not. The mechanisms must remain embedded in the spirit and intent of the framework we have discussed and animated by our commitment to educate for democratic citizenship. Our purpose must remain clear as a democratic imperative: Students must be afforded the opportunity to live the democratic experience if we are to expect them to serve the ideals of our democracy as adults.

SUMMARY

We have attempted to show that schooling and teaching have historically done little to capture the initiative of making democracy a lived experience. While we recognize that classes in civics and U.S. government are important, we also realize that the constitutional principles taught in such courses are generally irrelevant to students. Indeed, the federal courts have had the greatest impact in democratizing schools and classrooms.

We believe, however, that there is a significant foundation for our capturing the constitutional initiative as educators—we can create a teaching environment in which students can engage in understanding and practicing the goals and ideals of democracy. To do this, we must revisit the concepts, principles, and ideas of our Constitution. We must also recognize that we, as a nation and as a society of diversity, are continually striving to balance the interests of the individual with the interests of the collective. Rights and responsibilities such as freedom and control exist not as mutually exclusive opposites but on a continuum that represents the possibilities for balance.

Next, we need to consider mechanisms that can afford students the opportunity to engage in experiencing the necessities, subtleties, and difficulties of responsible, participatory citizenship. Concomitantly, we must understand that we seek the emergence of a democratic ethic in students as they engage in the activities. Implementing democratic experiences creates enjoyable learning environments in schools and classrooms.

LOOKING AHEAD

Chapter 7, "Social Power in the Classroom," examines the specifics of power dynamics in the classroom. Understanding power dynamics gives us great insight into the nature of the teacher–student relationship, which is requisite in our being proactive toward democratic discipline. Likewise, it gives us further insight into the origins of student misbehavior, thereby setting the stage for our reflective responses to such misbehavior.

❖ REFLECTIVE ACTIVITIES

1. Why is it so important that teachers take charge of educating for democracy? What principles can be used as a foundation for constructing democratic school communities? How do teachers' acts of discipline work for and against educating for a democratic citizenry?
2. Reflect on your own experiences in elementary and secondary school. What did you and your friends experience that helped or hindered your developing an understanding of the key principles and ideals of our democracy? What could have been done differently?
3. Assuming you have developed a commitment to developing mechanisms for students to learn democratic processes and values, what obstacles might you face and how could you deal with them? Be sure to consider the reactions of other teachers, administrators, parents, school board members, and, of course, your students.

❖ REFERENCES

Gathercoal, F. (1990). *Judicious discipline.* Ann Arbor: Caddo Gap Press.

McCutcheon, G. (1995). *Developing the curriculum.* White Plains, NY: Longman.

Novak, J. (Ed.) (1994). *Democratic teacher education: Programs, processes, problems, and prospects.* Albany: SUNY Press.

Chapter 7

Social Power in the Classroom

❖ Focus Questions

1. Teaching is basically a social activity. What social and group skills contribute to teacher effectiveness?

2. In what situations is legitimate power appropriately used? What caveats apply to its use?

3. Rewards, while generally considered a positive factor in the classroom, have an insidious aspect as well. How should an informed teacher approach the use of rewards?

4. How does an understanding of the three origins of student misbehavior help the teacher conceive personal strategies for addressing the challenge of establishing effective classroom discipline?

We, as human beings, are social creatures. In large measure our lives are defined by our social condition. We engage in social relationships to fulfill many of the needs and values we consider important, even essential, in our lives. These relationships include a wide range of possibilities, from intimate friendships and marriages to relatively impersonal activities such as attending a sporting event with thousands of others and participating as a member of an organization. Regardless of the type of social interaction we might scrutinize, we find that **social power**—the influence a person exerts on others—is involved.

THE SOCIAL POWERS

Max Weber (1947) was among the first to examine social power as a construct that helps define relationships. French and Raven (1968) adapted Weber's work in their study of supervisor power in the work setting. Their chief contribution was to identify five aspects of social power associated with supervisors that enable us to understand more clearly this pervasive phenomenon. Their work in turn was extended into the classroom setting by Richmond and McCroskey (1984) and Richmond (1990), providing us with insight into the teacher's role as the classroom leader, for the teacher is the supervisor of the students.

The five bases of social power identified by French and Raven, written as they apply to the teacher, are as follows:

Legitimate power. By virtue of their appointed position, teachers have the right to exert authority over students.

Reward power. Teachers may provide students with tangible or intangible awards, prized by students, for preferred behavior.

Coercive power. A teacher may invoke penalties, punishments, and sanctions upon students whom the teacher perceives not to comply with teacher expectations.

Expert power. Teachers elicit preferred behavior from students based on the students' perception of teachers as highly competent leaders.

Referent power. Teachers elicit preferred behavior from students based on the extent to which students identify with the teachers. This can be viewed in more common terms as "personality power."

To understand the dynamics of social power, one must realize that power does not inherently exist within the person from whom it emanates. Even legitimate power, which is ordained by the authority of the state government and exists as a legal entity, does not exist as a social force unless the student recognizes and accepts its legitimacy. Substitute teachers and student teachers sometimes have problems because their students perceive them to have status below some vague but functional threshold of legitimacy.

Legitimate Power

In most K–12 school settings, teachers are required to be licensed by the state government, so they have an ultimate recognition of their legitimate authority in the classroom. As state officials, teachers are charged with initiating, conducting, and controlling classroom instruction to achieve the school's—and ultimately the state's—intended learning outcomes. The authority of the teacher in this regard is so well established and understood that it is virtually unquestioned. Even in the many different sorts of teacher–learner situations that occur throughout society, the authority of the teacher is a given. The teacher–learner dynamic is a mainstay throughout our social structure.

The fact that a teacher is licensed as an officer of the state is not the operative source of power in the perception of students. Rather, children grow up in a society that values teachers and tacitly recognizes their authority as a necessary condition for effective education. This value is acquired along with many others that define our culture. Students do not consciously think, "My teacher is licensed so I need to do what he or she says." Rather, they sense that persons in certain positions—parents, teachers, clergy, police officers, lifeguards—exercise authority as an aspect of their roles. The question is not whether these persons have legitimate power but whether one will submit to it. In the past, students more readily accepted the teacher's position of authority as a sufficient reason to comply with classroom expectations. In recent years, students (especially at the secondary level) have felt less constrained by teachers' legitimate power. The media have frequently brought this to the attention of the public for many years.

Legitimate power imbues the teacher with the authority to direct learning activities that are deemed worthy and useful by the policy-making groups in the society. One likely source of school/classroom discipline problems actually originates with such groups because they do not necessarily include as members the students who are affected. The mantle of legitimate power lies specifically with teachers because they are quasi-government officials backed by legal endorsement. The police force is even more recognizable as an agency that utilizes legitimate power, sometimes at the expense of individual freedom. Certain other persons would be hard pressed to function successfully without the de facto power that attends their roles, such as ministers and scout leaders.

When students enter a classroom on the first day of school and meet the teacher for the first time, the teacher functions on the basis of legitimate power. Students arrive at a classroom where they are assigned, take a seat as directed, and await further instructions from the teacher. When the instructions come, the response is virtually unquestioning compliance. Directing classroom activities is simply the teacher's prerogative. Although other types of power will inevitably come into use in the classroom, the teacher's legitimate power is a pervasive factor necessary for the teacher–student relationship.

Other aspects of social power will eventually become operant as relationships are established and impressions are formed. But on this first day, students typically respond to the teacher's position more so than to the teacher as a person. For some period of time, from several days to a week or two, while impressions accumulate and familiarity grows, teachers usually experience something of a honeymoon, which may create a false sense of security for them. Teachers who do not use those early classroom meetings to establish a purposeful learning climate and inaugurate effective classroom management practices are likely to encounter discipline-related problems before many weeks have passed.

As part of legitimate power, the teacher establishes reasonable expectations for classroom order and efficient functioning—essentially, the classroom management function. Routines are established for attending to classroom regularities such as passing in homework, sharpening pencils, and entering and leaving class. Almost all of this happens as a matter of course in setting up an effective classroom. As teaching transpires, the teacher monitors the activity of the students, intervenes as necessary with cues to redirect students if misbehavior occurs or seems imminent, and generally manages the dynamics of the classroom. The smooth application of legitimate power proceeds without undue fanfare. It is what the teacher is supposed to do, in the students' perception, and they accept it in the course of events.

Legitimate power is not without its pitfalls. Some personalities are attracted to teaching because it provides access to such power and authority. These persons tend to impose more excessive demands for structure, conformity, and control than may be in the best interest of a democratic learning setting. Also, while legitimate power is a default posture available to teachers when other preferable power bases fail, teachers may resort too quickly to legitimate power strategies in the hope of quick results. So, although legitimate power is a useful source of teacher influence and control, it has negative consequences when not used with discretion or when overused.

Reward Power

Reward power is the construct through which teachers recognize and reinforce commendable performance or compliant behavior and encourage their continuation. Research indicates, however, that rewards have been overrated as an influence on students' motivation (Brophy, 1981; Richmond & McCroskey, 1984). Nevertheless, reward is useful and important where appropriately employed.

Reward power is used most commonly by teachers in the form of praise. Praise that is specific, personal, and clearly deserved is most effective. Praise that is habitual, insincere, and too general has little effect on students and may have a negative effect (Brophy, 1981). For example, if during classroom discussion or recitation the teacher follows each student's contribution with words such as "right" or "good," little impact occurs. On the other hand, if the teacher selectively responds to students' contributions with a deserved "That is an important point" or "You have introduced a whole new idea that we need to consider," the teacher has used a form of reward power that reinforces students to continue in a productive mode. Especially deserving students may be further rewarded by, for example, making them leaders of discussion groups when this assignment is clearly contingent on the quality of their prior contributions.

Students' grades may be perceived as rewards if they are high and, conversely, as penalties if they are low. Teachers should try to convey to students that grades are indicators of achievement as their primary function, even though high grades may secondarily have the effect of a reward. Students are more likely to own a grade when they perceive it as a measure of performance, not as a gift dispensed by the benevolent teacher. High grades, while they are ordinarily prized by students, should not be exploited as discipline ends by teachers in place of the learning outcomes the grades purport to measure.

A teacher's good intention in providing a reward may unwittingly emerge in the form of a bribe. The teacher who says, for example, "I'll give you two fellows money for a Coke after school if you'll promise not to bother Bobby on his way home," is actually offering a payoff to the bullies because of their unseemly intentions. In another case, we can imagine a teacher telling the students that if they are quiet when the principal visits the room, they won't be given a homework assignment that day.

Reward power covers a range of possible teacher motives/purposes. The subconscious motive in any given instance is not necessarily clear, a condition that complicates efforts to understand the use of reward power. The continuum of teacher purposes shown in Figure 7.1 helps make sense of reward power.

As one moves to the left of the midpoint of the continuum, award, there is increasing concern with addressing teachers' needs. These needs may be personal comfort and security, acceptance by students, and classroom order. As one moves right, there is increasing concern for students' needs, such as effective learning and students' self-esteem. Awards may involve both kinds of concern, perhaps simultaneously, for they are not mutually exclusive.

The continuum can also be analyzed in terms of teacher behaviors associated with the extremes and the midpoint. In situations of persuasion and bribery, teachers give students something the students value (such as candy, free time, and other special privileges) prior to their performance to increase the probability of the desired performance subsequently occurring. At the midpoint of the continuum but overlapping on both sides to some extent, teachers promise something of value prior to performance and make the promised award following the performance. On the right side of the continuum, teachers spontaneously give something of value (usually something nonsubstantive, such as praise and commendation) following performance. While one may take issue with the use and interpretation of certain of the terms on the continuum, there is nevertheless a change in tenor or meaning as one compares any two points that are in different segments of the continuum.

BRIBERY— - PERSUASION — — AWARD— — · INCENTIVE — — REWARD/REINFORCEMENT

←— —→

Figure 7.1

Reward power as such does not exist at the left side of the continuum; it begins to emerge only at the midpoint. In the very best of situations, students find satisfaction in the topics they study and the sense of purpose and accomplishment that ensues. The work essentially becomes its own intrinsic reward as students satisfy their needs for identity, stimulation, security, affiliation, and empowerment. Realistically, we know this happens with reasonable frequency to the more capable students, since they have the most opportunity to experience success and the self-esteem it engenders. Unfortunately, some students have few opportunities to experience success simply on the basis of their overall performance. For these students, the teacher's sensitive use of reward power can make a particularly worthwhile difference. Reward may come for them in the form of extra teacher attention, support, and recognition, with appropriate praise of incremental gains in learning or performance. In the class as a whole, reward power used intentionally affects positively students' general attitude and level of motivation.

Coercive Power

Coercive power is available to teachers when they need to take decisive, powerful action in response to student noncompliance. This type of power involves the teacher imposing authority in the face of resistance by students. The use of coercive power is necessary on occasions such as when physical danger is threatened or property damage is likely. The use of such power is evident when the teacher speaks stridently, engages in reprimands, assigns punishments, or physically intervenes.

It is unfortunate that coercive power is insidiously attractive to teachers who have strong needs for power or security. The misuse of coercive power, which may become manifest as verbal and sometimes physical abuse, occurs widely in schools as frustrated and misguided teachers attempt to deal with behavior problems. Richmond (1990) found in her research that

> efforts of the teacher to coerce students to engage in behaviors the teacher (or the system) prefers, while possibly effective in eliciting the desired behavior change, have very negative side effects both in terms of causing the student to dislike the teacher and, more importantly, in terms of reducing the cognitive and affective learning of the student. (p. 194)

Coercive power is not an inherent aspect of instruction nor of any other teaching strategy. But if during instruction some students do not respond to other more subtle and less powerful means to control intolerable behavior, the teacher must resort to coercive power. Students simply cannot be allowed to interfere with the class's right and responsibility to learn. Should coercive power be necessary during a learning activity, it should be used swiftly and decisively so that the class can return to the activity with as little disruption as possible. Removing the offending student(s) from the classroom is one effective intervention; other coercive measures may be appropriate as determined by the factors involved.

The sources of legitimate, reward, and coercive power are overt (i.e., one recognizes explicitly that power is being utilized when the teacher issues directives, provides incentives, or imposes sanctions). However, when students simply behave well without the clear expression of these direct uses of power, expert and referent power are operative.

Expert Power

Expert power is an implicit source of authority. Students recognize when a teacher is knowledgeable, well organized, businesslike and purposeful, and respected as a capable practitioner by other students and teachers. On the basis of these characteristics, such a teacher is likely to be treated with deference by students. They are likely to say something like, "She is tough, but you learn a lot in her class." The expert teacher often makes rigorous demands on students, and the students generally respond. Students sense that responding to a teacher who has expert power is the proper and, psychologically at least, comfortable thing to do. Research indicates that such teachers have a favorable impact on students.

Expert power during a learning activity is likely to be expressed through the teacher's management of the activity. The teacher will have established himself or herself with the students through all their prior classroom interactions, and this will carry over into the learning situation. The teacher will be well prepared for the class and will provide the students with a cogent rationale for the intended lesson. The conditions and procedures for an effective lesson will be made clear to the students, and they will be monitored to ensure that they are able to proceed successfully. If, for example, the lesson involves a discussion, the teacher will use expert power discretely through providing the appropriate level of structure, using questions wittingly, reinforcing appropriately, and summarizing and redirecting as needed yet allowing students the full measure of freedom and responsibility they can handle. Although expert power is largely subliminal, students sense it in terms of their confidence in the teacher, and they are reassured by it.

Referent Power

Referent power is another implicit source of authority. To some extent, expert power contributes to referent power, but referent power is more involved with the interpersonal dimension of the teacher–student relationship. Teachers who inherently display qualities that students admire are those that students identify most easily with and who therefore become role models for them. In the broad perspective, qualities that students admire are ones that they identify most readily with, and teachers who have such characteristics become role models for the students. Mode of dress and physical features attractive to the students contribute to referent power, but, more broadly speaking, qualities such as social maturity, a sense of humor, enthusiasm, and compassion are traits that attract students.

Referent power as it relates to any teaching strategy is difficult to separate out as a discrete influence on student attitude and behavior. Students respond to referent power in the generalized sense of liking the teacher. This translates into students participating and responding in ways they believe will please the teacher and earn the teacher's recognition and regard. Their enthusiasm and initiative allow the teacher the freedom to be flexible and creative and to be minimally concerned with structure and control, because students willingly make efforts for this type of teacher that often exceed expectations. In the final analysis, teachers who lack a critical mass of referent power are unlikely to be able to establish the conditions for the most effective classroom learning activities.

Based on a series of studies of classroom communication that she conducted, Richmond was able to state,

> It is clear that the development of positive relationships between teachers and students is critical. When such relationships are built, the availability of referent and expert power is much greater, thus opening many more communication options to the teacher for maintaining mundane control. (p. 194)

Teachers in whom a generous measure of both expert and referent power resides exhibit charisma, which is a powerful source of students' motivation. These teachers are effective in influencing students to achieve, but their impact on students in the affective domain is even more telling. They become, under the influence of these teachers, more positive in their attitudes about their schoolwork and about themselves. This results in a classroom climate in which intrinsic motivation is pervasive.

A CLASSROOM EPISODE

Social power occurs both overtly and covertly in the classrooms. Just which source of power is being used at any given time is not always easily determined, and different students may be responding simultaneously to different sources. Generally speaking, the best teachers are least dependent on the overt use of power—that is, their presence and their instructionally embedded management are sufficient to maintain classroom order. When the teacher must resort to overt measures to restore minimally acceptable learning conditions, a breakdown has occurred in the covert dimension.

The following scenario captures the dynamic quality of power interactions involved in the teacher–student relationship. This example of a class discussion will provide a setting for examining the dynamics more realistically.

Power Dynamics in the Classroom

Norma Cross teaches science and mathematics to two groups of sixth-grade students each day. Eight weeks into the first semester, she embarked on an astronomy unit in science. Her day began with the science lesson.

How the Episode Developed

The bell rang at 8:45, signaling the beginning of class for the day. Mrs. Cross rose from her desk at the side of the room and positioned herself in the front of the class. The students continued to talk for a few seconds, then gave her their attention.

"Thank you, class," she said. "It really helps us all when you get quiet and ready to go when the bell rings. Well, did you all read those pages I assigned in your science book for today?" The class generally murmured in the affirmative. "Well, in that case you probably won't mind a pop quiz this morning on some of the facts from your reading. Right?" Some readily audible groans and "Oh, no's" emerged throughout the class at the prospect of a quiz. "OK, no quiz," Mrs. Cross responded, "as long as you get your assignments done. But if I find you have been goofing off, well, you know what I have to do. Any arguments there?" She felt a bit guilty at the use of negative reinforcement first thing in the morning, but she had sensed some laxity over the past week.

"OK, you have all read the first few pages. What did you find out?" Many hands went up, and students recited some basic facts about suns, stars, and planets. Mrs. Cross was convinced, given the range of information they provided, that at least most of the students had read the material with sufficient understanding, and she complimented them. "You know, I think you should have asked for a quiz. It would have been an easy 'A' for most of you. I'm glad you didn't, though, because very honestly, I didn't have one ready. But don't you get too sure of yourselves—my name isn't Cross by accident you know."

"No," Bobby piped up, "it's because you married Mr. Cross." The class laughed loudly, and Bobby was pleased with himself. Mrs. Cross responded with good humor, "I guess you crossed me up on that one."

Then, more seriously, she said, "We are starting a new unit on astronomy this week. We could study lots of things, but I believe astronomy is something you should learn about this year in science. Rather than just plunge in, though, it might be useful if we took some time today to discuss why astronomy is important in our lives—if it is. So why don't we go ahead and circle our chairs for a discussion."

The class proceeded to form its chairs into a double-rowed U-shape as they had learned to do when directed. Some noise and confusion resulted as more students attempted to put their chairs into the rear row than would fit. Norma Cross intervened and directed several students on their chair placement. After about two minutes of shuffling and straightening, the move was completed.

"Now," Norma Cross began, "how do you see the study of astronomy being interesting and worthwhile to you?"

After a few seconds, Nancy offered hesitantly, "Well, it's just good to know about things like space. I mean, it's out there." "All right," Mrs. Cross said, "who wants to add something to that?" Jerry was sitting with his chin in his hands looking up at the ceiling. "Jerry, are you deep in thought? Share it with us." Clearly, Jerry's thoughts were not on astronomy and addressing him returned his attention to the discussion.

"Well," he offered rather lamely, "astronomy is interesting, I guess. I don't think I'd want to be an astronomer though."

Norma Cross picked up on that. "That's interesting, Jerry. Who does think you might like to be an astronomer?" A variety of responses followed, ideas such as wanting to have a comet named for you, being a college professor, and making space flights.

"Even so," Mrs. Cross intervened to redirect the discussion, "just a few of us, if any, will become astronomers. Should the rest of us know something about it?"

Jeannie answered, "Actually, we already know something. Everybody knows the sun and stars and stuff. Maybe that's enough, I mean, what do we need to know more for?"

Ricky caught Mrs. Cross's eye as he flicked his hand up, then began to answer Jeannie's question. Before he had a chance to make his point, Joel broke in with, "You're leaving out the most important thing, Rick. How about the—" At this point, Mrs. Cross, who was already up to get a pencil from her desk, stepped to the bulletin board, where a list of class rules was displayed, and tapped #3, which stated, "Allow others to speak without interrupting." Joel accepted this mild admonishment without protest and waited for Ricky to finish.

As Ricky continued his somewhat extended response, Carol and Joan struck up a rather animated conversation. Mrs. Cross caught Carol's eye with a stern look, and she broke off the conversation with Joan. As Ricky finished, Joel picked up the discussion and launched into a lengthy commentary. He used the term *scientific literacy,* to Mrs. Cross's surprise, and she made a mental note to come back to it. Meanwhile, Carol was again initiating a conversation, this time with Ginny. Mrs. Cross held up two fingers as she took a step in Carol's direction to get her attention, with the intent of signaling to Carol, "That's twice," for as the class knew, a third time meant going to the isolation seat in the far rear of the room.

"Thanks to Ricky and Joel for their thoughtful comments," Norma Cross said when Joel had finally finished. "I'd like to take a moment to say just a little more about scientific literacy, because I think Ricky and Joel really got at the heart of what we are about." As Mrs. Cross spoke, Ronnie and Jamie displayed a bit of commotion, which quickly erupted into a major disruption as Ronnie got out of his seat and began to struggle with Jamie. Mrs. Cross spoke both of their names sharply as she approached them; then she physically placed Ronnie back in his seat as Ronnie protested that Jamie had taken his pencil. In a controlled and purposeful tone, she told them she would see them in a few moments during the rest break.

"Sorry about this brief interruption, class. Remember a couple of weeks ago when we had a discussion something like today's on conflict resolution? Looks like Ronnie and Jamie and I are going to get a chance to see if it works," she said as she attempted to defuse the situation and continue the discussion.

The discussion went on until nearly the end of the class. Nearly all the students had participated. Mrs. Cross ended the discussion by summarizing the most important ideas. Her final words were, "You've convinced me with your eloquence that we should proceed with the astronomy unit, class." Then, with a wry smile, she added mischievously, "But you knew you would, didn't you?"

Analysis of the Episode

Even before the bell rang to begin class, social power associated with Mrs. Cross was affecting the children's behavior. The mere presence of an authority figure undoubtedly imposed a limit on their behavior. The students did not make conscious decisions about what was appropriate or possible. They simply sensed that under these conditions they could move throughout the room, talk with one another, sharpen pencils, or browse at the room library. They could not run or play roughly, nor could they talk or laugh excessively loudly. We can imagine that on occasion boisterous students who exceeded the tacitly understood limits had to be restrained.

Mrs. Cross's first overt act was to stand before the class when the bell rang. Her doing so, even on the first day of class, would have been a sufficient exercise of legitimate power to bring the class to order. By now, well into the semester, legitimate power was still available to her, but referent power had become the dominant source of controlling influence (i.e., the students had acquired respect for her in the role of teacher and would feel uncomfortable affronting her, notwithstanding the brief scuffle that occurred). If they had not acquired a critical level of respect, we could have expected Mrs. Cross to have had to shout above the din of the room to attempt to settle the students.

Legitimate power is continuously available to the teacher, and almost always students will initially accede to it. The first few days with a class are sometimes referred to as a honeymoon and provide the teacher an opportunity to begin to establish the referent and expert bases of power. The teacher who does not successfully do this during the first few days will find herself or himself tested increasingly by the students as they seek where the real, not just the stated, limits of behavior are. In these cases, the teacher finds it necessary to resort to legitimate power to maintain order. Overt interventions are needed more and more frequently. The students sense that the teacher is insecure and fearful or lacks expertise in group leadership skills and thus displays signs of impotence. Psychologically, the students are inclined to fill the power void with their own expressions of student power. The resulting situation would reflect varying degrees of anarchy. The greater the anarchy, the less comfortable the teacher becomes. Genuine discussion in such classes is impossible.

At some point, legitimate power is no longer sufficient to control students, and the teacher is forced into a militant posture involving the use of coercive power. This is a signal that things have gone too far; change must occur for the sake of the students' learning and the teacher's emotional comfort. Outside counsel and support are strongly recommended when the use of coercive power is required with increasing frequency. One of the most common mistakes made by teachers because of their reluctance to admit to their limitation (and by administrators because of their misplaced faith in the teacher's ability to work it out) is to allow matters to fester far too long without intervention. Struggles become irreversible when problems are not dealt with promptly.

Norma Cross made effective but low-key use of reward power on several occasions during the class. She did not simply take the class's positive behavior for granted but took a moment to recognize it by praising and specifying the reason for the praise. She expressed her appreciation to the class for its promptness in responding to the signal to start class and later for having come to class prepared. We can imagine that the class felt good about itself when the teacher they respected found reason to praise the students. This same feeling contributed to the climate that was being established, a climate in which increasingly lower levels of structure and higher levels of student initiative will exist.

Mrs. Cross used a mixture of legitimate power and expert power as she teased the class about a pop quiz. She recognized their apparent need for a reminder, and she resorted to the purposeful use of negative reinforcement to provide it. She felt a tinge of guilt as she considered the fine line between a reminder and a threat, but with the use of humor, she seemed to get her message across without ruffling feathers noticeably.

As a preamble to the discussion she planned, Mrs. Cross had the students recite based on their reading assignment. During the recitation, the class shared information that prepared them indirectly for what was to come—again a display of expertise by the teacher. After a good recitation, she praised the class, then indulged in a bit of humor based on her name. The class, especially Bobby, recognized the levity and felt free to call out a humorous reply. The teacher accepted it in the spirit of fun.

Through the skillful use of the power available to her, the stage had been set for a good discussion. Of course, there were no guarantees, but Mrs. Cross had done what she could to establish the optimum conditions for the discussion. She had used several kinds of social power in an unspectacular but purposeful way to accomplish her purpose up to that point.

The discussion mode was strongly signaled by the relocation of the students' seats. Mrs. Cross had to intervene modestly—again an expression of legitimate power—to expedite the movement of seats, but no real problems arose. In this new configuration, a different set of expectations was in place—a subtle and effective technique. In the U-shape, students generally faced each other, which diminished the teacher's power posture and transferred responsibility to the students. Nevertheless, the teacher's place at the opening of the horseshoe, even while sitting, imbued her with controlling influence. She relinquished only as much of her power as was judicious, for these were sixth graders still learning self-discipline. She hoped that one day she might even have a student be the discussion leader—but not yet.

Even as the discussion was getting well under way, Mrs. Cross noticed Jerry's attention lapse. She spoke his name first to make sure she had his attention, then asked an open-ended question to which he could make some response. It was a neat use of an instructionally embedded control measure. In fact, Jerry was rewarded by having his answer suggest the course of the class discussion for the next few minutes as the question of why people would or would not like to be astronomers was posed. Underlying this portion of the discussion was the teacher's expert power as students were drawn into discussion by her skillful handling of the group.

When Joel violated the rule about interrupting another speaker, the teacher gestured toward the statement of the rule being violated. Joel was clearly, but nonverbally, informed of his noncompliance, and other students were reminded of the rule as well. That minimal intervention, basically the use of legitimate power in this instance, was sufficient to reinstate the use of the rule. There was very little interruption in the flow of the discussion.

As the discussion progressed, Carol created a minor disruption by talking first to Joan, then a bit later to Ginny. In both cases, a nonverbal intervention was used, the second in a particularly purposeful way that was sufficient to terminate Carol's untimely socializing. A combination of expert and legitimate power again served the intended purpose.

The major disruption involved a mini-scuffle between Ronnie and Jamie. Ronnie is a boy with a quick temper and little patience. He simply couldn't tolerate Jamie's teasing, and in spite of the consequences he could anticipate, he took an aggressive measure. Mrs. Cross acted decisively. She spoke sharply, a use of coercive power, then extended the use of coercive power physically as she separated the two boys. She remained in control of her own emotions during the brief episode and followed it with what she intended as a constructive remark. The class's attention had obviously been drawn to the scuffle and the teacher's intervention. The tacit referent power she had developed over time with the class allowed her to return the class quickly to the discussion that had been interrupted. The discussion continued until the end of the session and apparently achieved its purpose.

SOCIAL POWER AND THE TEACHER

That teachers use social powers is a given. The manner in which they use the five kinds of such power will vary widely and will reflect the teacher's philosophy, personality, personal needs, social sensitivity, and professional maturity. In some ways, the manner of use of social power will be an extension of the teacher's intuition. Handwriting provides an analogy. There is a subconscious force that predisposes a certain style of handwriting, and while it can be overridden to some extent with overt affectations, its basic form remains in place. In a similar manner, the teacher's disposition within certain dyads (extroverted–introverted, structured–flexible, animated–passive, confident–tentative, autocratic–laissez faire, and others) will affect that teacher's interactive style.

So teacher behavior, while not preordained, is nevertheless strongly influenced by naturalistic factors. But there is a rational aspect of teaching that is subject to modification through reason and practice. The teacher who understands the five types of social power, makes a commitment to use the powers intentionally, and genuinely attempts to control the unwitting use of the powers in ways likely to have a negative outcome can markedly improve interpersonal relations and, therefore, the classroom climate.

The social powers can be used as a diagnostic tool to analyze the effectiveness of a teacher's discipline-related practices. While no prescription is possible from diagnostic information obtained in this fashion, suggestions for the direction in which change should occur will be evident. For example, teachers who rely heavily on legitimate and coercive methods for achieving classroom control need to find ways to diminish that overdependence and develop a more balanced use of the social powers. Remediation is unlikely to involve only finding better direct control methods; to incorporate a greater measure of expert and referent power into his or her practice, the teacher will also need to consider ways to improve classroom climate and the quality of instruction. For example, this could involve greeting students by name as they enter the classroom, having occasional classroom meetings to address class issues, giving students more opportunities to work in small groups, varying the classroom learning activities more frequently, and calling parents or even visiting the students' homes.

ORIGINS OF STUDENT MISBEHAVIOR

Misbehavior does not exist as an absolute, apart from other behavior. It is behavior that teachers judge not to comply with their expectations. But misbehavior in the classroom serves students in the same way that any behavior does—it reflects the students' effort to cope with the situations they confront in the course of conducting their lives. Any behavior is the outcome of the best decision the student can make at that point in response to the conditions he or she encounters. Behavior, and therefore misbehavior, from this perspective must have a cause. Of course, the causes are not always evident to students, nor do students necessarily even consider what the causes might be. They tend in many cases to react to conditions with actions that "feel right." As with any of us, what feels right at a given time may, in retrospect, be realized to have been ill conceived and may work to our disadvantage. As educators, we must try to understand behavior/misbehavior as a dynamic, complex entity and deal with it in an informed and compassionate fashion. To do less is to deny students the right to their humanness and to withhold from them unethically the benefit of the best professional service we should be capable of rendering.

Misbehavior has three sources, none of which is mutually exclusive from the others. Each source provides a different perspective on misbehavior in the classroom. These sources, as briefly introduced in Chapter 1, are the internally generated basic needs of students, the social dynamics that emerge within the classroom setting, and the conditions imposed within the classroom by the teacher.

Internal Needs

From one point of view, discipline is understood as the inclination of students to comply with the explicit expectations of the teacher and the more pervasive expectations within the group. Each student is a creature of free will who makes decisions about behavior from the range of available choices. The teacher does not directly change a student's behavior but provides the conditions intended to elicit a teacher-preferred choice. For example, by asking a question, the teacher sets up the expectation that the student will answer, but the student will decide whether to answer it based on his or her inclinations at that moment.

Where discipline is concerned, we are especially concerned about the students' compliance with the formal rules and tacit expectations regarding classroom order and decorum. The rules in the classroom in every case impose a restriction on the students' behavior. In general, students resist limitations on their freedom, but normally in classrooms, they accept reasonable limitations as a necessary condition of that setting. However, as students' needs for identity, stimulation, security, affiliation, and empowerment exceed some individually operative threshold, students will attempt to satisfy those needs. They may resort to misbehavior if necessary. In classrooms, students' needs as social creatures lead to many unsanctioned acts of communication, such as whispering and note passing. Their need for security may result in cheating on a test. Many other kinds of common misbehavior can be understood in this perspective.

When the teacher is aware of the normal inclinations of students, consideration can be given to establishing classroom conditions that reasonably accommodate them. If students' basic needs are being met by the sanctioned activities of the classroom, students have no classroom-induced reason to misbehave. If the topics studied are presented in an interesting and enthusiastic manner, if students are actively involved as participants, if they experience success, if they are respected and allowed freedom consistent with their acceptance of responsibility, if these and other conditions associated with effective and democratic teaching exist in the classroom, then the internal inclination of students to misbehave is largely defused. Teaching should not be conceived as a challenge to meet all the students' needs every moment. Realistically, teaching involves the more modest task of providing enough emotional comfort and motivation so that students' conscious behavior is directed for the duration of the class toward addressing the teacher's agenda for their learning. From this perspective, one readily realizes that the teacher must acknowledge and accommodate students' span of attention or risk imminent off-task behavior.

Social Dynamics

External to students individually but existing within the group collectively are factors that have implications for students' behavior. Students sense intuitively that the class, because it consists of a group, poses certain expectations for and limitations on their behavior. Factors that affect the way the group is perceived by individual students include class size, heterogeneous makeup, class leaders, cliques, compatibility within the class, and organizational structure.

In a setting that involves these factors, one readily recognizes the potential for student misbehavior. In a large class, the chance for a student to feel a sense of anonymity is evident. We can anticipate that some students who cannot tolerate anonymity will react in ways that range from the subtle to the bizarre to achieve some sort of recognition. Teachers cannot easily control class size directly, although some measures within the group may alleviate the effect. Some of these include careful monitoring, use of peer tutors, small-group work, and direct teaching approaches that actively and continuously focus students' attention on the learning activity.

Groups that are highly homogeneous confront the teacher with fewer kinds of conditions to accommodate. If the ability level of the students exists within a fairly narrow range, students are more likely to respond positively to a given teaching approach. If this is not the case, then more students are likely to be either bored or frustrated and thus prone to misbehavior. A number of strategies can help in such a classroom, including assigning differentiated assignments based on a temporary grouping plan, selecting peer tutors, and providing learning centers. These approaches make demands on the teacher, but they are well established ones that over time the competent and caring teacher can implement.

Intragroup dynamics pose a challenge to the teacher. Each class is a unique blend of personalities that gives rise to infinite possibilities. It helps make teaching interesting but does nothing to make it easier. Usually, certain students become prominent in terms of the influence they have within the group. While being careful not to have obvious "pets," the teacher does need to identify and acknowledge the special influence these students have and subtly solicit their cooperation in achieving the class objectives. The teacher is fortunate if these leaders are naturally good students. If not, the teacher's leadership skills will be especially challenged. But the teacher really has no choice, for if these students are not with you, they may eventually be against you, and they can take the class with them. Teachers should give these students leadership roles as appropriate and appeal to whatever sense of social responsibility they have. If their needs for identity and empowerment can be sufficiently met through these productive means, they will be there for you. If not, controlling the class and eliciting acceptably high achievement will be a far more demanding teacher task than otherwise.

When cliques are formed within the group, not only do students who share a mutual attraction congregate, but they may establish some level of xenophobia as well. A condition of the "insiders" and the "outsiders" occurs and plays havoc with the compatibility factor in the class. Students' concerns for their status within the cliques and their active rejection of the outsiders take precedence over the concern the teacher has for their learning. The teacher needs to address the situation head-on. A class meeting approach might be effective, following comments by the teacher informing the students of the nature of their social behavior, its likely reasons, and its detrimental effects. It should be posed as a problem that mature students should address and resolve, rather than a situation that should be allowed to linger and fester. Resolving such a problem within the class may in fact result in the most important learning outcome that occurs for that group. In other words, what emerged as a problem for the class can be reframed as an opportunity for intensely personal and meaningful learning.

Organizational structure is also a factor that affects the group. Classrooms are highly structured places designed primarily as sites for formal learning. As such, students' predicated need to learn subject content tends to be given the highest priority, while their psychological and emotional needs may be given only incidental consideration. Teachers need to recognize the possible stifling effect that overemphasis on structure can have in terms of students' feelings of anonymity, boredom, anxiety, alienation, and impotence. If in their well-meaning intentions to help students learn the content they ignore affective considerations, much of their teaching may be an exercise in futility. Teachers are either naive or insensitive who take the position that students' job when they come to class is to be ready to learn and the teacher's job is to present the material. Academically talented students who are highly motivated may arrive ready to learn, but the students who need the teacher most are those who have limited learning ability or, perhaps worse, those who have an "attitude."

In cases where students' motivation is insufficient for whatever reasons to support productive learning, the first priority of the teacher is to create the conditions that nurture motivation. How to accomplish this is a challenge to a teacher's creativity, initiative, compassion, and patience. Not all who attempt it are successful, despite their sincere efforts. Establishing a democratic classroom climate, helping students experience success and develop self-esteem, and using enlightened approaches to instruction are all involved. Only teachers who are able to use effectively the expert and referent sources of power have the potential to accomplish this task fully. Meanwhile, if the task is not accomplished at least to a minimally acceptable level, frequent behavior problems are virtually certain to occur. Teachers have searched for the means to directly control such classes, but they have looked in vain. More effective intervention is not the answer; more effective teaching is, including instruction and classroom management.

Teacher-Imposed Conditions

When most people think of discipline, they think of it in terms of teacher-imposed conditions. Discipline as they view it has to do with the approach taken by the teacher to deal with students' behavior. This is not wrong, but it is only part of the broader concept. For the teacher, instruction and discipline merge to constitute the act of teaching. In the best of cases, discipline is indistinguishable from instruction, for it is embedded within. The highly competent teacher has the quality that Kounin (1970) described as "withitness" that is part of expert power, and students are controlled through the subtle, all but imperceptible, discipline-related behaviors of the teacher. These behaviors include using time during the first class meeting(s) clarifying expectations and preparing students for successful learning in the class, moving purposefully about the classroom while teaching, sensing incipient misbehavior and defusing it, using a variety of classroom management techniques (e.g., passing papers, going to the library, using learning centers in the classroom) designed to make the classroom run smoothly, and having a democratically oriented comprehensive discipline plan in place that accommodates both developmental and remedial aspects of responsible student behavior.

Teachers should not take their approach to discipline for granted to the extent that they are unaware that they may be predisposing classroom behavior problems. Oliva (1993) comments that "it will take a complete change of thought before the point has been reached at which the majority of teachers are willing to admit that teachers themselves can be causes of pupil behavior problems" (p. 224). Some of the sources of such problems are insufficient firmness or consistency, personality or behavioral idiosyncrasies, lack of caring or respect from the students' perspective, unwarranted rules or expectations, and general incompetence. Students' chronic misbehavior is a signal that, at the very least, some investigation into the situation is warranted to determine the causes. If the teacher is culpable, then remedial help needs to be provided to improve his or her teaching to save a potentially productive teacher's career or to determine that the teacher may be better suited for a different career. Just as important, the students deserve the very best available teaching. While one may hesitate to justify misbehavior under any circumstances (other means of protest through due process should be available), one can nevertheless understand this source of student misbehavior. Finally, if it is determined that the teacher is competent but that the class is especially difficult to manage, even incorrigible, then support in some form must be provided. Otherwise, the class is a travesty of education in which everyone is a loser.

SUMMARY

Classrooms are generally settings that include a teacher who is the group leader and some number of students. By definition, social power—the influence one has on the other members of the group—is involved. By identifying the five types of social power, we can more readily deal with them. By diminishing our reliance on coercion and legitimate powers, by using discretion in our use of reward powers, we can shape in desirable ways our teaching strategies overall, particularly our classroom discipline strategies.

From our understanding of the classroom as a social setting, we can perceive the likely causes of student behavior/misbehavior in that setting. One source is the particular needs pattern that is idiosyncratic for each student, based on their individual personalities, perceptions, and experiences. A second source is the interpersonal relations that are characteristic of a given class based on the unique mix of students in that class. The third source is the teacher, including both teaching style and teacher personality. When we are aware of these influences on student behavior, we can, as with social power, work at shaping our teacher behaviors to create the conditions in the classroom that are optimal for productive learning.

LOOKING AHEAD

We have just discussed principles used for maintaining productive learning environments as well as for interpreting and understanding power relations as they play out in the classroom in terms of misbehavior and discipline. Chapter 8, "Establishing and Maintaining Optimal Classroom Conditions," will deal with some very specific considerations regarding the needs of students and the ways teachers can address these needs by effectively promoting democratic discipline while motivating students.

❖ REFLECTIVE ACTIVITIES

1. As was stated in this chapter, teachers who understand the five types of social power, make a commitment to use the powers intentionally, and genuinely attempt to control the unwitting use of the powers in ways likely to have negative outcomes can markedly improve interpersonal relations and therefore the classroom climate. As you vicariously project yourself into the teacher role (or as you critically reflect on previous or current teaching experiences), what insights emerge from this powerful way of thinking about your teaching? How does this guide your professional development?
2. How will you conduct yourself as a teacher not only to minimize yourself as the proximate cause of students' misbehavior but to minimize the possible deleterious effects of other sources of misbehavior?

❖ REFERENCES

Brophy, J. (1981). Teacher praise: A functional analysis. *Review of Educational Research, 51,* 32.

French, J., & Raven, B. (1968). The bases of social power. In D. Cartwright and A. Zander (Eds.), *Group dynamics* (3rd ed.). New York: Harper & Row.

Kounin, J. (1970). *Discipline and group management.* New York: Holt, Rinehart, and Winston.

Oliva, P. (1993). *Supervision for today's schools* (4th ed.). New York: Longman.

Richmond, V. (1990). Communications in the classroom: Power and motivation. *Communication Education, 39* (July) 181–193.

Richmond, V., & McCroskey, J. (1984). Power in the classroom II: Power and learning. *Communication Education, 33,* 125–136.

Weber, M. (1947). *The theory of social and economic organization* (Talcott Parsons, Ed.; A. Henderson and T. Parsons, Trans.). Glencoe, IL: Free Press.

Chapter 8

Establishing and Maintaining Optimal Classroom Conditions

1. What implications emerge from a teacher's commitment to employ a democratic teaching style?
2. Why is respect considered the most important condition—a sine qua non—for promoting a democratic climate?
3. What aspects of cooperative learning make it especially compatible with creating a democratic climate?
4. What principles of motivation are especially important as they relate to classroom discipline?
5. What niche do classroom management practices occupy within the discipline component of teaching?
6. What does a very successful veteran teacher mean when she asserts, "My definition of *teaching* is 'collaborating with students'"?

Classrooms are settings established for the purpose of engaging students in learning. Educators intend classrooms to provide the most fertile conditions for learning to occur; accordingly, we may assume that they make good-faith efforts to design such settings. The history of U.S. education reveals that the outcomes of such efforts have taken many forms.

We believe, based primarily on philosophical considerations, that U.S. classrooms should be designed to reflect the democratic principles that ought to form the economic, social, and political fabric of our society. Any other basis is incompatible with the intention schools have to prepare our children to become fully functional citizens in our society.

While the classrooms we envision have many dimensions, we examine three critical ones in this chapter: classroom climate, motivation, and classroom management as these dimensions are democratically construed.

CLASSROOM CLIMATE

Classroom climate is a pervasive but intangible factor composed of the sum of the perceptions and impressions about the classroom that exist in the minds of the students and teacher. As such, it affects the quality of the personal interactions that occur in the classroom. While individual perceptions and impressions will undoubtedly vary somewhat, the persons in the classroom will in general tacitly agree on its major features. For example, the extent to which a classroom is joyful, regimented, businesslike, chaotic, or austere will be sensed similarly by most students, as well as by the teacher.

Climate does not exist prior to when a particular group of students gathers on the first day of school, although some predisposing factors may be in place (e.g., the physical conditions of the classroom; the reputation of the teacher, which may already be known to many of the students). On that first day, the students perceive the arrangement of desks, the bulletin board, the window flowers, and the learning centers—and impressions begin to form. Then they hear the teacher's voice, take note of the initial classroom communications, observe the demeanor of their classmates—and further impressions form. It is crucial that these first impressions be positive. Achieving this outcome is a task that deserves diligent attention. Leaving first impressions to chance is an unnecessary and imprudent risk. Consideration of factors that will impress students on that first day needs to begin prior to that first class meeting.

Democratic principles deserve to be subscribed to by every educator in the K-12 school setting. Paradoxically, the schools, which have as a major purpose to prepare children to inherit the mantle of civic responsibility in this democracy, are often perceived as being among the least democratic of our institutions. The reasons for this, as we have asserted in previous chapters, lie within our history and tradition, but that does not justify them. Current and prospective educators have the moral imperative to eliminate from our classrooms the insidious inconsistency between what we believe and what we do.

People tend to think of the term *democracy* as having an essentially political connotation. When they apply it to the classroom, they infer that decision making should be determined by student vote or consensus. Having established this straw man, they quickly reject it as an untenable way to conduct a class. They remember their own experience in classrooms in which the teacher was an authoritarian presence and students were subject to the teacher's will. There was little conscious awareness of their own rights; likewise, their privileges were at the discretion of the teacher. Their preparation for living in a democracy occurred more as a topic of study in a political science course (often called "Civics" or "Problems of Democracy") than in any systematic way as a consequence of participation in the affairs of the classroom.

In middle and high schools, class officers, student councils, and even student courts may function, and they deserve to be commended when they function effectively. But in classrooms, there has been little expectation for teachers to observe democratic principles in an accountable way. This is not to say that teachers are necessarily averse to using practices that are compatible with democratic principles; this occurs as individual teacher choice or style rather than institutionalized practice.

More fundamentally, the term *democracy* is a philosophic one, as we have argued in preceding chapters. It does not prescribe any specific practice but provides tacit standards that affirm certain kinds of approaches to conducting classes and exclude others. Some of the principles that are affirmed include the following: respect, which is embodied in the ideal of every person's worth and dignity; freedom within reasonable limits; due process as an aspect of justice to provide students a means to address grievances; students' involvement in classroom decision making in matters in which their judgments are appropriate; and cooperative learning approaches that help students develop social skills. A brief commentary on each of these will clarify how they are applied in the classroom setting. If the teacher genuinely advocates democratic principles, the traditional roles of students and teachers become transformed, and power relationships are reconsidered; that is, students are empowered with greater freedom, but they must assume commensurately greater responsibility as well.

Respect for Students

Respect is the most important condition to democracy. Without respect, individual gamesmanship and one-upmanship thrive. Without it, powerful people establish the agenda and the weak are disregarded or marginalized. This is especially the case when the teacher has little respect for students.

If the teacher has no respect for students, his or her personal needs become the dominant factor that determines the tenor of the classroom. The students' needs—for identity (self-esteem), stimulation, security (mental comfort), affiliation (identification with a peer group), and empowerment (self-determination)—are not recognized by the teacher as factors in decision making. If the teacher's needs profile is normal (i.e., not unusually skewed toward any one characteristic), then the classroom may be a reasonably tolerable place for its students. But if a certain needs profile idiosyncrasy exists, the teacher's demands on the students may be exaggerated by his or her unconscious and misguided efforts to appease that irregular need.

If, for example, the teacher has a strong need to be accepted by students, he or she may bend too far in meeting their expressed or supposed wishes, although not necessarily their needs. The teacher may function with a popularity contest mentality. Possible outcomes include unchallenging assignments, low standards for achievement, unwillingness to enforce reasonable classroom rules, and deemphasis of the teacher's primary role as the leader in favor of seeking so-called buddy status with the students. If the teacher panders to the students, he or she will be exploited by them. The students, having no purpose or direction, may act in such ways that are merely temporary respites from the tasks confronting them. But such behavior is educationally unfruitful and over time will cause the students to view the teacher condescendingly, even resentfully. Their likely comment about the teacher will be something like, "We can do what we want in that class, but we don't learn anything." Students want and need the teacher to be an appropriate authority figure and to maintain the integrity of the adult role. Children from kindergarten through high school define their lives to a large extent in terms of their role as students. Whether or not they voice it unequivocally, they appreciate the teacher who helps them find integrity in that role.

Another example of a teacher with lack of respect is one who is inflexible and has an inordinate need for certainty and structure. This teacher will perceive the students as pawns to be controlled in all aspects of their student role. We can envision this teacher giving little evidence of a sense of humor, insisting that desks be arranged in precise order, having an extensive list of classroom rules and their associated penalties, verbally dominating the classroom and not tolerating student initiatives, and using a regimented approach to classroom management and learning activities. From the students' perspective, the classroom is not an exciting place to be, nor is it especially a kind and gentle place. The demanding teacher takes the students for granted and gives them little opportunity for self-expression and empowerment. The students' most frequently used metaphor for this type of classroom is likely to be one of a prison.

We can almost hear this teacher expressing the belief that children need lots of discipline. "Nowadays," the teacher says, "they get too little of it at home. Without it they cannot learn effectively. My job is to provide that discipline and to present the material. Their job is to learn it. Sure, I run a tight ship, but these kids aren't fooling around; they're learning."

Of course the students need discipline, and they need an authority figure. And of course the teacher is there primarily to present the material (that is, to conduct meaningful learning activities), and the children are there primarily to learn. The posture of this teacher is difficult to refute on the face of it because it is anchored in self-evident truths. If students were automatons, the case would rest at this point. But students need to be allowed the attributes of their humanity. They are sentient beings. Their lives are not defined exclusively by their response to their teacher's expectations. Rather, they continuously seek satisfaction and fulfillment on their own terms. Given this, the classroom is understood as a far more complex place than the simplistic one assumed by the inflexible teacher.

The two classrooms just described cannot be democratic ones because the teachers in each case lack an attitude of respect. The first classroom has a laissez faire climate in which respect is passively absent; that is, the teacher has not shown disrespect as much as he or she has just not attended to respect. The second classroom has an autocratic climate in which the teacher doesn't just ignore the respect factor but actively, if not purposely, suppresses it. The first teacher, through gaining confidence and teaching skill and becoming less dependent on students for affirmation, might eventually be able to incorporate respect for students as an integral part of his or her teaching style. The second teacher probably has a firmly established personality trait of inflexibility that makes it unlikely that he or she could accommodate students' needs except in the case of highly dependent students. Even then it would not be as much a case of accommodating needs as having a serendipitous needs fit; that is, dependent students would welcome the structure and certainty that other students would find stifling.

Do you know and consciously acknowledge your own personality- or habit-driven needs? Do you sincerely like students? Not only will you, but can you respect students? Can you develop an approach to teaching through which your own and your students' personal needs (not just predicated academic needs) will be simultaneously and adequately fulfilled? These are key questions to which your honest introspective answers are crucial as you contemplate a career in teaching.

Freedom in the Classroom

Freedom is a term inextricably associated with democracy. Without freedom, democracy cannot exist. It is a term used frequently in everyday speech with the assumption that its meaning is well understood. In general, we understand freedom to be our right as individuals to self-determination to the extent that it is consistent with the welfare of the group. As we are sometimes reminded, freedom does not sanction acts such as shouting "Fire!" in a crowded theater in which there is no fire.

A dynamic tension exists between the rights of the individual and the welfare of the group. Individuals seek to expand the limits of their rights to achieve their personal ends, while the social forces—the collective rights of the group, sometimes given formal expression as rules and laws—tend to restrict individual options. Thus we have the right to voice reasonable descriptions or opinions about others, but not to the extent that they are libelous. As parents, we have the right to control our children, but not to the extent that it constitutes abuse. As drivers, we have the right to drive on public roads, but we ignore the speed limits at the risk of penalty and danger to others.

This same sort of dynamic occurs in the classroom. In this setting the welfare of the group is understood primarily in terms of optimum learning conditions. This concept establishes the parameters of acceptable classroom behavior. The teacher's role vis-á-vis freedom in the classroom is interpreting what, in a particular classroom, constitutes the optimum learning conditions. Some general conditions are self-evident: that students will be attentive and that they will engage in the tasks (presumably reasonable and appropriate) the teacher assigns. Further, students may not distract other students from their work, nor may they leave class without permission. However, other conditions are not so evident within the context of freedom and optimum classroom conditions. Teachers are likely to perceive such conditions as appropriate, even necessary, whereas students may perceive them as unnecessarily restrictive, even oppressive. Here are some examples about which differences in perception may occur: using grades as a penalty, requiring students to be in their seats ready to work when the bell rings, needing permission to sharpen a pencil or use the class library, and reading a book of one's choice when the student is fully caught up on classwork.

How is the teacher to distinguish who has the more reasonable perception? The concerned, fair-minded teacher doesn't ask what will make him or her most comfortable or what will keep the students busy. More appropriately, the teacher asks: What is the greatest amount of freedom, with its attendant responsibilities and privileges, these students can handle, or learn to handle, as we address class goals? The teacher's job is to help students, as individual learners and as members of a group, grow in their ability to be responsible citizens in the class. This implies perceiving the students as more than passive recipients; they should be active contributors to the positive learning conditions. When everyone in the classroom has a positive, cooperative, self-determined role (or at least has the opportunity to have that sort of role) in the group's achievement, freedom exists in the most appropriate way.

To establish optimum learning conditions where freedom exists, you must first abandon self-serving approaches and expectations. Second, you must assume that the students have the potential to be responsible learners. Finally, talk with students in a class meeting format about freedom and responsibility. Negotiate with them. Cut them a little slack. Challenge them. Treat them with respect. Let your self-fulfilling prophecy be embedded in your faith in their potential. Remember, you are using some pretty powerful psychology when you do this, and you have every reason to believe it can work.

Now suppose you try it and it doesn't work? What will you do? Give up? No. Cry a little? Possibly. Retrench? Certainly. So keep the faith. Analyze. Be introspective. What dynamics occurred? Why? Who might be a sympathetic soulmate to help you think it through? Avoid anyone who is likely to be condescending or cynical about your concerns for democracy. What, then, is the most likely strategy for your next attempt to make the concept of freedom a positive factor in your classroom? Freedom is too philosophically fundamental to ethical and effective teaching to give up on it. Be as passionate about it as you are committed to it. There is no acceptable alternative to your commitment to freedom.

Due Process in the Classroom

Due process is a term not usually associated with classrooms.[1] On the other hand, as embedded in a democratic approach to justice, due process is a legal concept essential to the democratic process. This suggests that concern for due process has a deserved place in our thinking about life in a democratically run classroom.

Without question, children have all the legal rights afforded them by the Constitution consistent with their status as minors. These rights must always be observed at the risk of penalty to any violator, including educators. Hundreds of court cases involving children and educators attest to this. However, the focus of this commentary is not a matter of criminal nor tort law. Our concern is with the attitude reflected by the teacher who asserts: "I may not always be right, but I'm always the boss." Students should not have to tolerate such condescension and arrogance, yet virtually all of us from our own experience realize that this occurs commonly in classrooms, usually under the guise of requiring students to show respect. It occurs because many teachers do not make a good-faith effort to apply the principles of democracy in their classrooms.

The majority of teachers are decent, well-meaning people. But teachers are not exempt from questionable judgment and action. Their own experience as students will have disposed some of them to view classrooms in decidedly nondemocratic

---

[1] Refer to Chapter 6 for a more detailed explanation of due process.

terms. In the mentally and emotionally taxing conditions of the classroom, they some-times misunderstand students and misuse authority. When this occurs (or is alleged to have occurred) students deserve the benefit of due process for review and resolution of the perceived violation of their dignity or rights. In this context, we refer to due process in the ethical-moral sense more than in the legal sense.

Due process in the classroom may not look very much like due process in a legal setting, but it has the same intent in either case. It ensures a means of recourse to address a grievance. While student grievances in the classroom might have a variety of sources, discipline-related grievances usually involve alleged unfair, insensitive, or abusive teacher practices. For example, the teacher might threaten or use unusually harsh punishment, accuse students unjustly, demean students, or use physical coer-cion. Traditionally, teachers have been able to do such things with relative impunity. From both a professional and a democratic perspective, this cannot be condoned.

If the spirit of due process were applied in the classroom, how would it play out? The necessary basis is a commitment by the teacher to the use of democratic principles with a focus on justice. Everything else follows from that. Due process in the classroom begins with a set of reasonable expectations being established. Some of these expecta-tions may be codified in a list of rules; however, most experts recommend that such rules be held to a minimum and stated in fairly general terms (e.g., show respect for all persons in the class). Students may even be involved in developing the rules for the class in some cases, but in any event, the teacher is the final arbiter of the list. The list itself is not as important as the class discussion of it in terms of behaviors, their meanings, and their likely consequences. The spirit developed in the class is more critical than the rules, and it results in thinking and reflective patriotism (as discussed in Chapter 5).

Another component of this concept involves assuring (and periodically reassuring) the students that due process is operative in the class. Students must become con-vinced that the teacher is "for real" and that airing a grievance in an appropriate way will not be considered an affront by the teacher or a challenge to teacher authority.

Next, students must be made aware that due process is a two-way street. When the teacher has a grievance with a student or the whole class, he or she has the right to communicate that. For the most part, teachers have taken this right for granted. In the democratic teacher's classroom, students will be assured that this right will be exercised in a manner that respects the students' dignity, but it will be done as firmly as necessary.

From this point on, due process will need to be established in a manner that fits each respective classroom. In one sort of scenario, we might find the teacher encour-aging the students to personally discuss a grievance with him or her. However, if the matter affected the class as a whole and was not satisfactorily resolved, the student would be assured that the matter would be brought before the class. If the student was reluctant for any reason to confront the teacher directly, he or she would be advised to go to a counselor, the principal, or a designated ombudsman-teacher to present the case. If the school at large has a due process procedure in place, the stu-dents should be made fully aware of how to use it.

You should now realize that the particulars of due process are not as important as students being convinced that they genuinely have effective recourse as the need arises.

Student Decision Making in the Classroom

Democracy implies the participation of citizens. As a political construct, it embodies the ideal of government of the people, by the people, and for the people. While classrooms are not political or governmental entities, it is useful to think of students having a citizen role in that they are not only shaped by the classroom but help shape the classroom.

Most directly, constructive participation in the classroom involves complying with explicit expectations, such as attending regularly, completing assignments, and observing the established rules. Less directly, but in the spirit of democracy, students may be empowered by being involved in making decisions (to the extent feasible) about such things as units/topics to be studied, schedules of classroom events, ways to receive extra credit, classroom privileges, and the agenda for field trips. They may also be involved in developing cooperatively and endorsing as a class the behavior expectations to which they are willing to subscribe, and so create a sense of ownership in these expectations. Further, students may be asked for their impressions, opinions, and suggestions about any aspect of the class, including their assessment of the teacher's performance. In this latter issue, assessment should not be conducted in a pro forma way; students should know that they are involved in a genuine effort to improve the class.

We are not recommending here a token, tenuous nod toward student involvement. Kohn (1993) has observed that "few contrasts in education are as striking as that between students . . . taking responsibility for how they want their classroom to be, and students sitting in rows, having been bribed or threatened into complying with an adult's rules" (p. 14). Teachers should consciously involve students in every possible meaningful way. When opportunities arise for student decision making, the teacher is ready to use them to advantage. All this contributes to a classroom climate in which students learn about responsibility by being responsible and learn about democracy by engaging in the process.

Cooperative Learning in the Classroom

During the last several years, cooperative learning has emerged as a prominent teaching-learning approach. It has been shown in the balance to be at least as effective as other methods in achieving academic goals. A major reason for its increasing popularity is that it promotes interaction and interdependence among students (Slavin, 1991). Elementally, it is democracy in action in the classroom. Educators increasingly are adopting the position that social and affective growth are their legitimate concerns, along with academic achievement.

Cooperative learning takes a variety of forms (Stallings & Stipek, 1986). However, several elements are common to most cooperative learning settings. Some of the more prominent ones are selected from a list by Stahl (1994):

1. *Heterogeneous groups:* Teachers should organize three-, four-, or five-member groups so that students are mixed as heterogeneously as possible. . . . Students should not be allowed to form the groups based on friendship or cliques.

2. *Equal opportunity for success:* Every student must believe that he or she has an equal chance of learning the content of the lessons and the required abilities and of earning the group rewards for academic success.

3. *Positive interdependence:* Teachers must structure learning tasks so that students believe that they sink or swim together—that is, their access to rewards is as a member of an academic team wherein either all members receive a reward or no member does.

4. *Positive social interaction behaviors and attitudes:* Merely because students are placed in groups and expected to use appropriate social and group skills does not mean students will automatically use these skills. To work together as a group, students need to engage in such interactive activities as leadership, trust building, conflict management, constructive criticism, encouragement, compromise, negotiation, and clarifying.

5. *Individual accountability:* Students are placed in cooperative learning groups so that each can achieve higher academic success individually than were they to study alone. Consequently, each must be held individually responsible and accountable for doing his or her share of the work and for learning what has been targeted to be learned.

6. *Post-group reflection (or debriefing) on within-group behaviors:* Students spend time after the group tasks have been completed to systematically reflect on how they worked together as a team.

The teacher's role in cooperative learning differs substantially from his or her role in the other common methods such as exposition, discussion, and inquiry. Those methods address academic outcomes directly, and other effects are incidental (if they occur at all). The teacher is, to a large extent, the deliverer of information or the monitor of the students as they seek information. Much of what happens falls under the category of direct teaching. In the cooperative mode, social and affective outcomes are expressly sought and are complementary to academic outcomes. The teacher becomes the facilitator of the process while the students utilize small-group processes to achieve learning goals.

The success of cooperative learning depends on the extent to which students apply several of the key factors described in the previous sections: *respect* for each other, as they recognize each individual's necessary role and contribution; *freedom* within reasonable parameters, as they interact responsibly in their group and recognize the rights of counterpart groups; and *decision making,* as they reach consensus within the group on the issues they face. It becomes, in an immediate way, an object lesson in practical democracy.

Cooperative learning has been found to be effective for teaching in a wide array of subject areas and at every grade level from elementary school through college. This is not to imply that other methods are obsolete. Methods that have always been effective in the repertoire of skillful teachers should continue to be used when circumstances dictate that a particular one is the method of choice. However, teachers may want to consider cooperative learning (more so than recitation, interactive lecture, and individual seatwork) as their default approach; that is, cooperative learning should be used unless a conscious decision is made that some other method is preferable for a particular learning outcome.

In practice, there is likely to be an integration of methods in the course of a general learning activity. The teacher will need to lecture to deliver some useful information efficiently to the class; sometimes, a whole class recitation or discussion will be required; and when opportunity for genuine inquiry occurs, the alert teacher will be quick to engage the students. Nevertheless, in the class of the teacher committed to democratic principles, the general mode from which the teacher deviates to employ other modes is cooperative learning.

This represents a major departure from teaching as we have historically known it. But yesterday's answers are not a sufficient response to today's—and tomorrow's—conditions in any arena of our culture. This is as true of pedagogy as it is in the more obvious case of technology. So keep an open mind, and give cooperative learning a chance. The climate in your classroom will be enriched by it.

MOTIVATION

Motivation is just as important as the democratic social conditions of the classroom. For our purposes, **motivation** is considered the students' inclination and efforts to achieve the goals of the classroom. The very heart of teaching is creating the conditions that elicit motivation within students. According to this perspective, teaching is not just the delivery of subject matter. As professional educators, we often have difficulty communicating and justifying to noneducators our strategies and practices when slogans such as "back to the basics" have such prima facie appeal.

Our interest in motivation here is basic to our general approach to classroom discipline. Orderly and intentional behavior on the part of students is largely contingent on their being motivated to learn. Students who are engaged constructively in learning are unlikely to misbehave. Motivation is the most effective factor in deterring misbehavior. (If only it were a simple matter to acknowledge this proposition and apply it directly to our teaching behavior . . .)

Motivation does include several straightforward and generally accepted teacher characteristics and practices (such as being dynamic and enthusiastic, presenting material in an interesting way such that the students feel a need to get involved). But a more basic understanding of motivation is required of educators. As teachers, we need to approach motivation as the outcome of informed decision making, not as rote practice. We need to know more than how; we must also know why. To be fully functioning educators, we must engage in reflection on our beliefs and our practices regarding all aspects of our teaching, which certainly includes motivation and discipline. This requires a way of thinking about motivation and discipline that is especially pertinent to the classroom setting.

Maslow (1987) developed a hierarchy model of motivation based on human needs. He postulated these to be physical, safety, love and acceptance, esteem, and self-actualization needs. This model is the one most familiar to educators. Glasser (1986) also postulated a set of needs as the basis for his approach to motivation, which he presents in the context of control theory. His list includes the need "to survive and reproduce, . . . to belong and love, *to gain power,* to be free, and to have fun" (p. 23). Both Maslow and Glasser develop their ideas at length, and reading them would contribute to the professional development of any educator.

Ardrey (1970) developed a list of needs similar to those just cited. In our view, Ardrey's theory of motivation is most immediately applicable to the classroom setting and so is the basis we use to understand both students' motivation and teachers' motivation-related decision making. Ardrey's model was developed through observation of animal behavior, and his conclusion was that certain needs are common in animals ranging from laboratory rats through lions and baboons, and extending to human beings. His theory is all the more credible because it provides useful insights about behavior over such a diverse array of creatures. We as human beings are often arrogant regarding our place in the order of animal life, but Ardrey clearly made the case that we share with them not only similar physical characteristics but psychological ones as well. The needs he identified are identity, stimulation, and security. We have added to this the need for affiliation (peer group identity) and the need for power (or to be empowered). The deficiency conditions related to each of these needs are, respectively, anonymity, boredom, anxiety, alienation, and impotence. While animals of different sorts differ widely in the specifics of how they achieve satisfaction of their needs, the sources of those needs are quite similar. It is important to understand that when one or more of the needs are not met, we enter a motive state to satisfy the particular need(s).

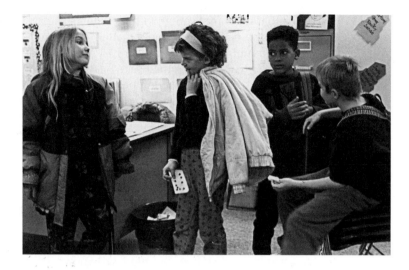

Identity Needs

Ardrey postulated *identity needs* to be the strongest of our psychological needs. His motivation theory does not deal with physical and safety needs to the extent that Maslow's does, but obviously where survival and fight-or-flight considerations are present, these are compelling first-order factors. In classrooms, these factors are not ones that typically must be dealt with. The school as an institution provides an ordered environment in which basic physical needs are met and in which threat to one's physical safety is minimal as compared with other settings. In any case, the teacher's main concern is with psychological factors far more so than physical factors.

Much of what was described in the previous section of this chapter affects students' identity needs. When students are respected, they feel worthy and appreciated as a part of the group. This in turn contributes to their awareness of self-esteem, the positive presence of which is an obviously comfortable and desirable psychological condition. When students are engaged in small-group cooperative learning activities, they have enhanced opportunity to be proactive simply because they compete for attention with far fewer cohorts; avoiding anonymity is easier to achieve.

Because identity is a basic and pervasive aspect of motivation, addressing it is an important concern for the teacher. Initially, the teacher should be aware that motivation occurs both as a long-term trait that endures as a more or less constant disposition and as an immediate condition triggered by a specific situation (Brophy, 1987). In the former case, motivation has an internalized stimulus, whereas in the latter the stimulus is external. Identity is likely to be associated with the internalized source. This, of course, is the most desirable sort of motivation because it is consistent and dependable, but it should not be taken for granted. Purposefully working at establishing and maintaining the students' disposition to long-term motivation through personal and social interaction is well worth the effort involved.

Some things the teacher can do to encourage long-term motivation are quite straightforward. Identity will be well served on an ongoing basis through the positive interaction that transpires regularly in a socially healthy classroom. In this happy and productive place, students have many opportunities for interaction, and their contributions are solicited and appreciated. The teacher quickly memorizes students' names and uses them. Further, the teacher tries to get to know students personally in terms of individual traits and interests. For example, Mark is already a good chess player; Julie is an anxious child who needs frequent reassurance; Ramon is already using men's cologne, though he does not yet shave, but don't tease him about it!; Surinder has an impressive baseball card collection; and so on for every student, even though there may be over 100 students a day in a secondary-level teacher's classes. In fact, in secondary schools the problem is further exacerbated by the alleged propensity of secondary teachers to be more content centered than student centered. An appropriate balance should be struck in a designed and purposeful way.

As was stated, self-esteem is inextricably a part of identity. The teacher needs to be continuously alert for ways to contribute to self-esteem; and, just as important, the teacher should avoid behaviors that unnecessarily undermine self-esteem. For example, the teacher need not be critical of wrong answers nor respond to a student negatively. Rather, an incorrect or hesitant answer is an opportunity to rejoin with leading questions until the student arrives at an acceptable answer. Meanwhile, the student has learned something about how to think through the issue at hand—and perhaps other similar issues as well.

Some children will arrive in class with inadequate social skills and limited or qualified acceptance in the classroom. These youngsters pose a certain kind of challenge to the teacher, for changing students' personalities—beyond helping them become more confident and aware—is not among the things that teachers can or should do. These are the unremarkable kids that the teacher must extend himself or herself for. Keep them in mind when the assignment needs to be written on the board, attendance needs to be taken, a note needs to be delivered, or a peer tutor can help a child who has been absent. Many such opportunities will occur (or can be contrived) that bring these "poor souls" into identity-enhancing situations.

Other children will arrive in class whose identities have been established through their assertive or brash, even intimidating, behavior. Early on, the teacher must realize that the outward bravado of some students, girls included, is often their response to their unfulfilled need for esteem. Teachers are not psychologists, and therapy is not their forte, but it is reasonably evident that many of these students could benefit from finding esteem through more socially acceptable behavior. One likely approach to the abrasive, potentially disruptive students is to talk with them in an open, nonadversarial, friendly way. They are likely to be emotionally disarmed by the teacher who takes a sincere and respectful interest in them, talks with them about mutual concerns, offers help in a noncondescending manner, and invites helpful suggestions in a problem-solving environment. When these youngsters begin to have new insights about their feelings and behavior, they may find reasons and ways to change their behavior. Keep in mind, however, that only the students can change their own behavior. Teachers can employ certain strategies, either professionally or intuitively derived, intended to elicit a particular response, but the influence of the teacher is through reflexive, never direct, channels. One of the common mistakes teachers make is to assume they can directly affect students' behavior while remaining blissfully unaware of any need to change their own.

What does the teacher do when insufficient change occurs on the students' part? First, keep trying. Perseverance will finally prevail in some cases. But more immediately, the teacher has little option but to enforce the consequences as appropriate, be certain the students realize the connection between their behavior and the consequences, and elicit the help of other school officials who are concerned with student behavior.

In cases in which identity is not effectively achieved on the part of the child, especially the "poor soul," feelings of anonymity occur. This condition is enervating. Professional teachers cannot tolerate its continued existence, for it is at cross-purposes with what the teacher is practically and morally charged to do. Teachers who make it their personal crusade to wipe out anonymity in their classrooms are alert to opportunities to raise students' levels of self-esteem and positive identity.

Stimulation Needs

The word *stimulate* is sometimes used as a synonym for the word *motivate*. For educators, *motivation* implies much more than *stimulation,* but the relationship is evident. Stimulation is involved especially with the short-term causal aspect of motivation and in this sense differs from the identity needs described earlier.

We are, in general, restless creatures. This certainly includes students in classrooms. Middle-school-age children especially have the reputation of being antsy, but the condition is actually pervasive throughout the K-12 years. Students become bored if they are insufficiently stimulated. Teachers are continuously challenged to find ways to channel restlessness and mental energy into productive educational activities that occupy students' consciousness and diminish their need to find alternative means to escape boredom. With widely varying degrees of success, teachers meet the challenge by, for example, selecting thought-provoking material, being enthusiastic, using variety in their presentations, encouraging students to be actively involved, using cooperation and competition selectively, and providing realistic opportunities for students to experience success. These and other means of stimulation are dealt with extensively in the professional literature.

Teachers are being naive when they assume that what they teach is self-evidently good for students, and for that reason, if no other, students should devote their mental energy to mastering the topic. Some students may, in fact, comply with the teacher's expectations because they value success for its own sake or because they have a strong need for teacher approval. But as many teachers will testify, students are less forgiving now than at any time in the past. They require ever more stimulating leadership on the part of the teacher. Is it unreasonable to expect that they should get it?

Effective teaching is, in the most basic sense, creating conditions in the classroom that genuinely arouse the students' interest in learning. Some teachers are especially capable of creating such conditions through the force of their personalities, their sense of "withitness," their communications and interpersonal skills, and their creativity and energy. The so-called born teachers are those fortunate enough to have many of these qualities—and there are others—in generous measure. For others, the task of eliciting motivation within students is not so readily achieved.

On athletic teams, the stars stand out from others who are cast as supporting players. But while the supporting players are necessary and valued, they need to use all their potential to make a sufficient contribution. The analogy helps make the point. Most teachers can't take themselves for granted any more than they can take their students for granted. We need to be introspective about ourselves, to define ourselves in terms of a profile of strengths and limitations. With this in mind, we set about purposefully developing ourselves to become the best teachers we can be within a framework of realistic expectations. There is no natural limitation on the extent to which we can engage in diligent work to achieve our worthy goals.

Our limitations are most evident in the task of stimulating students. To reprise the athletic team analogy, there are some who can't make the team at all, some who will have to work hard to be effective, and a few stars who are 'to the manor born.' And when the star teachers complement their talent with diligent effort, their impact on kids is likely to be truly notable. Is this discouraging? It isn't meant to be. If you honestly consider yourself to be blessed with some of the star talent, then go for it! Nothing is likely to give you more satisfaction in life than teaching. If you are realistically aware that you are not made of star stuff but you sincerely like kids and want to be there for them, then you go for it, too. You'll work hard in preparation, but there will be rewards. However, if in your moments of naked honesty you admit you lack the intuitively sensed critical traits of effective teachers, don't force it. Stimulating kids is not one of the things you were meant to do. You'll be especially susceptible to burnout as you find that classroom management and control of students consume your mental and emotional energy.

Security Needs

Security is not a discrete need apart from but rather an important component of motivation. Indeed, some of the factors that contribute to identity as described earlier promote security as well. For example, as particular students become increasingly accepted within a classroom group, their sense of security, because it is integrally related to their social status, rises accordingly.

Security involves an obvious physical dimension. In the world of the hunter and the hunted, security primarily means protection from predators. For example, when baboons are hunted, their troop organizes to protect the most vulnerable members; wolves hunt as a pack and so prey on much larger game than any individual could dare confront, and in this manner their availability of food and probability of survival are secure. But beyond very practical survival considerations, the group provides for social interaction that is absolutely essential to the psychic well-being of many kinds of creatures. It is this psychic dimension that is of most concern to teachers.

Anxiety, the deficiency condition related to security, is debilitating when it occurs beyond the level of tolerance, for it tenaciously imposes itself within one's consciousness. The affected person develops tunnel vision as he or she irresistibly focuses on the source of the anxiety and attempts to diminish or eliminate it. In the classroom, the most common source of anxiety is not fear of physical harm but rather the fear that one may not be able to cope successfully with assigned tasks, tests, or challenges. One's self-esteem is placed on the line, and this is psychologically unsettling. Survival of one's psyche and survival of one's body are closely related concerns. Just as in the case of physical threat, threat of psychological harm results in a reaction in the midbrain. Adrenaline flows, palms sweat, butterflies whirl in the abdomen, and the person becomes self-absorbed. A child in this condition is essentially unteachable. The teacher's concern, therefore, must be in promoting security and attenuating anxiety.

Teachers might begin by reassuring students of their awareness of the sources of anxiety and their intention to eliminate unnecessary causes. They need also to be continuously alert for signs of imminent anxiety and be ready to respond accordingly. Since a major source of insecurity is classroom evaluation, thoughtful consideration should be given to assessment practices. Here are some suggestions: use a portfolio approach to evaluation; teach students how to study, how to take notes, and how to take tests (it's amazing how infrequently this is taught!) so that they develop more confidence as scholars; use a mastery approach in which students may retake tests; use contracts in which students help define the intended outcomes; provide study guides at the beginning of a unit of study and conduct reviews regularly; involve students in developing the test questions; provide options to students when feasible (e.g., take-home tests).

While using some of these less threatening approaches to evaluation, teachers need to avoid the all too common practice of using tests as threats. It is one thing to inform or remind students about items that may appear on a test but quite another to resort to this as one's primary motivational strategy. Many students, especially so-called strivers, are already obsessed with grades; to exploit this further is unconscionable.

Security must also be addressed within the social structure of the classroom. Not every student has the potential to be a leader, but no student should have to accept isolate status. The teacher needs to be aware of the classroom dynamics and resist the efforts of aggressive or effusive students to dominate the class. There will inevitably be special friendships among the students, but when cliques emerge that are wholly devoted to their own self-interest, they should be neutralized. In other words, the teacher must be proactively in charge and work to promote open and comfortable relations throughout the class.

Teachers, through authoritarian, possibly intimidating, approaches can cause vulnerable students to feel insecure. Teachers who are inconsistent, moody, impatient, self-righteous, or lacking a sense of humor (sometimes these teachers simply don't like or respect children) cause stress in students that interferes with their ability to learn. Further, stress requires an outlet. If not in that teacher's class, then in another setting, the affected children must find release, and release frequently occurs in socially destructive ways. The travesty of this is that, in many cases, these martinet teachers claim they are running a tight ship or providing strong leadership. Rather, they are exploiting students essentially to satisfy their own distorted need for security and/or power.

Affiliation Needs

The need for affiliation is similar to the need for identity and certainly related to it. Affiliation refers to our effort to define ourselves, to establish a sense of self-worth through peer associations that function to validate (value) our sense of worth. The affiliation need is similar to the identity need in the sense that we define our personas in comparison and contrast with others—we are individuals who live in a collective. The degree to which we are motivated to fulfill our need for affiliation is a function of the degree of alienation we feel. When students cannot derive the basic psychological necessities such as mentioned previously, the drive to affiliate with some group that can provide even the minimum sense of worth is sought out.

Many adults are disbelieving when a gang member talks about love and acceptance as being the primary benefit of being in a gang. It is difficult (for some, impossible) to see the violence of gangs as a product of the desire of the alienated adolescent to get basic human gratification. However, as poverty, despair, and hopelessness expand across greater numbers of our population, alienation is felt by more and more people, and the motivation for any source of affiliation grows. Indeed, while gangs can be seen as abhorrent to our sense of civility, the individual members feel that their self-worth is affirmed through the affiliation.

Even when our basic needs are met, we still have a drive for affiliation. However, when our basic needs are met, including the need for identity, the groups we choose to fulfill our affiliation needs are far less spectacular than gangs. We join clubs, political organizations, or community service groups. For many of us in the general population, being a loyal and active fan of a sports team can satisfy a great deal of our need for affiliation. Students belong to such organizations as the pep club, the chess club, the football team, and the band. These groups enable us to meet our need for a sense of worthiness derived from others.

Understanding the need for affiliation can benefit the teacher and the students. Having students work in groups they are comfortable with, using partnerships for certain assignments like lab work, and using the principles of cooperative learning can aid in maintaining discipline and facilitate student achievement. On the other hand, teachers who conduct very rigid, traditional classrooms that allow for little or no group association or activity face a heightened probability of disruption from students whose sense of alienation is created by the structure. Minimally, teachers need to recognize that fulfilling the need for affiliation can facilitate discipline.

Empowerment Needs

Much of the foregoing sections has dealt with empowering students. Empowering is not something teachers do in isolation from other aspects of teaching. An observer in a classroom could not identify a particular teacher behavior as empowering students in the same way the observer could overtly view questions being asked or a lecture being given. Rather, the observer might judge that because of particular dispositions a teacher displayed, students were either being empowered or rendered impotent. When the teacher is disposed, for example, to respect students, to encourage their freedom, to engage them in meaningful decision making, and to provide them due process, students are being empowered. Empowering is addressed here not as a discrete idea apart from other needs issues but as an organizer that provides a thread to tie together the other concepts.

Traditionally, teachers have tended to view students as dependent children who are manipulated for their best interest. Given the nature of classrooms—which feature a mature and expert teacher who is invested with the authority of the state and 20 to 30 young people whose self-evident need is to acquire knowledge and skills—they by default may become places where the teacher is the deliverer of information and the director of activities, while students are essentially passive recipients of teacher services. But students, as we have said, are not automatons; they are sentient beings. Their needs to become knowledgeable and skillful are predicated ones, not the more basic ones that attend their essential humanness. The services that teachers provide in contributing to students' knowledge and skills are not being disparaged but rather placed in perspective. Students have, as we sometimes say, other fish to fry. Only by addressing the many needs of children—academic, personal, and social— can any needs be effectively met.

To empower students is to celebrate their wholeness, their complexity, the real people they are. In the classroom as elsewhere, they need to develop a positive sense of who they are, to realize that they have worth and dignity, and to control some aspects of their lives in satisfying ways. As an overriding factor, the teacher needs to realize this and do those things that are empowering within the framework of feasibility and productive learning.

How is this carried out in the classroom? As always, informed teacher judgment is the bottom line, for a prescription for one setting would likely be irrelevant for another; it is the spirit that counts most. Empowerment might occur in these ways:

1. Identify the natural group leaders, and allow them to assume their natural role within the group. Further, help these leaders develop and practice the skills of democratic group leadership.
2. Involve students in the process of conflict resolution so they can effectively resolve issues or disputes among themselves.
3. Use inquiry approaches to learning, which require students to take initiatives and engage in individually directed learning.
4. Use a cooperative learning approach that provides a heightened degree of autonomy within each established small group.
5. Allow students an appropriate decision-making role regarding topics, learning activities, and field trips.
6. Approach the class on a genuine basis that identifies the class as belonging to all the students; involve them in classroom management, including developing poli-

cies (consistent with democratic principles and school policies), routine activities, and expectations.

7. Take action that diminishes student empowerment only reluctantly and after dispassionate consideration.

8. Remain continuously alert for promising ways to empower students further in the interest of democratic climate and productive learning.

By their very nature, classrooms can work at cross-purposes to the outcomes for which they are intended. Classrooms are likely to include students who (1) are assembled as a large group, where each student has only limited opportunity for recognition and attention; (2) remain unnaturally passive for extended periods of time attending to tasks not of their choosing; (3) experience both academic and social conditions that create apprehension and even threat; and (4) feel little affinity for other students within the group or commitment to the purposes of the class. One can hardly design a setting more likely to result in the deficiency conditions previously identified: anonymity, boredom, anxiety, alienation, and impotence. As a teacher, you must counteract these deficiency conditions with your purposeful efforts to avoid the pitfalls they pose. To do this most effectively, you need a comprehensive, consciously conceived approach to motivation that targets identity, stimulation, security, affiliation, and empowerment. You can develop this through proactively addressing the five major components of motivation in ways we have suggested and complementing this with your own commitment, creativity, compassion, and enthusiasm.

CLASSROOM MANAGEMENT

We refer to classroom management as teacher behaviors intended to ensure that learning proceeds smoothly and effectively. There is no sharp demarcation between climate and management or, as will be discussed in the next chapter, between management and intervention. Some teacher strategies, such as establishing classroom rules and conducting class meetings, are shaped by the nature of the climate but have clear implications for managing the classroom. However, the focus changes as one considers the central meaning of each of these constructs. We address the constructs separately in this book, even though in practice the distinctions merge.

Both classroom climate and classroom management have as their purpose to establish conditions in the classroom that promote students' cooperative and productive behavior. In the case of climate, this is accomplished largely through affective means; for classroom management, through cognitive means. A familiar cliché in football is that the best defense is a good offense. This notion can be applied to managing student behavior if one thinks of the offense as effective instruction and management. When students are interested, they will be involved in the classroom learning activities; when they understand and accept the parameters for their actions, they are unlikely to engage in disruptive behavior. Teachers encounter relatively few discipline-related problems when they provide for students' motivation in ways described in the previous section and function in terms of expert and referent power (as explained in Chapter 7). This is perhaps the most constant and credible finding from all the research literature on classroom discipline.

Simplistically, then, we might say that if you want to have an orderly and disciplined classroom, use interesting instructional activities and reflectively derived managerial techniques. As an analogy, we might advise members of the swimming team to just stroke faster if they want to lower their times. Swimmers, of course, improve their times through working on conditioning and form, factors that are developmental. Similarly, teachers improve their effectiveness through deliberate efforts over time, but outcomes for teachers are less predictable than are outcomes for swimmers. So by all means, work at being the best teacher you can be, for as you improve your instructional and managerial skills, you will correspondingly attenuate students' tendency to noncompliant behavior. Your teaching should be composed of instructional/management behaviors on the one hand and controlling/intervention behaviors on the other. Your goal as a teacher is to be able to use as many of the former as possible so that you are required to use overtly the fewest of the latter.

Generally, when teachers anticipate and plan for their teaching, they do so in terms of lesson content and learning activities. Less attention is given to organizational and environmental factors. But these are essential parts of classroom management, and they deserve a substantial share of teacher attention, especially in the beginning days of the new class.

Classroom management involves a diverse array of factors, from establishing the regularities and routines of the class to monitoring individual and group behaviors. Books have been written on the topic, for it is an extensive and complex part of teaching.[2] No attempt will be made here to provide a comprehensive treatment of classroom management, but we will cite and briefly discuss a number of key aspects and give special attention to the first day the class meets.

Classroom Decor and Arrangement

Before the children arrive in your classroom for the first day of school, you will want to prepare an attractive setting for them—and, of course, for yourself. Most schools provide that walls and floors are cleaned, but beyond that teachers are largely on their own. The physical appearance is mostly at the discretion of the teacher. Greenery placed along the windows and in the corners adds a nice touch. Hanging plants are attractive; a sweet potato in water grows into an attractive and inexpensive hanging vine.

---

[2] Two books by the same five authors are noteworthy: Evertson, Emmer, Clements, Sanford, and Worsham, *Classroom Management for Elementary Teachers;* Emmer, Evertson, Sanford, Clements, and Worsham, *Classroom Management for Secondary Teachers.* Both of these books are in the 1994 third edition; the reference list in this chapter cites the 1984 first edition.

Pictures help, too. They can be selected to reflect learning topics or subject areas, or they might simply be attractive pieces of art in their own right. Artwork done by students is readily available, of course. While keeping the students in mind, you can still let your own personality and good taste be reflected in your selection.

Bulletin boards are a feature of every classroom. They may be used to provide current information to students, to complement instruction, to provide atmosphere by reflecting the seasons and holidays, and to suggest certain behaviors and values to children (e.g., avoiding drug use). Once the school year is in progress, enlisting interested students in developing bulletin boards is a way to help them evolve a sense of ownership in their classroom. Some teachers admit to not being artistic and being threatened by the expectation to have attractive bulletin boards. Many books on creating bulletin board displays are available in libraries, and every school's professional library should include some.

Classrooms at different levels and in different subject areas will require different facilities and equipment. They variously include learning centers, room libraries, laboratory desks and storage, chalkboards and audiovisual equipment, and file cabinets, as well as students' seats and the teacher's desk. How shall it all be arranged? The possible variations are almost endless, but several concerns need to be kept in mind. These include communication, traffic flow and efficiency of movement, frequency of use and accessibility, flexibility, and noise interference. For some teachers, having the teacher's desk in front of the room, the students' desks in straight rows, and the wastebasket near the door is always the way classrooms are. However, a lot of logic and a little creativity will result in classrooms that provide a different look to students, are flexible enough to accommodate a range of teaching modes and learning activities, and help to relieve boredom for everyone. The appearance of your classroom is the basis for the first impression students and others have of you as a teacher. You cannot directly control many of the subsequent impressions students and others have, so consider this important question: What is the statement I want my classroom to make? In answer to this question, decide how best to make your classroom your articulate and powerful agent of communication.

Classroom Routines

By the time students are in the second grade, they have begun to be aware that there are certain ways of doing things at school: entering and leaving class, having basic learning materials at hand, obtaining permission to speak, passing in papers, and sharpening pencils. But there is no guarantee that students will regularly and responsibly use these routines. The appropriate ways need to be taught and reinforced for students at all levels. As a teacher, you must determine how these regularities can be best accomplished in your classroom; then communicate this to students very early, provide practice as needed, and remind students when lapses occur. Teachers who do not systematically do this increase the risk of inefficiency and frustration.

One particular aggravation for teachers involves absent students and make-up work. Here again, the key lies in being systematic and keeping good records. Some teachers keep a folder for every student. When students are absent, materials pertinent to the day's lesson are placed in the folders. Students can readily retrieve these materials upon their return. In such a case, there is a certain assumption of student responsibility, and the realistic teacher understands the need to remain alert and to monitor students' make-up work. But to the extent that students are willing to be (or to become) responsible, the teacher is relieved of a lot of detail work.

In every social setting, rules exist. In some settings, the rules are mostly tacit, but in the relatively structured setting of the classroom, many of the rules are explicit. The recommendation by many knowledgeable educators is that formal rules be kept to a minimum number, usually about five. Following are two sets of examples. Evertson, Emmer, Clements, Sanford, and Worsham (1984, p. 22) suggest these rules for an elementary classroom:

1. Be polite and helpful.
2. Respect other people's property.
3. Don't interrupt the teacher or other students while they are talking.
4. Do not hit, shove, or hurt others.
5. Obey all school rules.

Emmer, Evertson, Sanford, Clements, and Worsham (1984, p. 42) suggest these rules for a secondary classroom:

1. Bring all needed materials to class.
2. Be in your seat and ready to work when the bell rings.
3. Respect and be polite to all people.
4. Do not talk or leave your desk when someone else is talking.
5. Respect other people's property.
6. Obey all school rules.

In any classroom, it is likely that the established rules will be different in some ways from these examples. You may, for instance, insist that all your classroom rules are stated in positive terms. In general, teachers should avoid long lists of very explicit rules covering everything from gum chewing to depositing scraps in the wastebasket. Rather, keep the rules fairly broad in scope, but spend some time in class discussing with the students the meaning of the rules and the reasons for them. At that time, examples of both complying with the rules and violating them can be given by the teacher or, even better, elicited from the class.

Regarding involving the students in actually establishing the rules, there is no clear-cut indication in the literature favoring either choice. It is, finally, a matter of teacher style and feasibility. Teachers who are committed to having a democratic climate may involve the students in setting rules because they believe that this is a way to genuinely empower students. However, secondary teachers who meet five or six classes every day would be hard pressed to try to conduct each class with a different set of rules. Each class could be allowed to express opinions about classroom rules, and the teacher, as the common factor among the classes, could then make a judicious resolution based on all the input. If this happens, all the classes should be given the benefit of hearing the rationale the teacher used.

Monitoring Student Behavior

Classrooms are dynamic and complex places. Usually they include 20 or more students, each of whom is a creature of free will with a variety of needs. There is an infinite number of possibilities for how this scenario might play itself out in the classroom. The wise and alert teacher can anticipate many of the more common possibilities and with a proactive stance be prepared to deal with them. This includes addressing climate, motivation, and classroom conditions in ways we have described.

Studies of classrooms make the point that classrooms are busy places (Good & Brophy, 1994). Although order, even tranquillity, usually prevails (some teachers would surely question this statement), the aura of decorum can change, sometimes quickly, into a scene of confusion as order breaks down. Discomfiture may be felt by the teacher as students resist his or her authority. Avoiding this experience is a high priority on the part of every teacher. So monitoring classes carefully and nipping the breakdown in the bud is clearly in the teacher's and the class's best interest.

Kounin (1970), in his seminal research on group dynamics in the classroom, identified four teaching strategies that contribute to classroom order. The first is "withitness," a term he invented to describe the teacher's awareness of everything that is happening throughout the classroom. Teachers who displayed this skill were said to have eyes in the back of their heads. They seemed to know what the students were thinking and what they were inclined to do before they did it. They are able to diffuse incipient misbehavior. For example, if a student were attempting to make eye contact with a neighbor, it is very likely that the first student wanted to say something surreptitiously to the second, or perhaps pass a note. The teacher might direct a topic-related question to the first student while giving a knowing look. Or the teacher might move purposefully to that area of the classroom, again making meaningful eye contact. When the students are familiar with the teacher's style, these unobtrusive teacher behaviors communicate that the teacher is on top of things. This use of expert power will, over time, discourage many students from even thinking about casual noncompliance.

"Overlapping" is the second strategy of effective classroom management. It describes the teacher's ability to do more than one thing at a time. The teacher does not always have the luxury of attending to just one thing and ignoring all else. One can envision a juggler keeping several balls in the air at one time and recognize how this analogy aptly applies to the effective teacher. The teacher who displays overlapping is able to write on the chalkboard while maintaining controlling eye contact with the class. And this teacher is able to keep the entire class on task while giving individual help to one child. The instance described above of a teacher proceeding with the lesson while tacitly diffusing noncompliant behavior is an example simultaneously of withitness and overlapping.

"Smoothness and momentum" constitute the third strategy. They are descriptive terms in their own right. Teachers who are well prepared are able to move through the lesson without awkward hesitations, without signaling to students their possible uncertainty or self-consciousness. They make smooth transitions from activity to activity. They use entries and closures for each learning activity, with appropriate bridges that maintain the flow, much as one might sense that turning a corner in a car changes direction but has purpose and continuity. Momentum refers to the teacher's ability to maintain pace without getting bogged down, thus losing students as spans of attention are exceeded. One particular student's question might be so specific to that student that answering it at length would cause most of the other students to tune out. An aware teacher would postpone an answer to that student until a more appropriate time or, perhaps, if feasible, ask a responsible student to quietly provide help to the questioner. In another instance, a lengthy discourse on some idea would result in wandering minds and lost momentum. Teachers' ability to have smooth, well-paced lessons contributes simultaneously to productive learning and effective management.

Kounin's fourth strategy is "group alerting." This involves giving cues to the students that encourage their participation in the class activities. Teacher questions are an important means of group alerting. For example, teachers should, in general, intersperse lectures with questions rather than engaging for extended periods in lecture alone. During discussions or recitations, calling on students randomly is a means of putting all students on notice that they cannot opt out simply by not taking the initiative. Other ways of alerting are to have a choral response when feasible, or to have every student write a brief response so that each has an answer ready if called upon. This is especially pertinent when important focusing or culminating questions are asked that every student should think about. Through gesturing, teachers may signal students to refrain from or continue with particular behaviors. Also, teachers may alert students about the importance of certain information by informing them that they are likely to encounter it on a quiz or that it is necessary to do certain homework problems. They might also challenge students: "You shouldn't have much trouble with the first ten problems, but if you get the last two right, you are really a star."

Withitness, overlapping, smoothness and momentum, and group alerting are not skills a teacher consciously thinks about instance by instance and then applies discreetly. Rather, these are habits of thinking and behaving embedded in the overall teaching approach. They are defining qualities of the teaching style within which they occur. They may emerge in the case of the so-called born teacher as a largely intuitive aspect of teaching, or they may have to be learned behavior for others, but in any case they are qualities well worth cultivating as you develop your teaching style.

The First Day

Students come to class with feelings of apprehension and curiosity. Is the teacher nice? Will the class be interesting? Will we have to do a lot of work? Will learning be fun, or at least not a real drag? Does the teacher yell at kids? Will we have homework on weekends? What are my chances of making good grades in this class?

By the end of the first day, many of these and other similar questions should have been answered for the class. Because this is the most critical of all the class meetings that will occur, it deserves to be the best planned class you teach. You may think of the first class as an exercise in applied psychology and approach it with strategies that have as much an emotional as an academic focus. Think of yourself as playing to a skeptical audience. Make every effort to assure students in ways that will leave them cheering (well, at least reasonably satisfied) by having their anxieties relaxed. Better to leave a positive first impression than to have to work at changing initial impressions later. Following is a list of items that deserve consideration as you plan that first class (Kindsvatter, Wilen, & Ishler, 1992, p. 267).

1. Conduct introductions, beginning with the teacher's, in which some appropriate bit of information is shared.
2. Present a course overview and rationale, highlighting interesting and relevant activities.
3. Present academic expectations and grading policy, accompanied by a rationale.
4. Present behavioral policies, expectations, and conventions, including a brief list of general rules and directions regarding how to enter and leave class, obtain a pass, be recognized to speak, use the pencil sharpener, pass papers in, obtain materials—whatever a comprehensive classroom management plan requires. This may extend over several days.
5. Provide opportunity for the students to express their expectations for the teacher, with the possibility of mutual verbal contracting.
6. Assure students that they will be successful in your class. Tell them how this will happen.
7. Begin studies during the first class meeting. The students will get the message that you consider class time to be precious and irretrievable, that it must be protected and used purposefully.
8. Attend to filling in seating charts, handing out textbooks, and making an initial study assignment.

These considerations will be more meaningful if they are examined within a context. The following classroom episode, while it presents just one setting, demonstrates the kind of thinking a teacher has done to address his concern that the first class meeting be a special time for the class. Teachers at other levels and subject areas will, of course, adjust their approach to the particular characteristics of their classroom.

A Classroom Episode: First Meeting of an Eighth-Grade Science Class

John Woods watched the students enter his general science class this first day of the semester. "Take a seat anyplace," he announced as the room filled. After the students had settled into seats, Woods told them his name and identified the class. "Uh oh," one student exclaimed, "I'm supposed to be in Mr. Davis's class," and he quickly exited.[3]

"Now that we're all here, let's get to know each other," Mr. Woods began as the last echo of the class bell died out. I'd like each of you to tell the rest of us your name because there are some new people here. Also, because this is science class, tell us the name of your favorite scientist—you know, a scientist you think has been a great example or has made a valuable contribution. I'll go first while you're thinking. Well, again, I'm John Woods, and I've been around here for a long time—actually 18 years. I've enjoyed teaching science to people like yourselves all these years. It's a great job, and I'm happy to be doing it again this year. Some of you know I'm adviser to the chess club and intramural program. I hope a lot of you are active in both this year.

"And my favorite scientist—I'll bet you never heard of him—a 16th-century man named Giordano Bruno. Eventually, we'll talk about him and many others in this course. Now, how about you?"

The 22 students in the class gave their names and, with some occasional prompting, named a scientist. Mr. Woods kept track of the scientist named by each student with the notion that, as their first written assignment, they would each do a brief report on the scientist they had named.

After introductions, Mr. Woods began to comment on the course. "This year you'll learn a lot about science. From your history courses, you know something of what life was like in the past. It's very different now—far more comfortable and, I think, far more interesting than at any time in the past. And the major reason for this? Science. Science has made it all possible." He elaborated on this theme for a few minutes, asserting that nobody could afford to be scientifically illiterate in today's world.

"In fact," he went on, "a large proportion of you will have science-related jobs and careers. What are some of these?" Almost every student responded as Mr. Woods recorded their answers on the chalkboard. "Good job, class," he complimented them when they had at least 15 occupations listed. "This should help you realize just how important science is in your life."

Then, making a transition, Mr. Woods described the science course. "This will be a course not just *about* science, but *in* science. Do you sense the difference? I'll be helping you to learn how to think like a scientist, and you'll find lots of ways to use that in your life—everything from appreciating the wonders of nature to staying healthy and deciding on a career. This will be a *doing* class, and we'll do some fun things. One thing will be a project you'll do for the science fair. Did I hear a groan from the back just now? Believe me, you'll be proud of your projects, especially if you come up with a winner. And, you know, one of our eighth-grade students gets to go to the American Students for Science meeting in Chicago for three days next April. How would you like to be that person? Also, you saw the science assembly put on by the eighth-grade students last year. We'll be doing that again." Mr. Woods went on to describe the cooperative learning strategy they would use and that they would have lots of choices about topics and activities during the course.

After describing the general approach in the course, Mr. Woods addressed some procedural matters. "I know you're all concerned with grades, so let's talk about that. Within a couple days, you'll receive a course outline that will inform you about things

---

[3] This episode was originally published in Kindsvatter, Wilen, and Ishler, *Dynamics of Effective Teaching* (White Plains, NY: Longman, 1992).

like grades, rules, and general expectations. But for today, let me just hit the highlights of these things. We'll have a unit test about every three weeks that will include both objective and essay questions. And you'll be graded on written reports, lab work, and your project. I'll also give credit to those people who participate and make valuable contributions in the class. But nobody will fail. If you should—heaven forbid—get a grade lower than C on any work, I'll ask you to redo it until it deserves a C or higher grade. However, I don't give higher than a B to any work that must be redone. The only way you can fail is not to turn in your work, but that hasn't been a big problem with my past classes. And because we're using cooperative learning groups, you'll get a lot of help from your classmates as well as from me when you need it.

"Perhaps one more thing I should say this first day is that I have just four nonnegotiable rules in my class. If you follow them as I intend to follow them, there isn't much chance that we'll give each other grief. If you don't—well, what can I say? We'll just have to talk it over and work it out the way reasonable people like scientists can. These are the rules: be on time, be prepared, be responsible, and respect the rights and feelings of others. If we eventually need more rules, we'll make them. Notice I said 'we.'"

John Woods paused momentarily as a signal that he was moving to another phase. "Well, I've been doing a lot more talking today than you have. I'd like to hear from you for the last few minutes today. I've told you what my expectations are for you; what are yours for me? You've been students for seven years—eight years counting kindergarten— so you have a lot of experience with teachers. What do you think I can do as a teacher and we can do as a class to make this a great year for all of us?"

The students were quiet for several moments thinking about what their teacher had requested. Then students brought up a variety of suggestions: "Don't give us homework on the weekends." "Don't yell at us like we're hard of hearing. Give us a chance to explain." "Write our assignments on the board." "Tell a joke now and then." The tempo picked up as students thought of more things to say. Mr. Woods acknowledged each suggestion in turn. As a closure to this segment of the class, he promised he would give their ideas consideration and respond the next day in class.

With only a minute or so remaining, Mr. Woods thanked the students for their attention this first day and for their thoughtful participation. Then he turned to the chalkboard and pointed to the assignment. "You see, I have written it as Joanie suggested. Do you see the textbook on your desk with the yellow slip inside the front cover? Hand the slip to me as you leave class, OK? Now, as the assignment on the board says, for tomorrow read the first short chapter on what it means to be a scientist. We'll have a discussion about that tomorrow.

Analysis of the Episode

Mr. Woods is one teacher in one class. No other teacher, not even an eighth-grade science teacher, will do things exactly as he had on that first day. For example, you might think Mr. Woods talked too much, and the students talked too little. And maybe they should not have taken any seat but rather have been assigned to seats for the purpose of getting to know them more quickly. John Woods crowded much activity into one

45-minute period. Was it too much to attempt in one day? Which things should have been given priority and which postponed until a later class meeting?

Mr. Woods demonstrated that he prepared with care for this first day, that he had specific objectives he intended to accomplish, that he conducted his class in a manner that would be unique compared with all the following days, and that he realized the importance of initiating momentum and providing the conditions for motivation early on.

SUMMARY

This chapter on democratic climate, motivation, and classroom management has not focused on discipline as much as it has on the key elements of effective teaching, although we mentioned discipline where it was pertinent. The most important proposition in this chapter is that discipline has far less to do with manipulating student behavior than with guiding students in a developmental process that has both academic and social components. This involves infusing constructivist teaching practices (encouraging students to be "meaning makers") to complement the behaviorist ones that usually prevail in U.S. classrooms. One very successful veteran teacher perhaps said it best: "My definition of teaching is 'collaborating with students.'"[4] Think about that. What are the implications for you if you accept that definition? Is it a challenge that enables you to transcend the commonplace in teaching and be a visionary?

LOOKING AHEAD

Chapters 7 and 8 have provided principles and concepts for understanding the classroom context and student psychology in terms of specific forces and factors that need to be reflectively considered in making discipline decisions. We must now move to the application of those principles in the service of establishing democratic practices in general while dealing specifically with student misbehavior.

Chapter 9, "Discipline-Related Intervention and Remediation in the Classroom," examines approaches to dealing with students who misbehave. Notions of "reasonable consequence" for misbehavior will be contrasted with the idea of punishment. We will introduce the idea of a behavior intervention and remediation plan and explore the principles of conflict resolution.

---

[4] Excerpted from a presentation by Joan Reha at Kent State University on April 13, 1994.

❖ REFLECTIVE ACTIVITIES

1. Commentary in previous chapters inclined toward helping you shape your belief system about classroom discipline. The focus in this chapter shifted somewhat toward teacher practices. As your ideas about classroom climate and management evolve, what practices suggested in or inspired by this chapter will likely become basic ones in your approach?

2. A powerful concept associated with classroom discipline is motivation. From an even broader perspective, how can motivation become the unifying theme that makes your approach to teaching internally cohesive and synergistic?

3. The proposition unequivocally presented throughout this book is that democratic principles must form the basis for classroom practices in general and discipline-related practices specifically. What problems, issues, or questions might you expect to encounter as you apply democratic practices in your classroom?

❖ REFERENCES

Ardrey, R. (1970). *The social contract*. New York: Atheneum.

Brophy, J. (1987). Synthesis of research on strategies for motivating students to learn. *Educational Leadership, 45*(2), 40–48.

Emmer, E., Evertson, C., Sanford, J., Clements, R., & Worsham, M. (1984). *Classroom management for secondary teachers*. Englewood Cliffs, NJ: Prentice-Hall.

Evertson, C., Emmer, E., Clements, R., Sanford, J., and Worsham, M. (1984). *Classroom management for elementary teachers*. Englewood Cliffs, NJ: Prentice-Hall.

Glasser, W. (1986). *Control theory in the classroom*. New York: Harper & Row.

Good, T., & Brophy, J. (1994). *Looking in classrooms* (6th ed.). New York: Harper Collins.

Kindsvatter, R., Wilen, W., & Ishler, M. (1992). *Dynamics of effective teaching*. White Plains, NY: Longman.

Kohn, LA. (1993). Choices for children: Why and how to let children decide. *Phi Delta Kappan, 75*(1), 8–19.

Kounin, J. (1970). *Discipline and group management in classrooms*. New York: Holt, Rinehart, and Winston.

Maslow, A. (1987). *Motivation and personality*. New York: Harper & Row.

Slavin, R. (1991). Synthesis of research on cooperative learning. *Educational Leadership, 48*(5), 71–82.

Stahl, R. (1994). The essential elements of cooperative learning in the classroom. *ERIC Digest*. Washington, DC: Office of Educational Research and Improvement, U.S. Department of Education.

Stallings, J., & Stipek, D. (1986). Research on early childhood and elementary school teaching programs. In M. Wittrock (Ed.), *Handbook of Research on Teaching*. New York: Macmillan.

Discipline-Related Intervention and Remediation in the Classroom

❖ Focus Questions

1. What principles of intervention and remediation should be included in an informed teacher's belief system?
2. What is the defining condition of punishment that renders it inappropriate for addressing misbehavior?
3. What are the necessary attributes of a reasonable consequence?
4. What is the particular difficulty in finding a reasonable consequence to fit particular kinds of misbehavior?
5. Why is conflict resolution the preferable approach to settlement of student problems?
6. What factors have deterred the more widespread use of conflict resolution?

In the popular book *I Know Why the Caged Bird Sings,* Maya Angelou's mother, in a moment of poignant insight, whispers to Maya, "See, you don't have to think about doing the right thing. If you're for the right thing, then you do it without thinking" (Angelou, 1993, p. 246). This expresses elegantly the philosophy of the authors regarding intervention into and remediation of children's unacceptable classroom behavior. As a teacher, your commitment to democratic and developmental discipline predisposes you to certain practices while it precludes others. Consideration of these practices until your predisposition is firmly established is a fundamental step in your preparation for leadership in the classroom. Your goal is to function within a consistent pattern of responses to students while you make a professionally sound decision in each instance.

There is no magic bullet where coping with misbehavior is concerned. Misbehavior presumably will continue to be inaccessible to preconceived, transportable solutions; each occurrence of misbehavior beyond trivial matters must be dealt with as a unique case.

The myth that "good control depends on finding the right gimmick" was explained in Chapter 1. We asserted that effective control is not achieved with any regularity by fortuitously stumbling upon something that "works" but rather through sound judgment grounded in an informed belief system.

In classrooms where a democratic climate, teacher leadership, and student interest exist in positive abundance, relatively little misbehavior is likely to occur. However, even in such classrooms, conditions sometimes are generated that precipitate misbehavior. Where democratic climate, teacher leadership, and student interest are less abundant, misbehavior will happen with greater frequency and severity. Every teacher must be prepared to intervene when misbehavior is detected.

Maintaining a productive learning mode in the classroom is a high priority, so teachers need to intervene in ways that least disrupt the learning activity while still redirecting the targeted students to resume appropriate behavior. Following intervention, there must sometimes be remediation of misbehavior in an effort to reduce the likelihood of reoccurrence. In this chapter we address these concerns. We have not found a magic bullet for dealing with misbehavior, but we believe that understanding the dynamics of discipline and the underlying causes of misbehavior is necessary for establishing and maintaining effective democratic classroom discipline.

INTERVENTION TO TERMINATE MISBEHAVIOR

When students misbehave in classrooms, especially in ways that interfere with learning activities, the teacher is obligated to intervene. Such an intervention is, by definition, a reaction—that is, a decision made quickly about what action to take in response to the misbehavior. In some cases, the misbehavior is casual and fleeting, and the teacher's reaction should be understated and routine. For example, the teacher might give the misbehaving student a meaningful look, call on the student to recite, or move to the vicinity of the student. When these incidents occur and the teacher's unobtrusive tactics reinstate appropriate behavior, they are matters of little consequence. Learning has not been disrupted, and little emotion is involved.

When misbehavior is more serious, or the offending student does not respond to the teacher's tacit efforts at control, the teacher needs to have a more elaborate plan in mind. In other words, while intervention is necessarily reactive, it should have a preconceived proactive dimension as well. The plan will vary among teachers, and even among different classes of the same teacher, in response to the many variables involved. The next section describes a general, seven-step plan that serves as an example and may be the basis for developing your own plan.

Step 1.   Have several unobtrusive tactics in mind for immediate use in cases of mild spontaneous misbehavior.

At this stage you are operating as much in the management mode as the intervention mode. You should develop a repertoire of readily applied unobtrusive interventions that you are comfortable using. Practice them by imagining scenarios in which you find yourself using them.

Step 2.   When misbehavior occurs, consider it in clear, dispassionate terms.

Disruptive behavior in the classroom frequently involves strong emotional overtones. You are likely to feel frustration or anger when students interfere with learning activities. Retaliation is the likely initial reaction tendency. However, instant self-control is absolutely necessary so that the democratic principles you subscribe to override any emotional surge and the analysis that is subsequently made is a thoughtful, objective one. Your first reaction must be to quickly size up the situation without making unjustified assumptions and to maintain a studied composure. Underreaction is by far preferable to hasty overreaction, which may violate your announced principles.

Step 3.   Move as quickly as possible to quell the disturbance and restore necessary decorum for learning to proceed.

You should have clearly in mind a graduated list of possible responses to as many types of misbehavior as may be anticipated. The minimum level of power (this is an application of legitimate power, described in Chapter 7) that is likely to suppress the misbehavior in question should be selected initially, with the option of moving through the list to increasingly stronger applications of power as necessary. Such a list may include these responses:

Make eye contact while continuing the learning activity.
Actively involve the student in the lesson.
Move to the location of the disturbance while continuing the learning activity.
Use a preestablished finger signal, with each additional finger (up to three, perhaps) understood as an indication that the student is closer to a penalty.
Say the student's name in a way that clearly indicates your intent.
Say the student's name and direct him or her back to the learning task.
If this is a secondary-level classroom, ask the student in as private a way as possible to remain after class.
Tell the student, if appropriate for the incident, to make a timely reparation or restitution.
Move the student's seat or ask the student to go to a previously designated time-out place.
Send the student to another location in the building, often the school office.

You should preserve the class time for learning activities through whatever reasonable measures are necessary. The time to pursue situations that require follow-up is after class. An inviolable rule is that the teacher must avoid an adversarial confrontation in the classroom. Meanwhile, when a discipline-related measure of some consequence is used, the student should be informed of the rationale for it.

Step 4.   As soon as possible after an incident, critically reflect on the conditions that precipitated the misbehavior.

Terminating misbehavior is in some cases not enough. If your discipline-related practices are to be educational, they must result in the student's understanding his or her behavior and finding alternatives to satisfy the need or condition that precipitated the misbehavior. Therefore, you must get pertinent information relating to the misbehavior. This information may be obtained through school records, the counselor or other teachers, the parents, the student, and sometimes from the school grapevine.

Having dealt with the symptom according to Step 3, you need to identify the source. If the behavior episode in question involves just one incident or very few students, it is helpful to determine the personal perceptions and needs of the student(s) that resulted in misbehavior. Why did the child act this way? What needs were sufficiently powerful that the child was willing to risk the consequences of violating the school/classroom rules? You will probably have to consider a host of variables, such as peer expectations and norms, personality and personal needs, the child's history of behavior, cultural orientation, values and priorities, home conditions, and pupil–teacher relations. At some point, your management approach and the school/classroom rule or code upon which the behavior is judged should be examined to determine their appropriateness.

If the behavior episode is a groupwide phenomenon, it will present more difficulty. This pervasive sort of misbehavior takes the form of students being continuously inattentive, unduly talkative and noisy, insubordinate, or unruly or engaging in complaining, mocking, or ridiculing. While it may be simply a problem of intragroup stress unrelated to you, it may also signal a structural weakness or breakdown in the climate or management aspects of your approach to discipline. If order cannot be restored and maintained with resolute teacher intervention, a systemic problem is apparent. In other words, the source of the problem probably lies more with you than with the students, for they have rendered you impotent. It is difficult for a teacher to admit and accept this. The human tendency is to blame the students and become increasingly assertive, even coercive. These tactics may have a temporary effect, but the underlying problem persists.

At the very least, a class meeting should occur, and the students should have the opportunity to be heard. An anonymous "opinionnaire" might also provide useful feedback, although you have to be prepared for some highly unflattering and outright profane comments on them. Your colleagues may have valuable advice for you and at least provide moral support. Through it all, sincere introspection is necessary. You need to go back to basic principles and rethink, using all the sources of sound information available to you, your approach to classroom leadership, discipline, and teaching in general. It is a gut-wrenching experience, for your identity and self-esteem are on the line, but it is the only way to possibly avoid failure and eventual burnout in your chosen profession.

We have described the worst-case scenario here. Few situations are so severe, but even when the problem is of lesser degree, it needs to be addressed by means such as those suggested here. The bottom line is that the students deserve the best teacher you can be, not one who must rely on students' tolerance and forgiveness while you remain complacent about your teaching shortcomings.

Step 5.   Determine what behavior expectations are appropriate, what remediation must occur, and what the optimum situation, realistically considered, should be.

You need to clarify what the terms *order* and *decorum* mean to you in your own classroom. How will you balance your expectations between structure and flexibility, student initiative and teacher directives, and student responsibility and specific classroom rules to achieve optimum conditions? These expectations should be clearly communicated to your students at least verbally and preferably in writing. The expectations can be the topic of a very meaningful discussion with the students as they offer their suggestions about the factors that create the optimum classroom. Then, in most cases when exceptions to those expectations occur, remediation (if this is remediation at all) occurs simply as students discontinue the deviant behavior when reminded of the expectations.

When misbehavior is induced by more deep-set psychological motives or by intragroup factors, remediation is a much more complex matter. Special provisions may need to be made for students who have personal adjustment problems such as overaggressiveness or attention deficit disorder. Specialists are usually available to teachers in these cases. When the problem is one of group dynamics, suggestions made in Step 4 are pertinent. The success of the strategies you use will ultimately be measured by the extent to which optimum conditions previously described by you are achieved.

Step 6.   Select the response from the set of alternatives that has the greatest promise of resolving or mitigating the discipline-related problem, while conforming to the tenets of your belief system.

As the most critical part of your strategy, you must select from your list the most appropriate tactic—the one that is least stringent yet has the potential to restore order.

Cases of minor misbehavior may need no further attention. Just a tacit reminder or mild reproof from the teacher is sufficient. Most misbehavior in most classrooms falls into this category. Instances are inattentiveness, private whispering, note passing, talking out inadvertently, and typical "messing around."

More serious misbehavior or undue persistence in minor misbehavior requires teacher follow-up. You have at your disposal such strategies as these:

Confer with the student after class or, if necessary, at a later designated time.
Call the parent to exchange pertinent information, and try to arrange a cooperative approach to the problem.

Arrange a conference involving whatever parties have an interest or a contribution to make, including possibly the parents, counselor, psychologist, or administrator.

Refer the case for more specialized attention.

Recommend in-school suspension, especially if counseling attends that suspension.

Confer with a colleague or supervisor for advice and support.

Involve the class in an examination of the problem if intragroup factors are a major contributing factor.

Establish more realistic or democratic classroom expectations, or clarify existing appropriate ones.

The selection of the appropriate strategy or strategies is, of course, a matter for your professional judgment. The extent to which you use an ill-informed belief system and faulty judgment, or you do not have sufficient skill to implement a selected strategy effectively, you can expect to have only limited success in coping with the more serious discipline-related problems.

Step 7. Evaluate the effectiveness of your strategy in resolving or mitigating the discipline-related problem in question.

As suggested in Step 5, you must determine the extent to which your selected strategy has achieved the optimum conditions you have established as the ideal situation. In cases of serious or complex discipline-related problems, the strategy may need considerable time to take full effect, so you may have to settle temporarily for progress toward rather than achievement of the optimums. However, when the strategy is not sufficiently effective, you must reconsider the whole problem. First you must reexamine the underlying conditions, then determine why the initially selected strategy was ineffective, and finally decide on and apply an alternative strategy. An "action research" approach, as implied in this description, is recommended so you can address in a systematic, data-based manner what may be an emotionally charged procedure.

REMEDIATION OF BEHAVIOR

Each phase of discipline—establishment of a positive climate, classroom management, intervention, and remediation—blends into the adjacent one in the sequence. Remediation was thus initiated in Step 4 of the intervention process.

Remediation may be thought of as the measures taken to guide students who have misbehaved to adopt teacher-approved ways to deal with the tasks and stresses of the classroom. In some classrooms, remediation—in the active and purposeful sense of the term—does not occur by design. The follow-up to misbehavior in these classrooms is limited to **punishment** (i.e., imposing an aversive condition that is so unpleasant that it presumably will deter future misbehavior). Examples include giving

harsh reprimand or ridicule, having the student perform onerous tasks such as writing a phrase repeatedly or copying from the dictionary, reducing a grade, or having the student serve time in a detention location.

In democratically conducted classrooms, remediation is applied in accordance with the concept of reasonable consequences. A **reasonable consequence** is a measure with a developmental focus that targets a personal learning outcome for the student. Ideally, when a reasonable consequence is applied, the child will recognize more than a simple chronological connection between the misbehavior and the consequence. For example, two students who persist in having a private conversation may be separated, but it should be clear that this is happening because a previous reminder has been ignored. In practice, a punishment and a reasonable consequence may be indistinguishable to the casual observer. The most important difference between them is the spirit and purpose with which each addresses misbehavior. Punishment and a reasonable consequence differ in several important ways. The following comparisons will help clarify these differences.

1. *Punishment* implies taking action against the child. A *reasonable consequence* implies taking action for the child (i.e., in the student's interest as much as any other concern).

A teacher should be the child's advocate in a proactive way. To deal with a child in a manner that is hurtful and without redeeming developmental features violates democratic principles. There is no place in a classroom for a vindictive teacher whose motivation for punishing a child is revenge or retaliation.

2. *Punishment* is an authoritarian approach; it is based on the legitimate and coercive powers of the teacher. A *reasonable consequence* is a humanistic approach; it is based on human-relations principles, especially expert and referent powers.

Punishment is carried out with the singular focus of terminating an unacceptable behavior, without particular regard for the possible negative emotional effect of reprimands and penalties. In using a reasonable consequence, the teacher takes into consideration the overall impact of the discipline-related measure and minimizes unnecessary negative emotional effects.

3. *Punishment* involves a teacher-wins–student-loses outcome. A *reasonable consequence* intends a judicious resolution and avoids dealing in a winner–loser context.

A teacher-wins approach is self-serving. A teacher's reason for being in the classroom at all is to contribute to the learning and development of children. If the teacher's personal need to win a power struggle takes precedence over a concern for students, then the ends and means of teaching are being reversed. Teachers' satisfaction should come from the positive things they do for children. Even when penalties are assigned by the teacher, as they sometimes must be, effort should be made to present this reasonable consequence as an outcome related to the misbehavior, not simply a demonstration of who has more power.

4. *Punishment* is a short-term end in itself; serving the sentence ends the incident. A *reasonable consequence* is a means to a more important end.

In cases of mild incidental misbehavior, a tacit response or verbal reminder by the teacher may, in fact, end the incident. But when the child's misbehavior is indicative of more serious causes, that child's need for introspection and reconsideration of the behavior in question is self-evident. To ignore this is to lose the opportunity to help the child in a way that may be more important for him or her than any immediate subject-related outcomes of the lesson.

5. *Punishment* is based on the assumption that it establishes an aversive condition that will deter future similar acts of misbehavior. A *reasonable consequence* is based on the assumption that many students can ultimately be persuaded by principles such as reason, justice, consideration, fair play, social responsibility, and the golden rule.

Conventional wisdom informs us that if we make a penalty sufficiently repugnant to a child, that child will avoid the behavior that triggers it. Up to a certain point, this is so. A child who is not strongly motivated to a particular misbehavior will not engage in that behavior if the behavior is not worth its price. But the fact that misbehavior is a frequent occurrence in classrooms despite the interventions used regularly by teachers is evidence of the limited effectiveness of penalties in their own right. So while interventions must be used to terminate unacceptable behavior, changing students' predisposition to misbehave by patiently using personal and social persuasion is a more promising and democratic approach.

6. *Punishment* addresses only observed symptoms of behavior. A *reasonable consequence* transcends symptoms and responds to apparent causes.

This highlights a principle already alluded to in statements 2 and 4. A genuine concern for the child requires the teacher to recognize that serious or chronic misbehavior signals that the child has a problem needing to be addressed, not simply that the child is a nuisance to be suppressed.

7.　*Punishment* is not necessarily directly related to the misbehavior it follows. A *reasonable consequence* is related to the incident of misbehavior in a recognizable way and often involves the principle of restitution.

When possible, the teacher should insist that the child make atonement for a wrongdoing in a way that relates the atonement to the behavior. When using a punishment, the teacher is essentially saying, "You misbehaved, now you suffer." Mere suffering has no remediating effect; the child's problem, and therefore the disposition to the behavior, continues.

8.　*Punishment* has emotional overtones; anger, frustration, and venting are often exhibited by the teacher. A *reasonable consequence* is essentially rational; problem-solving approaches are employed when appropriate.

Students who are disruptive or disrespectful anger teachers. The response by the teacher often reflects that anger. It is pointless to advise a teacher not to get angry or not to feel any negative emotion; human beings feel such emotions when they encounter uncivil behavior in others. But when anger is allowed to control behavior, it results in behavior that strikes out at the source as retaliation. This often takes the form of harsh punishment in the case of teachers. This might bring momentary relief to the teacher, but it undermines the teacher's commitment to professional behavior. In contrast, a reasonable consequence involves a learned response characterized by detachment and directed toward resolution of the problem. This is undoubtedly the most difficult aspect of teaching, but fully professional teachers learn to do this.

9.　*Punishment* is effective as a deterrent only with students who value the teacher's approval. A *reasonable consequence* depends for its effectiveness on the teacher's informed and professional judgment.

Children who are unruly obviously do not value the teacher's approval very much. Yet these are the very children teachers need most to help with their coping skills. So punishment without follow-up remediation may be effective for the friendlier and less willful students, but it fails in its most critical task, which involves developmental effects. The principles of human relations will serve the teacher—and the students—far better in the long run, but the proverbial patience of Job is essential.

10.　*Punishment* serves primarily the teacher's needs, especially the needs to assert power, protect one's self-esteem, and reaffirm one's role as the classroom authority. A *reasonable consequence* involves the teacher and the student in an interactive mode; some negotiation may be part of the process.

If misbehavior in the classroom is viewed as a problem to be cooperatively addressed and resolved to the greatest satisfaction of everyone involved, then the democratic principles of mutual respect and due process must be applied. The idiosyncratic needs of the teacher must defer to these principles.

11. *Punishment* has likely negative side effects, especially resentment and anger, on the part of the student. A *reasonable consequence* may have some unintended side effects, but these are mitigated because determining a reasonable consequence involves participation, reflection, and understanding on the part of the student.

Punishment, with its primary intent being to impose aversive conditions, virtually always will be resented by students. However, over time, students become aware of a teacher's demeanor and behavior pattern. When they realize (and this is the ideal case) that the teacher is consistently evenhanded and respectful, that the teacher's motives are based on the best interest of the students, that the teacher is neither arbitrary nor humorless, and that students are genuinely involved in determining consequences for their misbehavior, then reasonable consequences are likely to be palatable. This is not to say that students will always accept with perfect equanimity whatever penalty may be assigned. Still, many students will be inclined to be introspective about their behavior and may arrive at useful insights about it rather than only feeling the anger and resentment that inevitably accompany punishment.

Presenting principles of discipline and ways of thinking about students' behavior is the primary function of this book. Ultimately, you must make decisions about your own approach in general and about specific interventions in the busy classroom setting. You will want to share cases, real or envisioned, and talk them through with peers, associating with each incident the endorsed principles that are becoming part of your belief system. Consider the application of reasonable consequences in the following brief episode.

A Classroom Episode: Application of Reasonable Consequences

Davey uses class time to surreptitiously read books of his choice, but he often fails to complete assignments. The teacher, on the first occasion the incident is detected, asks him to put the book away and attend to the class assignment. She also adds, "Are you OK with the assignment? Do you need some help to get started?" This reminder and offer of support might solve the problem in some cases. However, Davey is caught repeating the act, and, after redirecting his behavior to the assignment, the teacher asks him to see her for a moment after class. At that time, she spends a few moments apart from the other students reminding Davey firmly but evenhandedly that he needs to attend to his assignments and that he should realize that further similar behavior will require more stringent measures. Thus far, no penalty as such has been assigned, and again, this may solve the problem. On the third occasion, the teacher must assume that reminders, gentle and firm, are insufficient, and the time has come for a more in-depth talk with Davey to help him examine his behavior and discuss its consequences. Ultimately, Davey agrees that it is reasonable that when he illicitly reads books brought to class the books should be confiscated, and he realizes that should there be a reoccurrence, his parents will be called and requested to use their influence.

The application of reasonable consequences in this episode was straightforward, and the consequence clearly fits the misbehavior. But this is not always the case. What will you do when one student punches another and causes a bloody nose? You might use eye-for-an-eye reasoning and punch the perpetrator in the nose—at the risk of a law suit. Or you might assign noon detentions for a week, but how would that be construed as having even a remote connection to the misbehavior? Consider the student caught cheating on a test. Should you lower the grade or even tear up the paper? This distorts the measure of the student's achievement, for grades are properly employed as indicators of achievement, not penalties or rewards. Should you reprimand the student in front of the class, even though you know that demeaning a student causes resentment? (You should realize that the majority of students will cheat if given the opportunity.)

Finding immediate, specific, appropriate consequences to many sorts of misbehavior is not possible, even for creative, well-informed veteran teachers. Every teacher should talk with students about their misbehavior, give the students an opportunity to be heard, involve the students in working problems out, and keep an accurate record of the incidents. In schools where misbehavior is minimal, such action may be sufficient. In schools where misbehavior is a serious problem, increased systematic attention to behavior is necessary. However, once again, do not default to raw power and punitive measures that address symptoms but ignore causes. Only when causes are dealt with through thoughtful and purposeful remediation will school and classroom discipline-related behavior measurably improve.

As recommended in Step 6 of the intervention plan, when misbehavior is not successfully treated with routine management-type interventions, you should select from a set of preconceived alternatives the most appropriate measure. In cases where alternatives are more punitive and less remedial than you might prefer, a generalized systematic approach is recommended. As an illustration of such an approach, a behavior intervention and remediation plan is presented here. It has six phases, each of which describes a reasonable action at that point in the sequence. Teacher judgment must take precedence over predefined action; that is, the behavior plan is suggestive and should be applied judiciously. Further, the plan requires the teacher's willingness to forego the crutch that punitive measures have traditionally provided. This might be an intimidating prospect to the novice teacher, but you should at least work toward a student-centered approach such as this.

The behavior plan is based on using a generalized response to misbehavior. This response involves the issuance of notices of misbehavior as a reasonable consequence. In the six phases of the program, the consequence becomes increasingly stringent. The behavior plan can in part be applied by a teacher individually, but in the secondary school especially it is more effective if it is a schoolwide, democratically based program. Actually, every school should have a sound and systematic plan in place for dealing with discipline. Every teacher, but new teachers especially, can benefit from it. An advantage of this schoolwide plan is that teachers and students get help quickly and assuredly by design in cases of serious and chronic misbehavior. The plan as presented here is quite elaborate and admittedly idealistic in some of its provisions. Its full implementation would require a high level of commitment by the school as a whole, and by each teacher, to achieving decorum and helping problem students. But any teacher and any school could adopt parts of it and, in any case, the spirit of it. Phases 1 and 2 especially, which make use of notices of misbehavior, can be straightforwardly adopted even by the novice teacher, and this would make provision for applying the concept of reasonable consequences in a basic but effective form.

Behavior Intervention and Remediation Plan

PHASE 1—FIRST NOTICE OF MISBEHAVIOR

1.1   The teacher issues a written notice as a reasonable consequence for misbehavior that exceeds the routine classroom management level.

1.2   Following the issuance of the notice, the teacher engages in a brief private conference with the student, stating the nature of the misbehavior and the reason for the notice. The child has the opportunity to explain and clarify the behavior in question.

1.3   The teacher encourages the child to think about the behavior and its implications and to make a verbal commitment to refrain from it.

1.4   A copy of the notice is kept by the teacher, and another is filed in the school office if the program is schoolwide.

PHASE 2—SECOND NOTICE OF MISBEHAVIOR

2.1   In addition to again following the steps outlined in Phase 1, the student develops cooperatively with the teacher a written commitment, or contract, for improved behavior.

2.2   Because this is at least a somewhat serious or persistent misbehavior, the student may be advised to talk with a counselor or other designated school official.

2.3   If appropriate, the parents are notified. However, this is a matter for teacher judgment.

PHASE 3—THIRD NOTICE OF MISBEHAVIOR

3.1   A meeting including the child, the teacher, and others as appropriate is convened to examine the pattern of misbehavior.

3.2   Special disposition may be made at this time if the situation warrants it based on due process (e.g., the student could be transferred out of that teacher's class, especially if the student requests it).

PHASE 4—FOURTH NOTICE OF MISBEHAVIOR

4.1   A discipline seminar is conducted by a specially trained faculty member, perhaps at noon three times a week. Students with four notices must attend these sessions for a week. All pertinent aspects of discipline are discussed with the intent that the students acquire insights into their behavior.

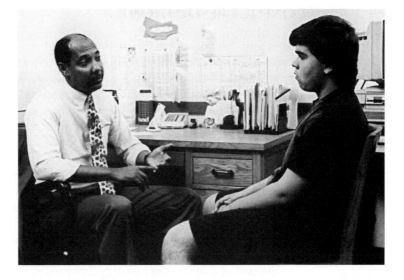

4.2 Each student is provided the opportunity to state his or her side of the situation in a nonjudgmental setting.

4.3 Suspect disciplinary practices on the part of a teacher may be identified, and that teacher may be helped with constructive suggestions from a nonadministrative expert in that area.

PHASE 5—FIFTH NOTICE OF MISBEHAVIOR

5.1 The failure of the seminar to prevent further issuance of a notice to a student results, subject to individual consideration in each case, in an assignment to in-school suspension conducted by the specially trained faculty member.

5.2 Students continue to keep up with classroom assignments but also spend considerable time discussing behavior from a remedial perspective.

5.3 Students are required to provide substantive assurance that behavior in the regular classroom will subsequently improve prior to their release from suspension.

5.4 A parent conference may be helpful but is not mandatory before the student is released from in-school suspension.

PHASE 6—INDIVIDUAL DISPOSITION

6.1 Failure to improve behavior sufficiently through the preceding five phases will result in referral or other administrative action.

6.2 Cases of flagrant misbehavior or violation of civil law are handled administratively as a Phase 6 matter exclusively.

CONFLICT RESOLUTION

Within any classroom, conflict between children inevitably will emerge. Traditional approaches to this occurrence require the teacher to intervene in the conflict, examine the behaviors and probable causes, and make a judicious resolution. Children learn in the classroom that teachers settle conflicts among students. Outside the classroom, in their own groups, they learn that the more powerful among them, socially or physically, resolve conflicts by imposing their will. Neither of these approaches is appealing from a democratic perspective.

A more democratically appealing approach is the use of peer negotiation and peer mediation. This places the expectation and responsibility on the students to confront differences among themselves of many sorts and arrive at a mutually acceptable plan or settlement. Students are empowered as they attain and use the social skills involved. Persons who have not purposefully learned the basic skills of negotiation and mediation are unlikely to acquire them otherwise, and they resort to power approaches when dealing with conflict.

The use of conflict resolution techniques in classrooms does not involve a plan the teacher can immediately implement. Considerable preparation is required. First, teachers themselves must acquire the skills, then the children must be trained in them. Teachers typically acquire the skills through workshops and inservice programs, although any teacher might, through private study, acquire knowledge about and understanding of the process. However, practice in using the skills is important, and this can most safely and assuredly occur in workshop and clinical settings. The time required to learn the necessary skills and the programs in which they are embedded is considerable, although it varies from report to report in the literature. A typical program requires 15–20 hours during eight weeks.

By the end of 1993, at least 5,000 schools at all levels were reported to be using formal conflict resolution programs (Willis, 1993). Most programs occur in elementary schools in which children remain together as a cohort for the largest part of each day. In middle schools and high schools, conflict resolution tends to be incorporated into the curriculum, usually in the social studies courses, or presented through group guidance.

Negotiation is the first step of conflict resolution. When two people have a conflict, they need to avoid engaging in a power struggle and, instead, enter into a mutually understood process of negotiating their differences. "To negotiate solutions, students need to define their conflict, exchange positions and proposals, view the situation from both perspectives, invent options for mutual gain, and reach a wise agreement" (Johnson, Johnson, Dudley, & Burnett, 1992). The process seems straightforward enough when one views it as these readily understandable steps. But when conflict does occur, so does emotion, and rationality gives way to more basic instincts. Thus, the parties involved (i.e., our students) need to learn these steps well and practice using them so negotiation can proceed even in the context of heightened emotion.

Whether in the case of individuals or groups or nations, we know that differences are not necessarily negotiated to settlement. When settlement cannot be reached, mediation needs to occur. Mediation requires specially trained student mediators in the classroom and throughout the school to aid in reaching an acceptable settlement. As described by Johnson and Eisele (1994),

> Peer mediators learn many skills before they are put on the job. First, they learn how to listen carefully, restate and clarify what they hear, and ask neutral yet pertinent questions. They then learn to shift through differing perceptions to the underlying cause of a conflict, how to defuse anger, and how to develop empathy between the disputants. Finally, they learn to maintain confidentiality (unless they hear allegations of abuse or threats of violence—then they must report this information to a teacher). (p. 27)

Willis (1993) estimates, based on a practitioner report, that 80–90% of peer-mediated agreements hold; this is a better success rate than that for teacher-imposed settlements. But he also comments that not all student conflicts lend themselves to student resolution (e.g., illegal activities, violence, and weapons display or use). But when mediation does apply, it is the preferable approach to settlement, for empowered students not only resolve their conflicts in a democratic way, they learn important life skills while they make peace.

Learning conflict resolution skills is similar to learning effective study skills. Both are self-evidently good for children, yet both are often ignored or taken for granted by educators. While our main task as teachers is to guide children in learning topics that are the official part of the curriculum, we serve students best when we recognize that they do not learn in a vacuum. An important part of our task is providing optimum conditions within which our objectives can most successfully be attained by students.

As a teacher committed to democratic teaching, and therefore to democratic discipline, you need to consider eventually making conflict resolution a program that you initiate in your classroom. If you teach at the secondary level and your school discipline program does not include conflict resolution, you should take the initiative in advocating it. If children do not learn it in school, where will they learn it? Can you suggest a more worthwhile topic or skill that they might learn in your classroom?

SUMMARY

We have taken the position in this book that classroom discipline is essentially a neutral concept, although in practice it may incur both positive and negative teacher feelings. In classrooms where a positive climate exists and students' demeanor is in accordance with the teacher's expectations, discipline is a tacit but satisfying aspect of teaching. Typically, we do not even consciously associate discipline with this situation, but actually it is operating optimally.

On the other hand, certain instances require teacher intervention and remediation. A teacher has to be prepared for the negative aspect of discipline by realizing that most students are pretty decent and likable young people even though they have their bad days, as we all do; that most of their behavior is actually orderly and respectful; that having a sound, proactive discipline intervention and remediation approach in place has a powerful preventive effect; and that acquiring discipline-related skills (experience is an important consideration here) will diminish the frequency with which intervention is necessary.

We began Chapter 1 with the statement that "discipline is the bane of the teacher." Realistically, we know that some teachers never get beyond that. But most teachers who have been around for a few years find ways to cope confidently with this aspect of teaching. In general, they find other aspects of teaching, such as the ever-increasing paperwork, to be more aggravating than dealing with behavior problems. With this book as a whole, and this chapter in particular, we hope we can help you move quickly to those practices that will enable you to find far more that is positive than negative in discipline.

LOOKING AHEAD

Chapter 10, "Developing a Discipline Plan," will afford you the opportunity to apply the principles discussed so far through the examination and critique of an actual discipline plan. From this point, you will pursue the development of your own plan as a major step forward in the quest to be a reflective practitioner.

❖ REFLECTIVE ACTIVITIES

1. In the minds of many teachers (and most noneducators), intervention is the essence of discipline. How would you respond to an educator who maintains that kids are to be told what the rules are, that if they violate them they are just asking for trouble and the teacher is there to see that they get it?
2. How will you prepare yourself to remain level-headed and outwardly dispassionate when confronted by particularly offensive student behavior?

❖ REFERENCES

Angelou, M. (1993). *I know why the caged bird sings*. New York: Bantam Books.

Johnson, D., & Eisele, M. (1994). Playground peacemakers. In *Innovative discipline*. West Haven, CT: National Education Association Professional Library.

Johnson, D., Johnson, R., Dudley, B., & Burnett, R. (1992). Teaching students to be peer mediators. *Educational Leadership, 50*(1), 10–13.

Willis, S. (1993). Constructive solutions that stuck. *ASCD Update, 35*(16).

Chapter 10

Developing a Discipline Plan

This book has introduced you to a spectrum of ideas that relate to classroom discipline in terms of ideology, principles, propositions, and practices. You should now be prepared to conceive a personal approach to discipline. If you reflected in a critical and developmental way as you read, your belief system has begun to take on a distinct profile as ideas gel, tentative commitments to principles are made, and particular practices are targeted.

In this chapter we will review the book's major ideas to provide you with a ready reference. We will then share with you a discipline plan created by a teacher for use in her classroom. It may well include features that you will consider incorporating into your own plan, but, more important, it is an example of the thinking process that attended the systematic creation of a practical plan for classroom discipline.

REVIEW OF MAJOR IDEAS

In general, the term *discipline* refers to students' classroom demeanor. It also has at least three more specific meanings. It may refer to the tacit conditions within classroom climate that are disposed to orderly behavior; it may refer to students' inclination to comply with teacher expectations; and it may refer to the expectations and measures the teacher imposes within the classroom. All these aspects must be addressed in a comprehensive approach to discipline.

The issue of discipline has not been well understood by teachers. It is often perceived as having an aura of mystique, which in turn creates a fertile medium for the emergence of the myths of discipline. Recognizing the myths as the misguided assumptions they are is important in developing an informed approach to classroom discipline. Professional teachers must subscribe to the knowledge base of the profession and order their behavior accordingly.

All professions necessarily have a knowledge base; education is not an exception. Our knowledge base includes examined theories and pertinent principles of teaching. As professional practitioners, teachers are ethically required to engage in highly informed practice (praxis) consistent with our professionally endorsed knowledge base. The use of conventional wisdom, which is a basis for practice that is unscrutinized and accepted on faith, is not sufficient to sustain the integrity of the profession. Further, teachers can expect to be empowered (i.e., recognized for their expertise and given commensurate autonomy) only if praxis typifies their teaching.

Ideology refers to the set of assumptions we make individually about our personal world, and it becomes the lens with which we interpret our world. It is dangerous to hastily acquiesce to the values and norms of the dominant ideology, which may not serve the best interest of students. Regarding classroom discipline, this may refer, for example, to the sort of traits teachers often ascribe to their "best" students, traits such as obedience and respect, which essentially function to please the teacher.

Current students have lived their entire lives in the postmodern culture. Their lives have been markedly influenced by technology and media in a way that their teachers' generation has not. They have transcended the generation gap, as differing generational perspectives were previously described. Now there exists a true cultural gap, for the difference between the lived experience of teachers and that of students has continued to increase. Because schooling and teaching function to reproduce the dominant culture, postmodern students are immediately at odds with teachers, the propagators of that culture. However, students are what they are through circumstance more than choice. Teachers need to make concerted effort to understand students, including their expectations, preferences, and icons. Otherwise, intolerant teachers may contribute to the problems arising from differences, which will result in discipline incidents occurring in classrooms.

Schools exist to impart to students knowledge that meets their predicated needs. Albeit less evidently, schools prepare students to be citizens in a democratic society. But schools are not agencies apart from society. They have the potential to be microcosms of society. The lived experience of students in classrooms should be of the same genre as the lived experience of citizens in the normal course of living. Understanding the role of democratic principles in the functioning of society should lead to understanding the role of those principles in classrooms.

We support the proposition that the role of schools in society, and therefore of teachers in classrooms, is to incline students to be predisposed to think and act democratically. Key ideas in thinking and acting democratically are civic concern, civic caring, and tolerance. Concern addresses our conscious interest in justice, integrity, fair play, and equal opportunity. Caring focuses on human dignity and the action, participation, and service we perform on behalf of our democratic system. Tolerance involves our conscious, reflective decision to allow, even respect, postures and behaviors with which we do not personally agree.

The hidden curriculum teaches students little about democratic ideals, while it teaches a great deal about nondemocratic, authoritarian governance. Where discipline is concerned, control and containment of students are predominant teacher motives, while formative considerations consistent with democratic principles have low priority. Being a good citizen in the classroom is more associated with unquestioning obedience than with thinking loyalty. The guiding principle in this book has been that schools should educate for an ethical, reflective, critical, and informed citizenry. The discipline dimension of the classroom, especially as this involves concern, caring, and tolerance, provides the opportunity for authentic citizenship education in the form of lived experience.

Constitutional law, the template for our democratic society, has powerful implications for the way curriculum and activities in schools are conceived. While the U.S. Constitution has remained highly stable over time, interpretation of its provisions has varied as is reflected in certain key lawsuits. A major ongoing issue is the alliance between the rights of the individual and the rights of the collective. The principle of compelling interest is central to this tension; citizens' individual rights are limited only to the extent that the greater good of the society must be served. Schools have not regularly recognized this principle and have traditionally imposed a rigid regimen in classrooms. In this postmodern era, schools should take the initiative in providing students the opportunity to experience democratic living through activities that apply in a purposeful way certain key tenets of the Constitution. This is especially pertinent to discipline insofar as students' rights and due process are concerned.

Social power, the influence a person has on other persons in a group setting, is a necessary component of interpersonal action in the classroom. Five types of power have been identified: legitimate, reward, coercive, expert, and referent. The teacher's intent in a democratic classroom should be to use expert and referent power as much as possible, use reward power selectively, and use legitimate and coercive power only when pressed to do so, such as in the case of intervention to terminate misbehavior.

Student misbehavior occurs for three often interrelated reasons. One of these is that students' internal needs for identity, stimulation, security, affiliation, or empowerment are not met. The second is that intragroup dynamics introduce stress among the students. Third, students may resist the teacher's (sometimes misguided) classroom discipline policies. All these reasons should be considered in any instance of misbehavior, and the teacher response should be framed accordingly.

A classroom in which optimal conditions exist is one in which the teacher is unconditionally committed to democratic principles and competently translates those principles into teaching practice. The most pervasive component of the classroom that is affected by democratic principles is climate. Several factors (including respect, freedom, due process, and decision making) must purposely be infused in that classroom, while authoritarian approaches are avoided on principle.

Optimal conditions in the classroom include a substantial measure of motivation. Democratic principles do not produce positive motivation directly, but they do create the climate within which opportunities for intrinsic motivation are maximized. And when students are motivated (i.e., when they identify with the classroom learning objectives), the inclination to misbehave is minimized.

Effective classroom management practices are also necessary in a classroom characterized by optimal conditions. In practice, the most effective management strategy is solid instruction. But the teacher must be proactive in matters that are specifically managerial, such as establishing routines and monitoring continuously.

No matter how thorough your preparation for classroom discipline or how skillfully you apply the pertinent principles, instances of misbehavior will sometimes occur. You don't control students in the most immediate sense; you only manipulate certain variables in the classroom to which students respond. You know you will need to intervene on those occasions of unacceptable behavior to terminate it and restore optimal conditions for learning. When applied, intervention should be based on a systematic plan designed in terms of measured steps and informed teacher judgment. Remediation following serious or chronic misbehavior should be thoughtfully conducted, again in terms of a systematic plan, using reasonable consequences rather than punishment as a referent. As you become more sophisticated in matters of classroom discipline, introducing a program of conflict resolution is recommended. It conforms nicely with democratic principles as it empowers students in terms of trust, responsibility, and decision making.

If these ideas are viewed atomistically, they may be thought of as defining features within a belief system. If the review is interpreted holistically, a comprehensive and cohesive concept of discipline emerges. The views are complementary, each contributing to an understanding of discipline. From these ways of viewing discipline, its underlying humanistic spirit is sensed. It is important for you to grasp and integrate this spirit into your belief system and teaching style. In this way your approach to discipline is predispositionally democratic and always in the service of your students.

DEVELOPING A PERSONAL DISCIPLINE PLAN

In Chapter 8 we presented methods of creating a democratic climate and initiating effective classroom management. Chapter 9 set forth guidelines for systematic approaches to intervention and remediation. These strategies are not plans in themselves, but they should contribute substantially to the discipline plan you develop.

Your plan will be unique and personal. It will include, always implicitly but preferably explicitly as well, your philosophy, beliefs, priorities, and perspectives. It will be the best design that you are currently capable of producing to meet the needs of you and your students in your classroom.

The following is a discipline plan outline that will provide a framework for developing your own plan. It may serve you well as is, although you may wish to add features that are pertinent to your particular situation.

Discipline Plan Guidelines

Premises of My Approach to Discipline
a. What are the democratically and organizationally assured rights and conditions of my students?
b. What are my discipline-related responsibilities and rights as a teacher?
c. What discipline-related beliefs, propositions, and principles will guide the development of my discipline plan?

d.   What aspects of my own character and personality need to be considered as I develop my own discipline plan? That is, where do I place myself along the continuum in the following dyads?
     passive–active
     reactive–proactive
     dispassionate–compassionate
     independent–dependent
     extraverted–introverted
     structured–flexible
     controlled–turbulent
     patient–quick tempered
e.   What approach to classroom discipline will satisfy my personality-driven needs for identity, acceptance, security, and power (authority and control) while preserving my democratic integrity and satisfying my students' academic and emotional needs?
f.   What are some promising features of the plans of my respected colleagues (or, in a student teaching setting, mentor teacher) that I feel comfortable incorporating into my own plan?

Techniques and Strategies in the Four Major Aspects of Classroom Discipline
a.   Establishing a positive climate (i.e., creating conditions within which students learn effectively and will have no classroom-induced reasons to misbehave)

b.   Maintaining order during class (i.e., classroom management)
c.   Intervening when order must be restored
d.   Remediating the behavior of students who seriously or chronically misbehave

---

The following plan was edited for content only where confidentiality required. Put yourself in the place of the student teacher who wrote it and think through the situation with her. As you will realize, a teacher's discipline plan is not a dispassionate discourse; it is a personal and passionate essay.

Discipline Plan

Section 1—Premises of My Discipline Plan (Sowd, 1995)
As I reflect on my first week of student teaching, I am keenly aware of the importance of classroom control in creating a productive and instructive environment. Because of this experience, I read the articles on effective discipline plans with added interest. One entitled "Don't Let Them Take You to the Barn" (Hanny, 1994) was of particular interest as I had nearly visited that fine farm facility and was in great need of advice. I found myself ambivalent about the proper way to establish and enforce rules and [my plan] could be labeled what Phelps (1991) termed the "sailboat" form of management style, which "goes with the flow" and assumes that no problems will arise. This may be okay for a teacher who has *history* with students, those teachers with previous reputations, but it did not work for me as a student teacher. The most obvious issue in my mind is that a true educational experience can only be realized if there is some semblance of control in the classroom. Teachers can teach and students can learn only in an atmosphere conducive to learning.

Students' Rights
Students in a high school classroom have the implicit right to an environment where learning is a priority item. By this I mean that students are treated as individuals, that their thoughts, feelings, and abilities are considered in classroom planning, and that there is a reasonable assurance of safety for all students. Students should feel that they are valued and that their best interests are being served. They should feel that they are respected by the teacher and by their fellow students. They also should be assured that the subject matter is presented in a manner that is understandable and relevant. They should be assured the right to learn in an environment that is conducive to that endeavor.

Teacher's Responsibility and Rights
Teachers, on the other hand, have a responsibility to their students to provide an atmosphere that is conducive to maximum learning for all students and an atmos-

phere in which they can teach their students effectively. Teachers should provide for the individualized success of all students in their classroom, regardless of individual student abilities. In order for this to happen, teachers need to develop sound classroom management skills that provide students with classroom procedural structure as well as standards for their behavior. The ultimate goal of teachers should be to provide students with a discipline plan that can guide and encourage student-centered self-discipline that functions not only in the classroom but outside it as well. Teachers also have the responsibility to effectively plan their discipline policy and daily lessons as preventive maintenance against problems that might arise.

Teachers have the right to expect respect and compliance with reasonable and fair discipline policies. They have the right to establish and enforce these policies in a fair, individualized, and democratic manner. They have the right to the same respect from students that they themselves practice. However, they must earn and establish that respect, and one way in which that is done is by prethinking and enforcing a fair and reasonable discipline plan.

Personal Beliefs

My view of discipline is deeply rooted in my experiences as a parent. Discipline is like a necessary evil. Just as we teach children to walk, talk, and read, we need to guide them in the proper way to behave. This is not only for the sake of producing a sane learning environment, but also so that students can learn to function as productive citizens. I want students to enjoy learning, feel challenged, and want to be in my classroom, but first they must realize that there are ground rules that exist in every society, including the society of the classroom. No two classrooms are alike, just as no two communities are alike. All persons need to feel their way in a new situation. They need to learn the guidelines. Therefore, it is important for the rules of the classroom to be set immediately and firmly so there is no doubt how this classroom society will function. Once this basis is set, students can feel comfortable and safe. It is important to me that students feel safe and unthreatened in my class. Unfortunately, this feeling is not guaranteed if there is anarchy in the classroom. Once an environment of student self-control is established, real learning opportunities can happen.

I feel very strongly, however, that discipline plans should never include any element of embarrassment or humiliation for the student. Also, the many should not suffer for the few. Punitive measures should be avoided at all costs. Once rules are established, infractions of rules should be handled on an individual basis in a nonobtrusive manner. Group punishments are inappropriate and unfair. Firm consequences for infractions of the rules should be enforced, but, generally, threats of detention are ineffective and useless.

No one orientation to discipline makes an ideal classroom manager. Instead, the ideal classroom manager is one who understands and applies a number of principles and practices. [Classroom managers] understand the purpose of effective classroom management. They recognize the relationship between teacher behavior and student behavior, that teachers themselves may often be the cause of student misconduct. They also identify those variables that are within their control. Cognitive variables are within the teacher's control and include thorough preparations, formulating specific rules, determining responses prior to the occurrence of off-task behaviors, and adopting preventive approaches to discipline. In the affective dimension, the teacher recognizes the importance of positive relationships and projects enthusiasm for learning. In terms of psychomotor variables, teachers can make changes and improvements in the physical environment to prevent opportunities for misbehavior. They can move around the room, make eye contact, and use vocal variation to discourage student boredom (Phelps, 1991).

Personal Considerations

My own character and personality define how I will function as a classroom manager. It has been my limiting factor in my first week of teaching. I hope to have an interactive, cooperative atmosphere for learning, where students view me as a facilitator. I think that students should play an active role in their education. I find myself to be an active, extroverted person. However, I also like to work within the confines of order and structure. I am not sure I feel as though cooperative activities can be properly carried out if some understanding of order and cooperation are not established. Again, once the ground rules for function within a classroom are set, there is a framework for cooperative work, but not until. I don't care for chaos, and I am afraid cooperative activities can be interpreted as that by pupils. I also am a patient and compassionate person. It is one of the forces that took me to the field of education. There is a fine line between showing this side too early to students and preventing them from seeing it at all. This is an area [in which] I will need experience to work out. In my first week of student teaching, my patient side jeopardized my ability to control the classroom. What ensued was an attitude that I was not in control. It was a learning experience I hope to rectify immediately. I am unclear still how to be firm without appearing rigid. Experience must be the key. My instincts as a teacher coincide with my instincts as a mother. I will need to be clear and consistent with the rules that are important to me if I am to have the teaching atmosphere I desire. Only when this has been accomplished do I feel I can *let up*.

Ideas Acquired from My Mentor Teacher

My mentor establishes strict authority early in the first two days of the school year. She is very firm in her expectations. She then lets up as the year progresses. She has a good reputation with students and is well liked. I believe her strong point is that despite her extroverted style, students feel comfortable confiding in her. She does not pretend to be perfect. She is true to herself, and students recognize this. What works for her would not necessarily work for someone else. I have taken her advice to heart though. She told me that I should ignore students talking if it did not bother me, but that if it did, I should sit on it early. She turned out to be correct in her assessment. I do believe as the literature states that rules need to be established early and enforced to ensure a successful school year. I did not understand the implications of this statement until I experienced my first week of student teaching.

Section 2—Four Phases of Discipline
Establishing Climate

Establishing a positive academic climate for students is essential in a comprehensive discipline plan. In such a climate, students are on task and have no classroom-induced inclination or opportunity to misbehave. Teachers who have mastered techniques for promoting on-task behaviors are successful classroom managers. These teachers provide structure for the classroom and the lesson (McDaniel, 1994). Students should be focused from the moment they enter the room. Classes may begin with a settling task. Students can be taught to routinely begin work on a review drill, a focusing event for the new lesson, or a board-work assignment. These activities focus students on the work at hand. Teachers can communicate to students at the beginning of the lesson the objectives and activities planned for the day. It is important for teachers to provide a variety of activities in their lesson plans and to utilize techniques that help students make smooth transitions from one activity to another. These techniques include establishing routines for distributing and collecting materials and rearranging furniture for cooperative learning activities (Reis, 1988). Teachers can also provide positive classroom climate by arousing interest in the lesson by relating what students know and have experienced to the day's lesson. In a comprehensive discipline plan, teachers use a repertoire of techniques to focus students and keep them on task.

The teacher's personal relationship with his or her students also provides for a positive classroom environment that minimizes behavior problems. First and foremost, teachers must learn students' names. Calling on students by name and giving personal references during class communicates to students a caring demeanor. Teachers also should circulate around the classroom during problem-solving sessions to give individual help to students and provide cooperative practice and learning opportunities to encourage student success. Teachers can avert many behavior problems by maintaining a warm, supportive learning climate where academic success is emphasized and genuine interest is shown in the student as an individual (Kindsvatter, Wilen, & Ishler, 1992). A final note to avert discipline problems and promote a positive climate is to treat students kindly and with respect, much the way we all want to be treated. Demonstrating positive expectations toward students and providing a personalized learning environment is key to effective classroom management.

Classroom Management for Establishing and Maintaining Order
Maintaining order in a classroom seems to be a relatively simple procedure that can be complicated by inconsistency and misconceptions. The first step in effective management is setting clear, firm, and specific rules on day one. It is most effective to set a minimal number of rules and to set only those that are important to the teacher's needs and that the teacher intends to enforce. Each rule should be specific enough that each student has a clear understanding as to its meaning. Rules should be stated in a positive manner. Positive rules suggest a solution to a problem rather than a feeling of restraint. Teachers should give rationales for each rule and describe consequences following the infraction of each rule. Students can give a hand in making the rules. They are more apt to comply with rules that they have helped formulate. Perhaps the place where classroom management is most likely to break down is in the enforcement of classroom policies. Inconsistency with rules, assignments, and consequences breeds behavior problems (Wasicsko & Ross, 1994). Teachers should mean what they say and follow through with consequences. Meaningless threats are useless. Teachers should also learn to ignore. By giving credence to each minor incident (e.g., gum chewing, note passing), teachers create discipline problems.

Teachers can maintain order by their physical movements. Many problems can be averted if a teacher moves about the classroom and monitors activities, keeping students on task. They should maintain eye contact with students and demonstrate *withitness* by unobtrusively correcting problem behavior before it gets out of hand. Students should be praised for good behavior and willing responses to encourage positive attitudes. Finally, teachers should demonstrate positive expectations toward students. They should assume that every pupil, if given the chance, will act properly. If students don't meet these expectations, the teacher should not give up. Some students require much attention before they will begin to respond (Wasicsko & Ross, 1994).

Intervention to Restore Order
Intervention involves the use of action, not anger, to control behavior (McDaniel, 1994). Action should be swift and firm. It implies movement rather than talk. Instead of raising their voice, teachers should walk over to the student involved and correct, and provide consequences for, the infraction. Teachers should employ the *soft reprimand* when a student's in-class behavior needs correction. It is more effective to

move toward the student and in a lowered voice give a specific, quiet, direct command because this personalizes a directive and causes minimal disruption to other students. This private communication does not create a public issue where a student cannot back down because of peer attention. The teacher should be assertive and employ body language to communicate authority. Slowly walking up to a child, facing him or her directly, and making eye contact will make a definite impression of compliance for most students. Using the broken record approach where a teacher keeps repeating the request for compliance, refusing to be diverted or ignored until the request is obeyed, is also effective. Using the least obtrusive reminder of noncompliance is always the preferred method of intervention, but firmness and consistency are always prudent in maintaining classroom order.

Remediating Problem Behavior
In an ideal world, teachers monitor behavior and enforce rules agreed upon by the teacher and students alike, and there is no need for remediation. However, since school is a slightly less than ideal place, there are times when students seriously infringe on the rights of others and when remediation is necessary. Teachers should only resort to extreme measures when the infraction is of serious nature or is chronic and cannot be ignored—that is, when it interferes with the rights of other students. When *teacher looks* and *soft reprimands* fail to convince a student to cease a misbehavior, consequences must be enacted. These can run the gamut from changing the student's seat or enforcing a time-out, to an individual conference after class or after school when the teacher addresses the problem and tries to resolve the situation with the student. When this fails, the teacher might develop a contingency contract with the student, which would be an agreement of behaviors to be developed by the student, the responsibilities of others (teachers, parents) in helping the student achieve the goals of the contract, the pleasant consequences available to the student for meeting the behavioral criteria of the contract, the unpleasant consequences that will result from the student's failure to meet the behavioral criteria, and a maintenance goal to encourage the learner to sustain progress. The contract would then be signed by all parties concerned with its success (Reis, 1988).

For chronic behavior problems, a call home might induce a change. Additionally, after-school or lunch-time detentions might be in order. When all other measures fail, expert advice should be sought. A meeting with a counselor or a school psychologist might be of help in dealing with a difficult situation. I personally would save referrals to the assistant principal as a last resort. I don't really even like the idea of detention as a punitive measure. For the most part, I would try every resolution before I brought in any authority figure other than a parent. I am not convinced that in-school suspension is a deterrent for students. Sometimes, being out of the classroom is exactly what they want. So I consider anything after seeking professional advice as a last resort measure. In general I believe that teachers should do every feasible thing in their power to resolve classroom conflict themselves before resorting to extreme methods.

Ultimately, each teacher must develop a discipline plan with which he or she is comfortable. Some teachers have a higher tolerance for noise and confusion than others. The most important point to remember is that you must be the *teacher* and that you must be yourself and be comfortable with the classroom environment. If problems do arise, it would be prudent to seek advice from an experienced teacher and to remember that by caring about students, a teacher can develop techniques that lead to good classroom management and a more satisfying teaching experience.

CRITIQUE OF THE DISCIPLINE PLAN

At the very outset of the discipline plan, the student teacher, Ann, acknowledged her awareness of the importance of classroom control and her lack of confidence about it. Because of this, she procured and read several articles about discipline to help her think it through. That was a rational and appropriate response to her concerns. In this matter, as with many other teacher concerns, the professional knowledge base is a useful source for information and suggestions.

Ann has taken an organized approach to the task of developing her plan. Her premises (Section 1) include five subcategories: students' rights, teacher's responsibilities and rights, personal beliefs, personal considerations, and ideas acquired from her mentor teacher. Section 2, the application section of the plan, is subdivided into four parts: establishing climate, classroom management, intervention, and remediation. This has resulted in a comprehensive plan.

In the students' rights section, Ann unequivocally states that her students must be respected and their best interest should be served. In the following section, on the teacher's responsibility, she commits herself to establishing a classroom within which her discipline strategies would be administered in the interest of students. Student centeredness apparently is the organizing theme of her discipline plan.

Ann believed that her experience as a parent was useful in understanding her students' behavior. Not everything about teaching is learned from books. Personal experience will inevitably inform you and be a factor in how you cope. But personal experience serves one best if it is examined, as it appears Ann realizes.

Ann was adamant, and rightly so, about setting rules early and enforcing them firmly. But does a teacher forgo an opportunity to empower students if rules are arbitrarily imposed on them? This is, as much as anything, a philosophical issue. Democratic considerations would suggest involving students, although Ann hasn't made this an explicit intention.

Teachers themselves may be a significant contributing factor to misbehavior, but they do not routinely accept culpability. As Ann explored her personal beliefs she expressed concern about this and was prepared to make a conscious effort to avoid being part of the problem. She deserves to be complimented for this.

In the personal considerations section, Ann is introspective and honest with herself. She expresses concern about the level of order in her classroom and questions whether students were ready to work cooperatively. She also wonders how she could be firm without appearing to be rigid. These kinds of matters must be consciously raised if they are to be rationally addressed as the problems they are.

The mentor teacher in this instance had a personality markedly different from Ann's, and therefore she was a different sort of teacher than Ann could be. Ann realized she could not simply adopt her mentor's ways but that she would have to find those ways that were compatible with her own personality and student centered philosophy.

As one of her approaches to establishing climate, Ann planned to have an assignment for students the moment they entered the classroom. This businesslike expectation not only avoided wasted precious moments and possible horseplay, it also communicated to students the teacher's sense of purpose. Ann accepted her responsibility, from both an instructional and a discipline perspective, to use a repertoire of techniques to provide for students' motivation and keep them on task.

Ann intended to give a rationale for each rule and describe the consequences for each infraction. Students certainly deserve to be presented with rationales. The reasonable consequences should not be preordained in a mechanical way. We can't be sure about the consequences in Ann's case, for she is vague on this point. If she has reasonable consequences in mind, then we can be assured she is examining causes and giving students individual consideration. However, it is not uncommon to find lists of infractions and their associated penalties (punishments, really) posted in classrooms. This "no-brainer" approach bypasses teacher judgment. But isn't teacher judgment the heart and soul of professional teaching?

Ann has thought about her approach to intervention when misbehavior occurs. Having thought about it ahead of time, and having committed herself to reasonable actions, she is far less likely to employ hasty, ill-conceived responses based more on anger that on professional decision making. Ann apparently realized that the ability to handle the stress of the classroom with studied calmness is learned behavior.

As part of remediation, Ann suggests that detention might be in order. However, she also states that she does not like the idea of detention. Her ambivalence is understandable, but she probably should come firmly to grips with it; either determine that it is effective and appropriate or abandon it on efficacious or philosophical grounds.

Finally, Ann takes a tentative, but on the whole positive, view of her responsibility for discipline in the classroom. She understands the challenge that managing students presents and realizes that she doesn't have all the answers; in the first week she had already taken a few licks, but she was learning. She has a philosophy she believes in, she is very much in touch with herself, and she has a good discipline plan. She'll be okay.

CONCLUSION

Ann's discipline plan is not perfect. However, it is a fine start. It is serviceable even though we know it will change with experience and professional maturity. Those of you who are anticipating student teaching or are novice teachers can probably find appealing aspects of it to include in your own plan. We wish it had democratic principles more explicitly cited as its organizing concept. On the other hand, Ann's ideas are generally compatible with democratic principles.

We hope that this book has provided more than just an intellectual experience. It could be the instructive stimulus for the generation of your own informed, comprehensive, theoretically grounded discipline plan. As Ann did, you need to make a philosophic commitment, identify and organize core ideas, and speculate about how they will play out in terms of the four phases of classroom discipline. Like your instruction, your classroom discipline will evolve over the years. A solid foundation at this early stage will provide the basis for your continuing development as an ever more effective teacher.

❖ REFLECTIVE ACTIVITIES

1. What lasting impressions are you left with from reflecting on democratic discipline as presented in this book? How has your belief system been substantially affected? Are you more comfortable or less comfortable than before regarding the challenge of discipline to the teacher? Do you feel the need to pursue in greater depth some of the ideas and issues that were raised?
2. At the end of Chapter 1, we suggested that you identify the bedrock principle, the most basic proposition, upon which your approach to classroom discipline will be or is built. Has that principle remained the same? If not, what has it become as you have considered and reconsidered the many facets of democratic classroom discipline?
3. The most obvious task at this point is that you write a draft of your personal discipline plan. While some details may have to wait for your immersion in an actual classroom setting, the basic philosophy, propositions, principles, and practices can be shaped in broad strokes. Committing words to paper (or to screen) is necessary for selecting, organizing, and critically reflecting on your ideas.

❖ REFERENCES

Hanny, R. J. (1994). Don't let them take you to the barn. *The Clearing House, 67,* 252–253.

Kindsvatter, R., Wilen, W., & Ishler, M. (1992). *Dynamics of effective teaching.* New York: Longman.

McDaniel, T. R. (1994). How to be an effective authoritarian: A back-to-basics approach to classroom discipline. *The Clearing House, 67,* 254–256.

Phelps, P. H. (1991). Helping teachers excel as classroom managers. *The Clearing House, 64,* 241–242.

Reis, E. M. (1988). Effective teacher techniques: Implications for better discipline. *The Clearing House, 61,* 356–357.

Sowd, A. (1995). Personal document.

Wasicsko, M. M., & Ross, S. M. (1994). How to create discipline problems. *The Clearing House, 67,* 248–251.

Glossary

Note: The following terms and definitions are particular to their usage within the context of this book.

Care The disposition to act upon our concern for others.*

Civic Obligation See *Concern*; *Care*; and *Tolerance*.*

Classroom Management The aspect of classroom discipline that is especially concerned with establishing and monitoring classroom rules and regulations. (In some professional literature, the term is used as a synonym for *discipline* or in reference to teacher intervention behaviors only. In other professional literature, it refers to the wider scope of teacher activities, including planning and monitoring instruction as well as discipline.)

Compelling Interest The legal condition by which schools have reasonable responsibility to restrict individual freedom to protect the rights of the many.

Concern The felt need or motivation to think and act on something. As a civic obligation or virtue, it is the motivation for care and tolerance.*

Constitutional Initiative An active plan to incorporate basic principles of the U.S. Constitution in the activities of teaching and schooling such that students have the opportunity to experience the rights, responsibilities, and activities of democratic living within the school community.

---

* *The Civic Imperative: Examining the Need for Civic Education* by R. Pratte, 1988, New York: Teachers College Press.

Conventional Wisdom Assumptions, beliefs, and principles that are widely held by practitioners but have not been validated through a professional or scholarly knowledge base.

Craft Knowledge See *Conventional Wisdom*.

Critical Reflectivity The process of engaging in continual discovery and critique of ideas and actions to achieve optimal understanding, interpretation, and judgment for the greater good of all members of a community. It is also the catalyst for praxis that enables the educator to be a reflective practitioner.

Curriculum The elements that students have the opportunity to learn. (See also *Hidden Curriculum, Null Curriculum,* and *Overt Curriculum*.)

Democratic Discipline The activities of school and classroom discipline that operate within a framework that is reflectively defined by the ideals of democracy and ethics. It is humanistic and provides for addressing the worth and dignity of all students through consciously incorporating the basic principles of freedom, equality, and justice across the activities of teaching and schooling. It promotes students' experiencing the foundational elements of our democracy, including but not limited to due process, equal opportunity, free speech, participation in governance, right to grievance, and inclusion.

Democratic Ethic A set of principles that serve as the catalyst for our society to act democratically. (See also *Civic Obligation*.)

Discipline The dimension of teaching that addresses student demeanor. It is especially concerned with promoting behavior that conforms to teacher expectations and changing behavior that does not. More explicitly, classroom discipline may have its focus on the following elements: the classroom climate (discipline is seen as intragroup standards embedded within the classroom that encourage and shape purposeful behavior); the students (discipline is the disposition of the students to comply individually and collectively with classroom standards for preferred behavior); and the teacher (discipline includes the teacher's expectations for student behavior presented in the classroom in the form of rules and regulations).

Discipline Mystique   An assumed quality, usually involving awe or apprehension, attributed irrationally to discipline.

Discipline Myth   A belief about discipline that seems to be valid but is unsupported or wrong when reflectively considered using the professional knowledge base.

Due Process   The right to fairness in the application of official actions and the freedom from being treated arbitrarily in a discriminatory or unreasonable manner.

Educational Philosophy   A construct that represents a set of beliefs, or assumed truths, about how the world operates.

Empowerment   The act of teaching such that students know where, when, why, and how to use and think with the knowledge taught.

Enfleshment   The idea that we embody the elements of the dominant ideology such that they are internalized to the point that we take them for granted as being part of the essence of our being.

Ethics   A set of reflectively derived principles that guide interpersonal relations such that all people are treated with respect and dignity for the good of the community.

Hegemony   The noncoercive process by which the belief systems of the dominant ideology are acquired.

Hidden Curriculum   Elements that the student has the opportunity to learn but are not formally taught.

Ideology   The basic (acquired) belief system used to make meaning of events and experiences.

Misbehavior   Any student behavior that violates the teacher's expectations of what is appropriate in a given situation. Misbehavior is relative to the teacher's perception and may or may not be thought of as such by the student.

Motivation   The human inclination and disposition to meet a felt need. Motivation is needs driven and is marked by a feeling of interest in putting forth a directed effort.

Mystique   See *Discipline Mystique.*

Myths of Discipline   See *Discipline Myths.*

Null Curriculum   Elements that the student has no opportunity to learn.

Overt Curriculum   Elements that the student has the opportunity to learn that are formally taught.

Postmodern Culture   The social and cultural conditions that reflect the formative influences of media, technology, and sensation on the students of today (also referred to simply as "the postmodern").

Pragmatism   Thought and action that have powerful yet practical results. *Critical pragmatism* refers to the outcome of praxis with very conscious inclusion of ethics and values in terms of the human consequences of an action. *Vulgar pragmatism* refers to concern only for the immediate, practical solution, with no use of reflectivity.

Praxis   The reflective merger of theory and practice. Praxis is the professional goal of reflective practitioners.

Professional Knowledge Base   The collective literature of education, including research findings, scholarly treatises, theory, and examined practice.

Punishment   An aversive condition imposed by a teacher in response to student misbehavior that is intended to deter or prevent future misbehavior.

Reasonable Consequence   A teacher's reflective response to student misbehavior that has an ethical and democratic developmental focus— that is, a response that targets a positive personal learning outcome for the student.

Social Power   The influence one has on others within a group setting. The five types of social power we refer to in this text are legitimate, reward, coercive, referent, and expert.

Tolerance   The capacity to disagree with the act or idea of another while having the power to do something about it but choosing not to out of respect for the legitimacy of differences as a valued democratic principle.*

Index

About the Authors

Randy L. Hoover is Professor of Education at Youngstown State University where he has served as Chair of the Department of Secondary Education for 10 years. Before receiving his Ph.D. in teacher education from The Ohio State University in 1984, Dr. Hoover taught social studies at the secondary school level for 12 years.

Professor Hoover has a wide range of interests in education, including critical issues in democratic teaching and schooling. He has published articles dealing with cognitive style, philosophical foundations of education, and critical reflectivity, and is currently writing a book on empowering teaching methods. His current work focuses on democratic practices, postmodern culture, and instructional methods that facilitate student empowerment. Specifically, his work deals with the development of a professional culture for teachers that reflects the idea of *praxis:* a tight link between theory and practice in all activities of teaching and schooling.

From his professional beginning, he has focused on education, citizenship, and ethics as they relate to educational institutions. He is an advocate of understanding postmodern culture and its effects on students, teachers, and institutions.

Richard Kindsvatter received his Ph.D. in teacher education from The Ohio State University in 1966, then joined the faculty of Kent State University until his retirement in June 1996. During his career at Kent State, he was at various times an instructor, student teacher supervisor, assistant dean, director of student teaching, and department chair.

As a student teacher supervisor early in his career, he realized that the student teacher's most difficult challenge was classroom control. His efforts to help his students led to a career-long interest in discipline. He has published book chapters and monographs on the topic as well as articles in professional journals such as *Phi Delta Kappan, Educational Leadership,* and *Clearing House.*

Professor Kindsvatter also has an abiding interest in classroom instruction, having taught math and science at the junior high level for several years. He is co-author of *Dynamics of Effective Teaching,* now in its third edition.

DATE DUE